THE HULK WILL ALWAYS BE A PART OF DR. BRUCE BANNER, BUT BANNER WANTS TO BE REMEMBERED FOR HIS CONTRIBUTIONS TO SCIENCE AND NOT FOR TURNING INTO A BIG, GREEN FORCE OF RAGE AND DESTRUCTION. TO ACHIEVE THAT GOAL, BANNER HAS STRUCK A MUTUALLY BENEFICIAL DEAL WITH MARIA HILL, THE DIRECTOR OF S.H.I.E.L.D. SHE PROVIDES BANNER WITH A LAB, STAFF AND ALL OF THE RESOURCES HE NEEDS TO BETTER MANKIND, AND BANNER PROVIDES S.H.I.E.L.D. WITH THE HULK FOR ANY MISSIONS THAT MIGHT NEED EXTRA MUSCLE.

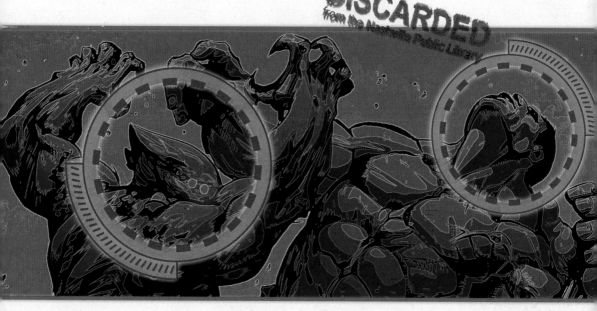

INDESTRUCTIBLE HULK

HUMANITY BOMB

VOLUME 04

INDESTRUCTIBLE HULK VOL. 4: HUMANITY BOMB. Contains material originally published in magazine form as INDESTRUCTIBLE HULK #16, #17.INH-19.INH, #20 and ANNUAL #1. First printing 2015. ISBN# 978-0-7851-8949-7. Published by MARVEL WORLDWIDE, INC., a subsidiary of MARVEL ENTERTAINMENT, LLC. OFFICE OF PUBLICATION: 135 West 50th Street, New York, NY 10020. Copyright © 2013, 2014 and 2015 Marvel Characters, Inc. All rights reserved. All characters featured in this issue and the distinctive names and likenesses thereof, and all related indicia are trademarks of Marvel Characters, Inc. No similarity between any of the names, characters, persons, and/or institutions in this magazine with those of any living or dead person or institution is intended, and any such similarity which may exist is purely coincidental. **Printed in the U.S.A.** ALAN FINE, EVP - Office of the President, Marvel Worldwide, Inc. and EVP & CMO Marvel Characters B.V.; DAN BUCKLEY, Publisher & President - Print, Animation & Digital Divisions; JOE QUESADA, Chief Creative Officer; TOM BREVOORT, SVP of Publishing; DAVID BOGART, SVP of Operations & Procurement, Publishing; C.B. CEBULSKI, SVP of Creator & Content Development; DAVID GABRIEL, SVP Print, Sales & Marketing; JIM O'KEEFE, VP of Operations & Logistics; DAN CARR, Executive Director of Publishing Technology; SUSAN CRESPI, Editorial Operations Manager; ALEX MORALES, Publishing Operations Manager; STAN LEE, Chairman Emeritus. For information regarding advertising in Marvel Comics or on Marvel.com, please contact Niza Disla, Director of Marvel Partnerships, at ndisla@marvel.com. For Marvel subscription inquiries, please call 800-217-9158. **Manufactured between 12/19/2014 and 1/26/2015 by R.R. DONNELLEY, INC., SALEM, VA, USA.**

10 9 8 7 6 5 4 3 2 1

WRITER
MARK WAID

#16
ARTIST: **MAHMUD ASRAR**

#17
ARTISTS: **CLAY** & **SETH MANN**
(PGS 1-10, 12-13) AND
MIGUEL SEPULVEDA
(PGS 11, 14-20)

#18
ARTISTS: **JHEREMY RAAPACK**
(PGS 1-10) AND
MIGUEL SEPULVEDA WITH
TOM GRUMMETT (PGS 11-20)

#19
ARTISTS: **JHEREMY RAAPACK**
(PGS 1-12, 16, 19-20), **JOE BENNETT** &
RUY JOSÉ (PGS 13-15) AND
TOM GRUMMETT WITH
KARL KESEL &
ANDREW HENNESSY (PGS 17-18)

#20
PENCILER: **JOE BENNETT**
INKERS: **RUY JOSÉ** WITH
SCOTT HANNA

COLORIST: **VAL STAPLES**
LETTERER: **VC'S CORY PETIT**

ANNUAL #1
WRITER: **JEFF PARKER**
ARTIST: **MAHMUD ASRAR**
COLORIST: **NELSON DANIEL**
LETTERER: **VC'S CORY PETIT**

COVER ARTISTS: **MAHMUD ASRAR**
& **DAVE MCCAIG**

ASSISTANT EDITOR: **EMILY SHAW**
EDITOR: **MARK PANICCIA**

COLLECTION EDITOR: **ALEX STARBUCK** • EDITORS, SPECIAL PROJECTS: **JENNIFER GRÜNWALD & MARK D. BEAZLEY**
SENIOR EDITOR, SPECIAL PROJECTS: **JEFF YOUNGQUIST** • SVP PRINT, SALES & MARKETING: **DAVID GABRIEL**
BOOK DESIGNER: **NELSON RIBEIRO**

EDITOR IN CHIEF: **AXEL ALONSO**
CHIEF CREATIVE OFFICER: **JOE QUESADA**
PUBLISHER: **DAN BUCKLEY**
EXECUTIVE PRODUCER: **ALAN FINE**

PREVIOUSLY

AFTER DELIVERING A PUNCH STRAIGHT TO THE FACE OF TIME ITSELF, HULK HAS SAVED THE PAST. EVERYTHING WENT BACK TO NORMAL. FOR THE MOST PART. SOMETHING WAS CHANGED...

BUT HULK'S JAUNT THROUGH TIME MEANS BANNER IS BEHIND IN HIS WORK.

HULK DESTROYS, BANNER BUILDS.

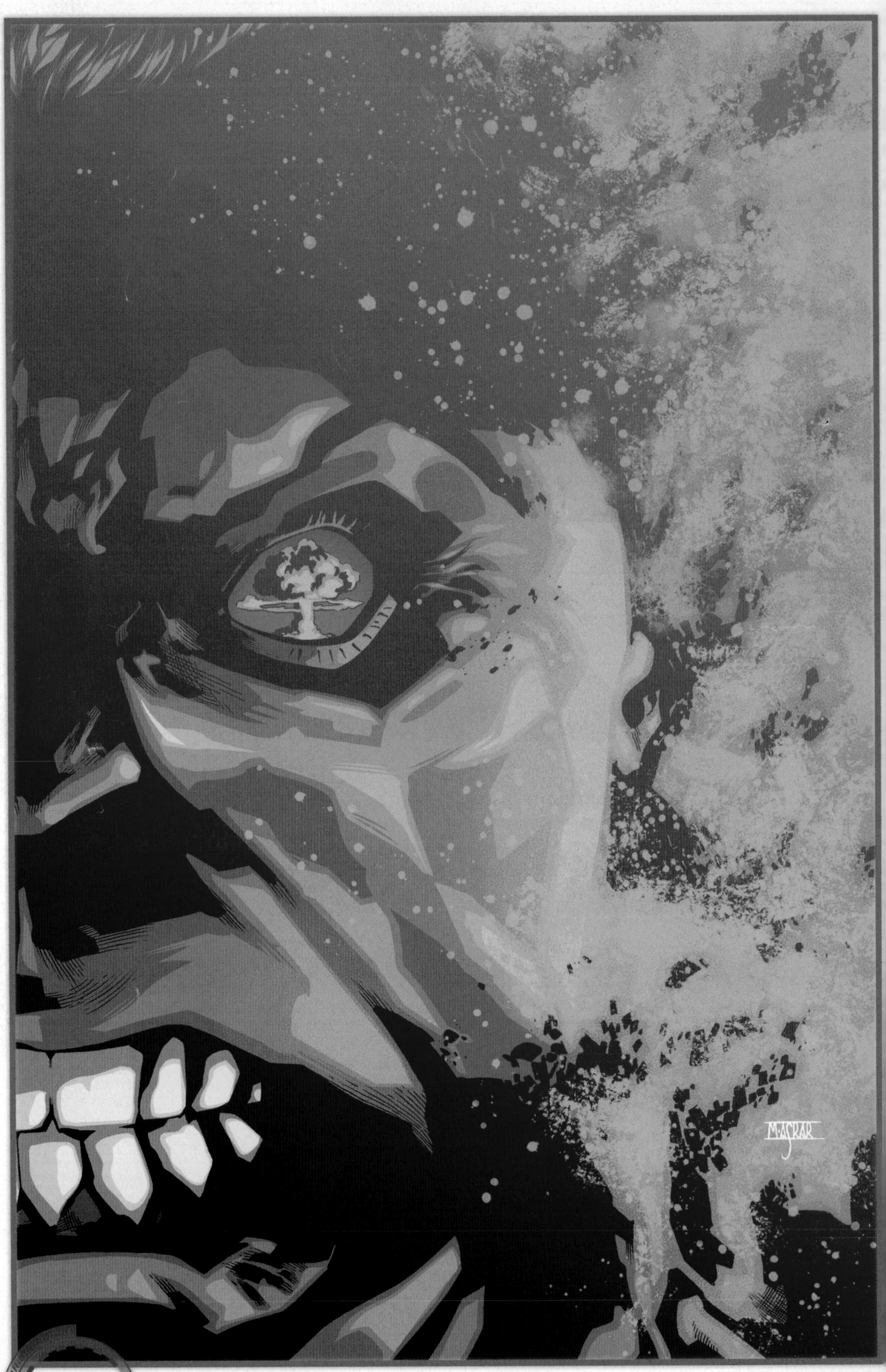

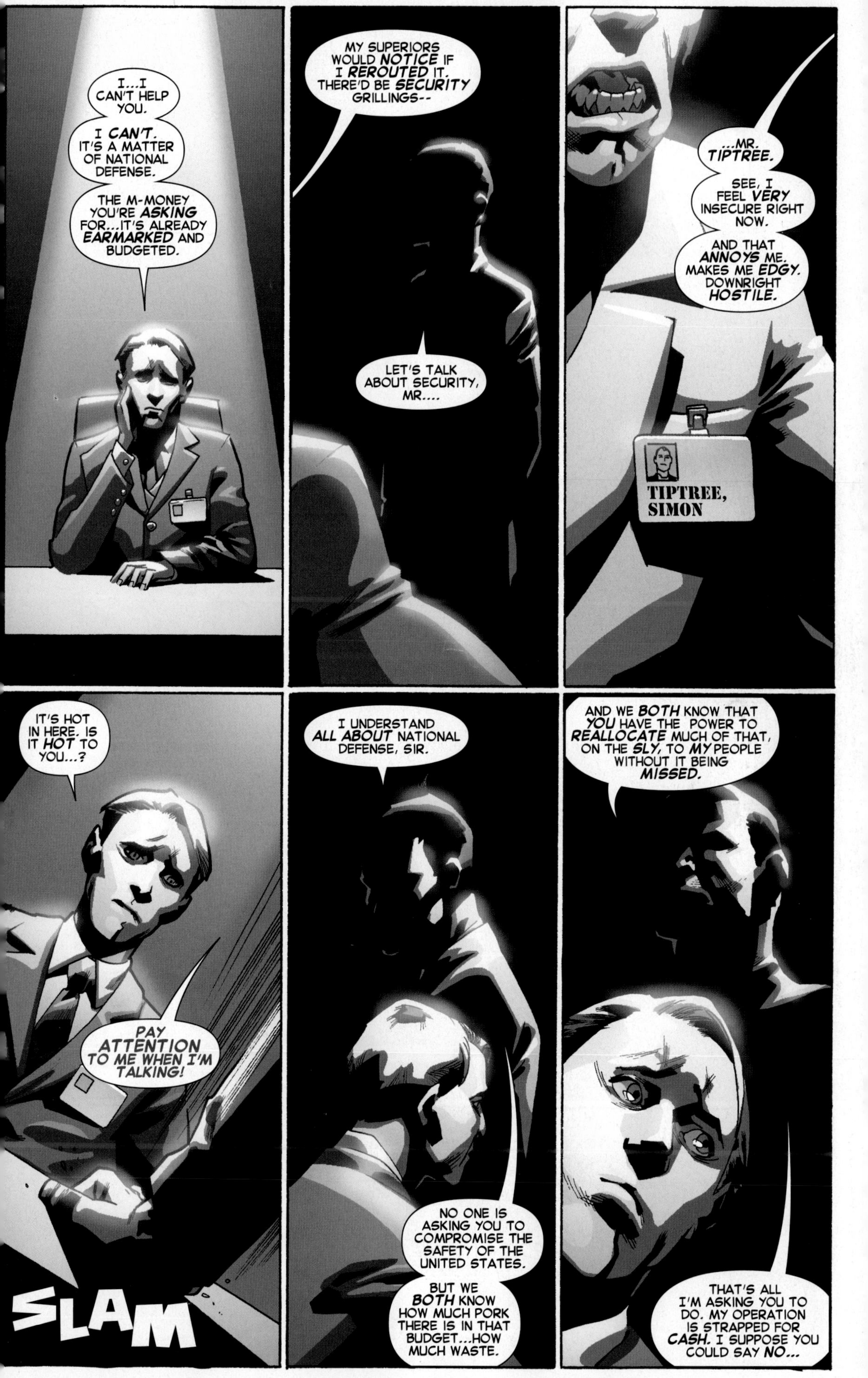
I...I CAN'T HELP YOU.
I CAN'T. IT'S A MATTER OF NATIONAL DEFENSE.
THE M-MONEY YOU'RE ASKING FOR...IT'S ALREADY EARMARKED AND BUDGETED.
MY SUPERIORS WOULD NOTICE IF I REROUTED IT. THERE'D BE SECURITY GRILLINGS--
LET'S TALK ABOUT SECURITY, MR....
...MR. TIPTREE.
SEE, I FEEL VERY INSECURE RIGHT NOW.
AND THAT ANNOYS ME. MAKES ME EDGY. DOWNRIGHT HOSTILE.
TIPTREE, SIMON
IT'S HOT IN HERE. IS IT HOT TO YOU...?
PAY ATTENTION TO ME WHEN I'M TALKING!
SLAM
I UNDERSTAND ALL ABOUT NATIONAL DEFENSE, SIR.
NO ONE IS ASKING YOU TO COMPROMISE THE SAFETY OF THE UNITED STATES.
BUT WE BOTH KNOW HOW MUCH PORK THERE IS IN THAT BUDGET...HOW MUCH WASTE.
AND WE BOTH KNOW THAT YOU HAVE THE POWER TO REALLOCATE MUCH OF THAT, ON THE SLY, TO MY PEOPLE WITHOUT IT BEING MISSED.
THAT'S ALL I'M ASKING YOU TO DO. MY OPERATION IS STRAPPED FOR CASH. I SUPPOSE YOU COULD SAY NO...

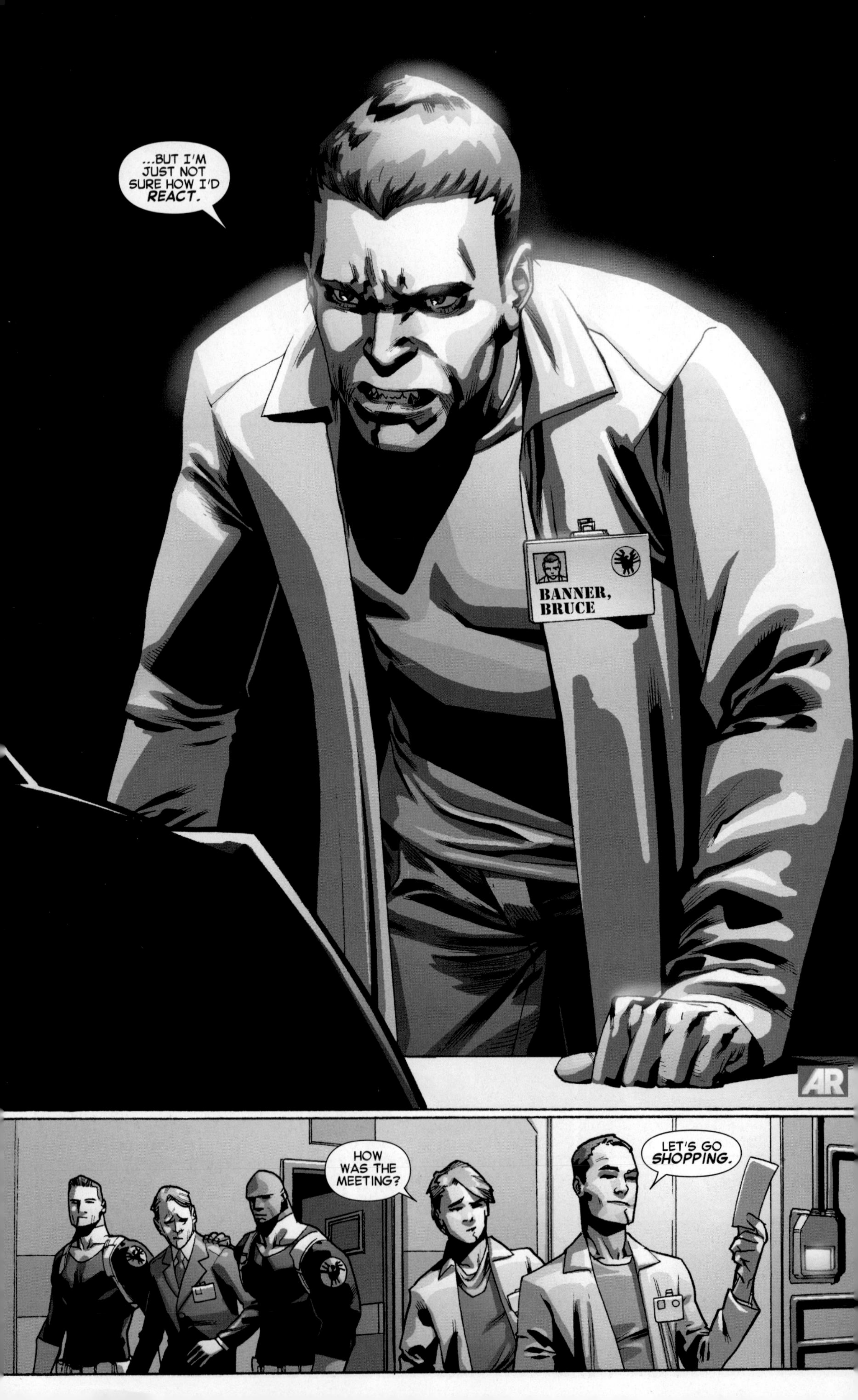
...BUT I'M JUST NOT SURE HOW I'D *REACT.*
BANNER, BRUCE
HOW WAS THE MEETING?
LET'S GO *SHOPPING.*

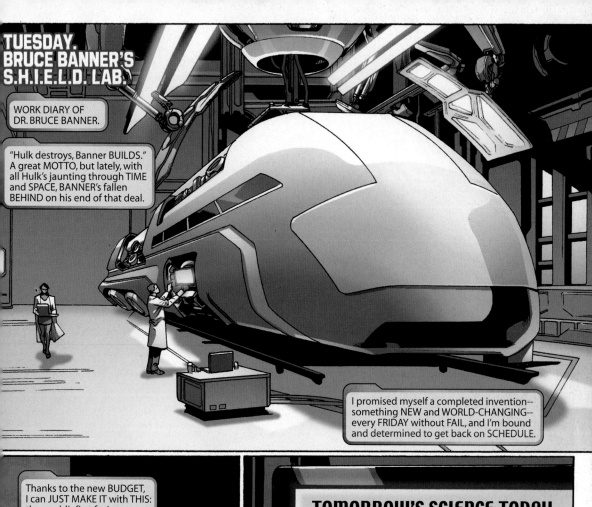

**TUESDAY.
BRUCE BANNER'S
S.H.I.E.L.D. LAB.**

WORK DIARY OF
DR. BRUCE BANNER.

"Hulk destroys, Banner BUILDS."
A great MOTTO, but lately, with
all Hulk's jaunting through TIME
and SPACE, BANNER's fallen
BEHIND on his end of that deal.

I promised myself a completed invention--
something NEW and WORLD-CHANGING--
every FRIDAY without FAIL, and I'm bound
and determined to get back on SCHEDULE.

Thanks to the new BUDGET,
I can JUST MAKE IT with THIS:
the world's first fusion-
powered HIGH-SPEED RAIL...

DOC,
YOU SHOULD
SEE THIS...

TOMORROW'S SCIENCE TODAY
TONY STARK DELIVERS
GAME-CHANGING FUSION-POWERED RAIL ENGINE

...engine...

STARRRRRK--!

AR

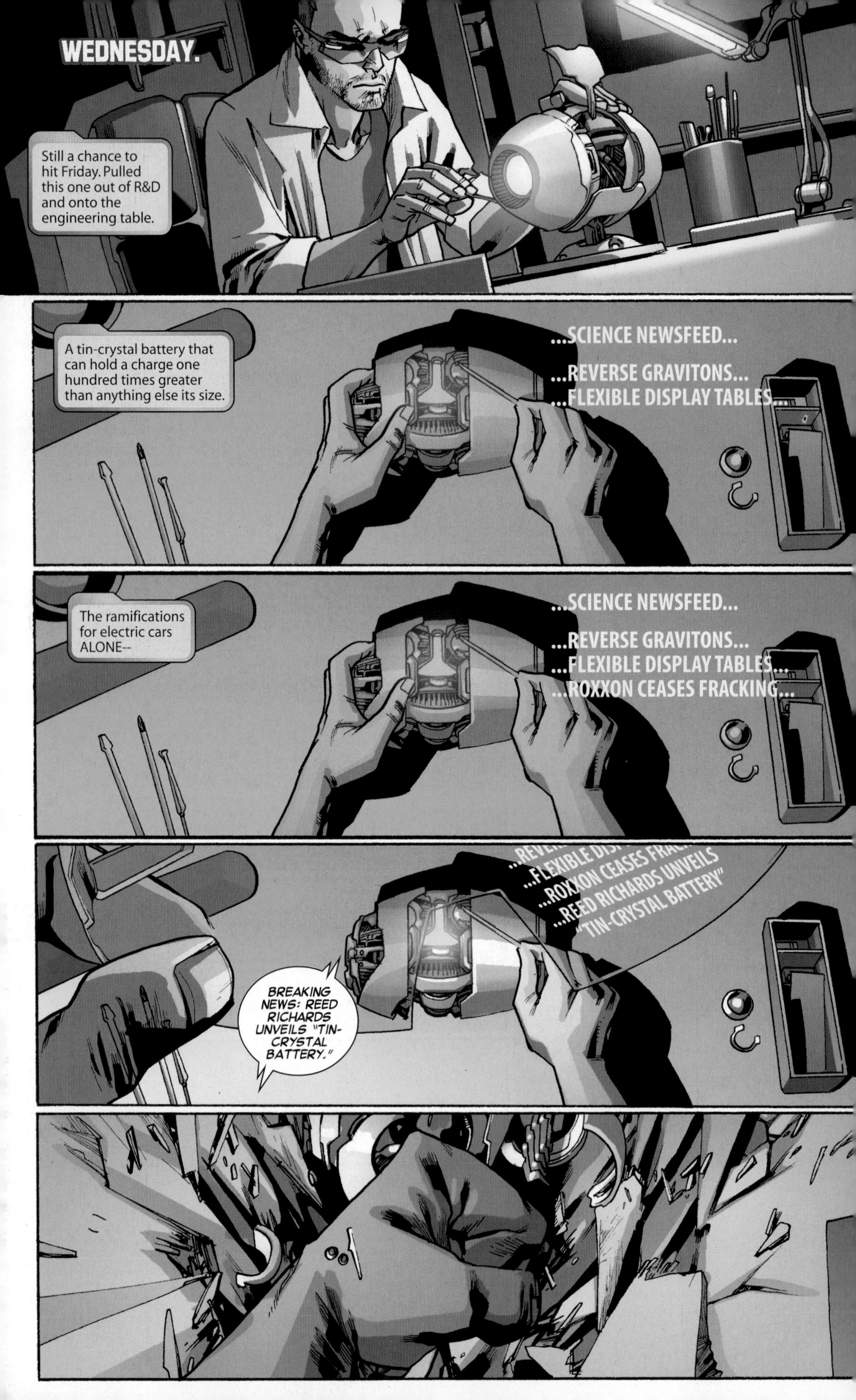
WEDNESDAY.
Still a chance to hit Friday. Pulled this one out of R&D and onto the engineering table.
A tin-crystal battery that can hold a charge one hundred times greater than anything else its size.
...SCIENCE NEWSFEED...
...REVERSE GRAVITONS...
...FLEXIBLE DISPLAY TABLES...
The ramifications for electric cars ALONE--
...SCIENCE NEWSFEED...
...REVERSE GRAVITONS...
...FLEXIBLE DISPLAY TABLES...
...ROXXON CEASES FRACKING...
...FLEXIBLE DIS
...ROXXON CEASES FRAC
...REED RICHARDS UNVEILS
"TIN-CRYSTAL BATTERY"
BREAKING NEWS: REED RICHARDS UNVEILS "TIN-CRYSTAL BATTERY."

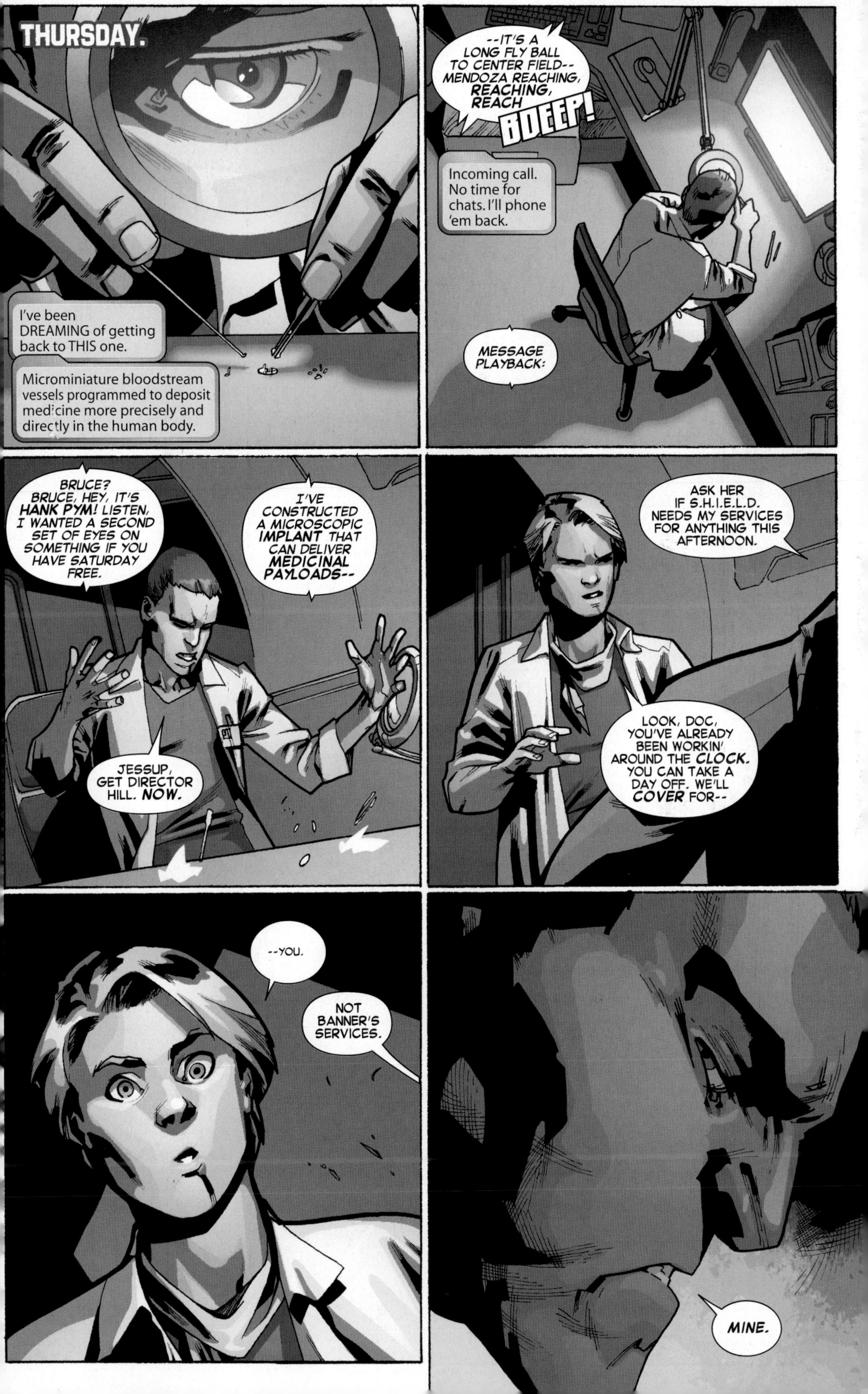

THURSDAY.
I've been DREAMING of getting back to THIS one.
Microminiature bloodstream vessels programmed to deposit medicine more precisely and directly in the human body.
--IT'S A LONG FLY BALL TO CENTER FIELD-- MENDOZA REACHING, REACHING, REACH
BDEEP!
Incoming call. No time for chats. I'll phone 'em back.
MESSAGE PLAYBACK:
BRUCE? BRUCE, HEY, IT'S HANK PYM! LISTEN, I WANTED A SECOND SET OF EYES ON SOMETHING IF YOU HAVE SATURDAY FREE.
I'VE CONSTRUCTED A MICROSCOPIC IMPLANT THAT CAN DELIVER MEDICINAL PAYLOADS--
JESSUP, GET DIRECTOR HILL. NOW.
ASK HER IF S.H.I.E.L.D. NEEDS MY SERVICES FOR ANYTHING THIS AFTERNOON.
LOOK, DOC, YOU'VE ALREADY BEEN WORKIN' AROUND THE CLOCK. YOU CAN TAKE A DAY OFF. WE'LL COVER FOR--
--YOU.
NOT BANNER'S SERVICES.
MINE.

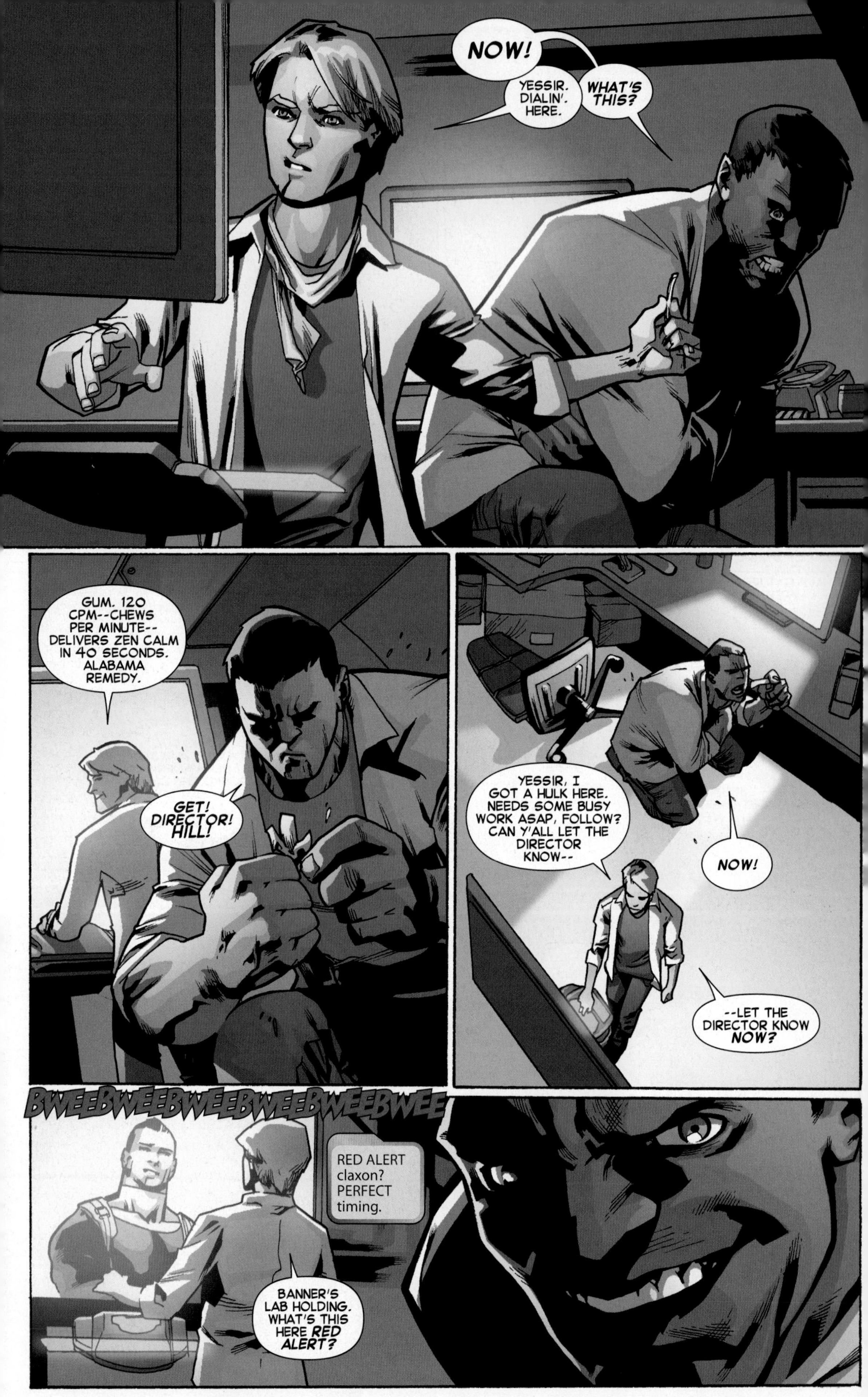
NOW!
YESSIR. DIALIN'. HERE.
WHAT'S THIS?
GUM. 120 CPM--CHEWS PER MINUTE--DELIVERS ZEN CALM IN 40 SECONDS. ALABAMA REMEDY.
GET! DIRECTOR! HILL!
YESSIR, I GOT A HULK HERE. NEEDS SOME BUSY WORK ASAP, FOLLOW? CAN Y'ALL LET THE DIRECTOR KNOW--
NOW!
--LET THE DIRECTOR KNOW NOW?
BWEEBWEEBWEEBWEEBWEEBWEE
RED ALERT claxon? PERFECT timing.
BANNER'S LAB HOLDING. WHAT'S THIS HERE RED ALERT?

ALL HANDS. SAYS SOME UNKNOWN ENERGY IS RADIATING FROM A MESOAMERICAN PYRAMID DOWN IN MEXICO...?

TELL THE DIRECTOR I'M ON MY WAY!

WEEBWEEBWEEBWEEBWEEBWEEBWEEBWEEBWEEBWEEBWEEBWEEBWEE

NOT YOU, BANNER!

WHAT? WHY NOT, HILL?

THIS SITUATION CALLS FOR DAMAGE CONTROL. WE NEED SOMETHING BROKEN, WE'LL CALL.

DOCTOR!

AAAH!

WEEBWEEBWEEBWEEBWEEBWEEBWEEBWEEBWEEBWEEBWEEBWEE

SHUT ME OUT? JUST FOR GOIN' AFTER A KID LOOKED SUSPICIOUS! AN' THEY TAKE MY BADGE AN' GUN FOR THAT? FOR DOIN' MY JOB?

I WAS A DEPUTY THIRTEEN YEARS! THAT COUNT FOR NOTHING?

GUM?

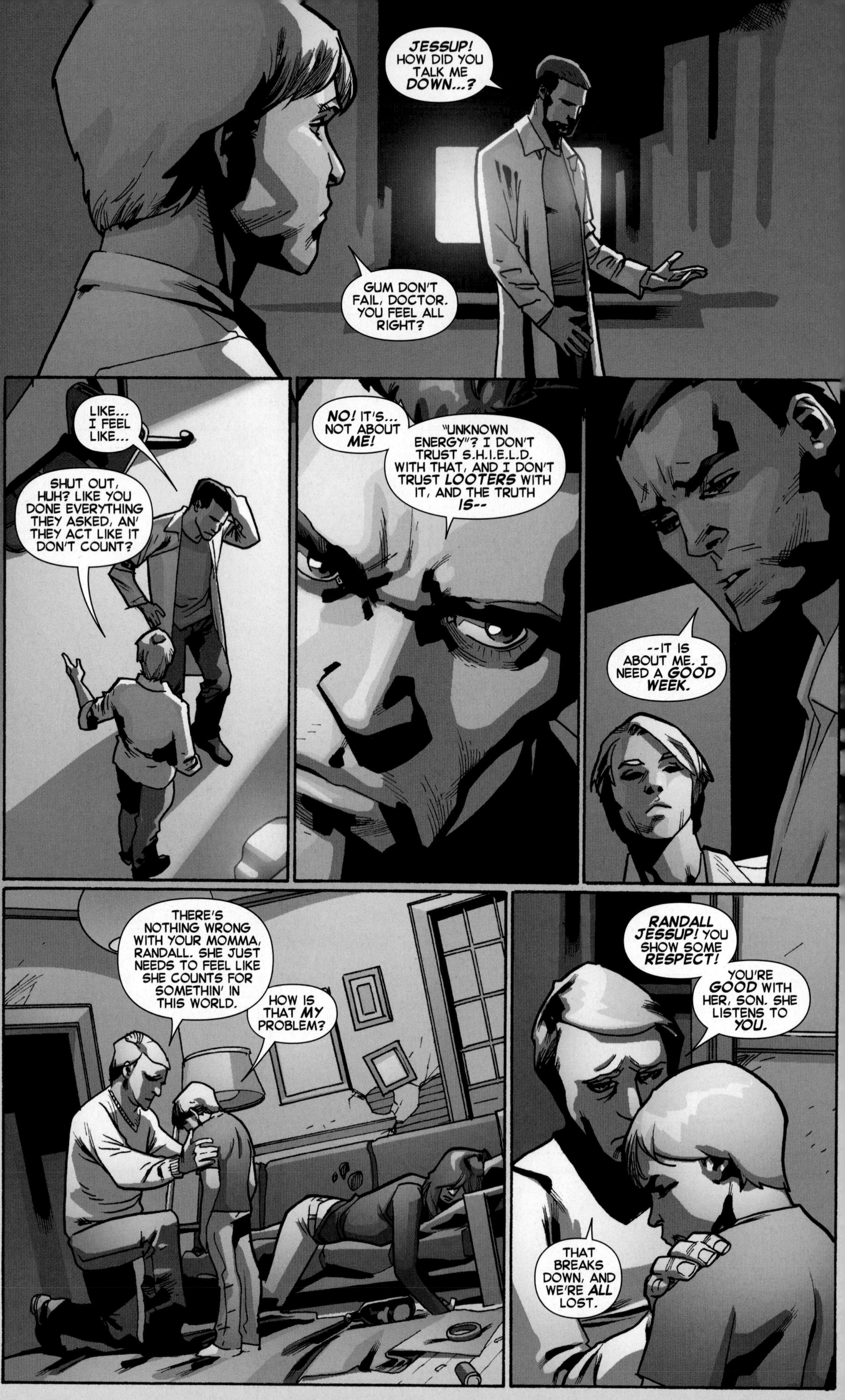
JESSUP! HOW DID YOU TALK ME DOWN...?
GUM DON'T FAIL, DOCTOR. YOU FEEL ALL RIGHT?
LIKE... I FEEL LIKE...
SHUT OUT, HUH? LIKE YOU DONE EVERYTHING THEY ASKED, AN' THEY ACT LIKE IT DON'T COUNT?
NO! IT'S... NOT ABOUT ME!
"UNKNOWN ENERGY"? I DON'T TRUST S.H.I.E.L.D. WITH THAT, AND I DON'T TRUST LOOTERS WITH IT, AND THE TRUTH IS--
--IT IS ABOUT ME. I NEED A GOOD WEEK.
THERE'S NOTHING WRONG WITH YOUR MOMMA, RANDALL. SHE JUST NEEDS TO FEEL LIKE SHE COUNTS FOR SOMETHIN' IN THIS WORLD.
HOW IS THAT MY PROBLEM?
RANDALL JESSUP! YOU SHOW SOME RESPECT!
YOU'RE GOOD WITH HER, SON. SHE LISTENS TO YOU.
THAT BREAKS DOWN, AND WE'RE ALL LOST.

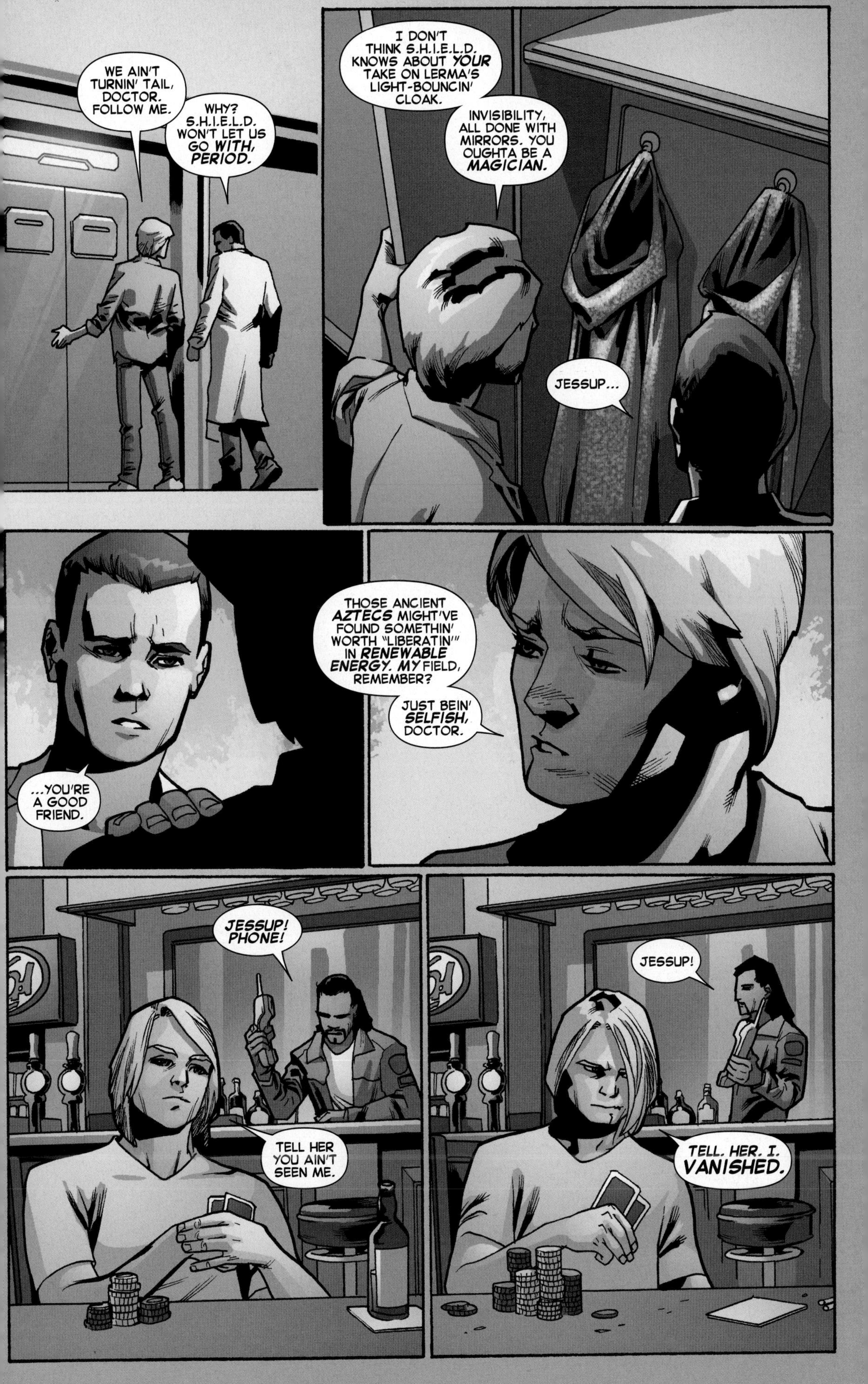
WE AIN'T TURNIN' TAIL, DOCTOR. FOLLOW ME.
WHY? S.H.I.E.L.D. WON'T LET US GO WITH, PERIOD.
I DON'T THINK S.H.I.E.L.D. KNOWS ABOUT YOUR TAKE ON LERMA'S LIGHT-BOUNCIN' CLOAK.
INVISIBILITY, ALL DONE WITH MIRRORS. YOU OUGHTA BE A MAGICIAN.
JESSUP...
...YOU'RE A GOOD FRIEND.
THOSE ANCIENT AZTECS MIGHT'VE FOUND SOMETHIN' WORTH "LIBERATIN'" IN RENEWABLE ENERGY. MY FIELD, REMEMBER?
JUST BEIN' SELFISH, DOCTOR.
JESSUP! PHONE!
TELL HER YOU AIN'T SEEN ME.
JESSUP!
TELL. HER. I. VANISHED.

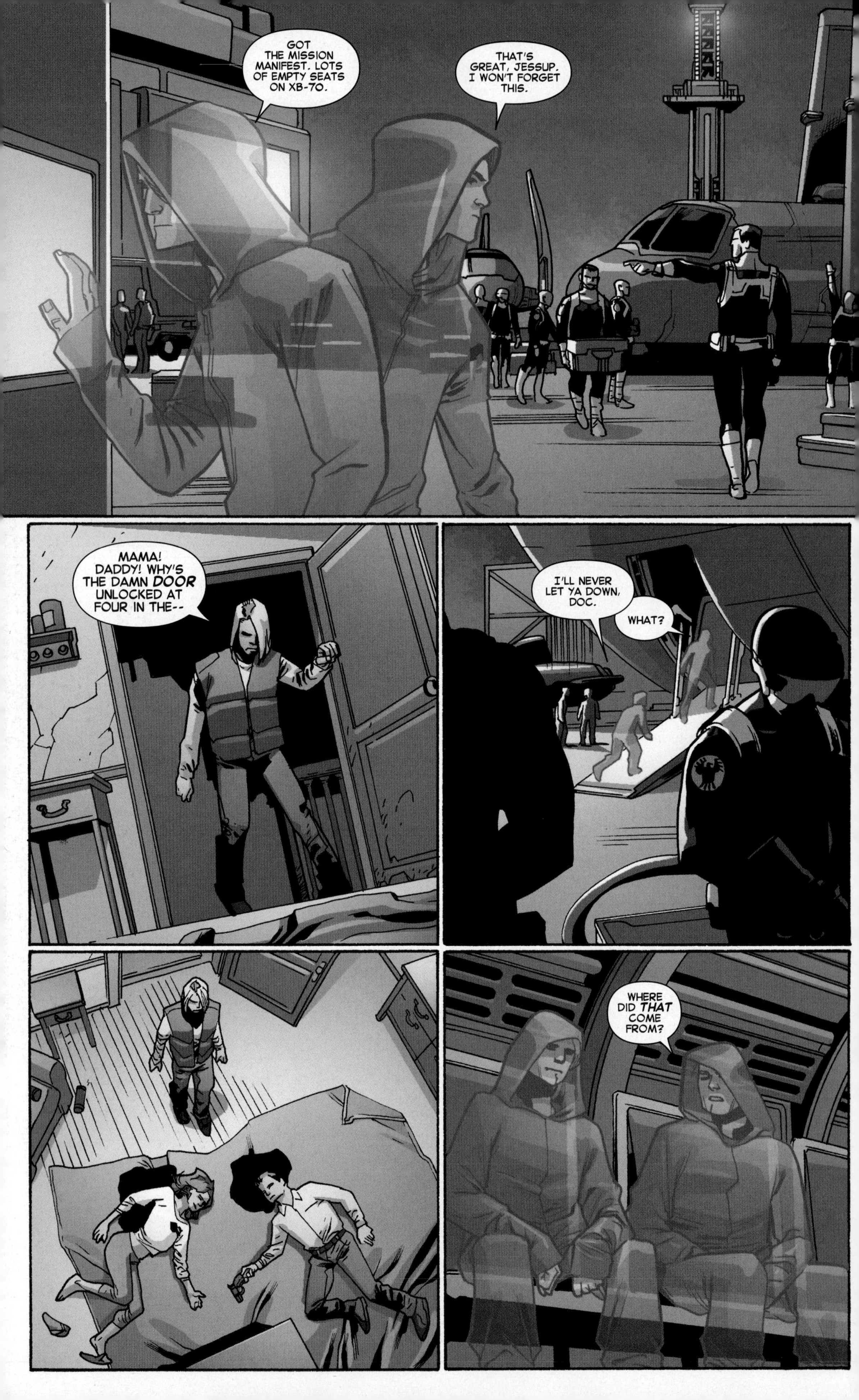
GOT THE MISSION MANIFEST. LOTS OF EMPTY SEATS ON XB-70.
THAT'S GREAT, JESSUP. I WON'T FORGET THIS.
MAMA! DADDY! WHY'S THE DAMN DOOR UNLOCKED AT FOUR IN THE--
I'LL NEVER LET YA DOWN, DOC.
WHAT?
WHERE DID THAT COME FROM?

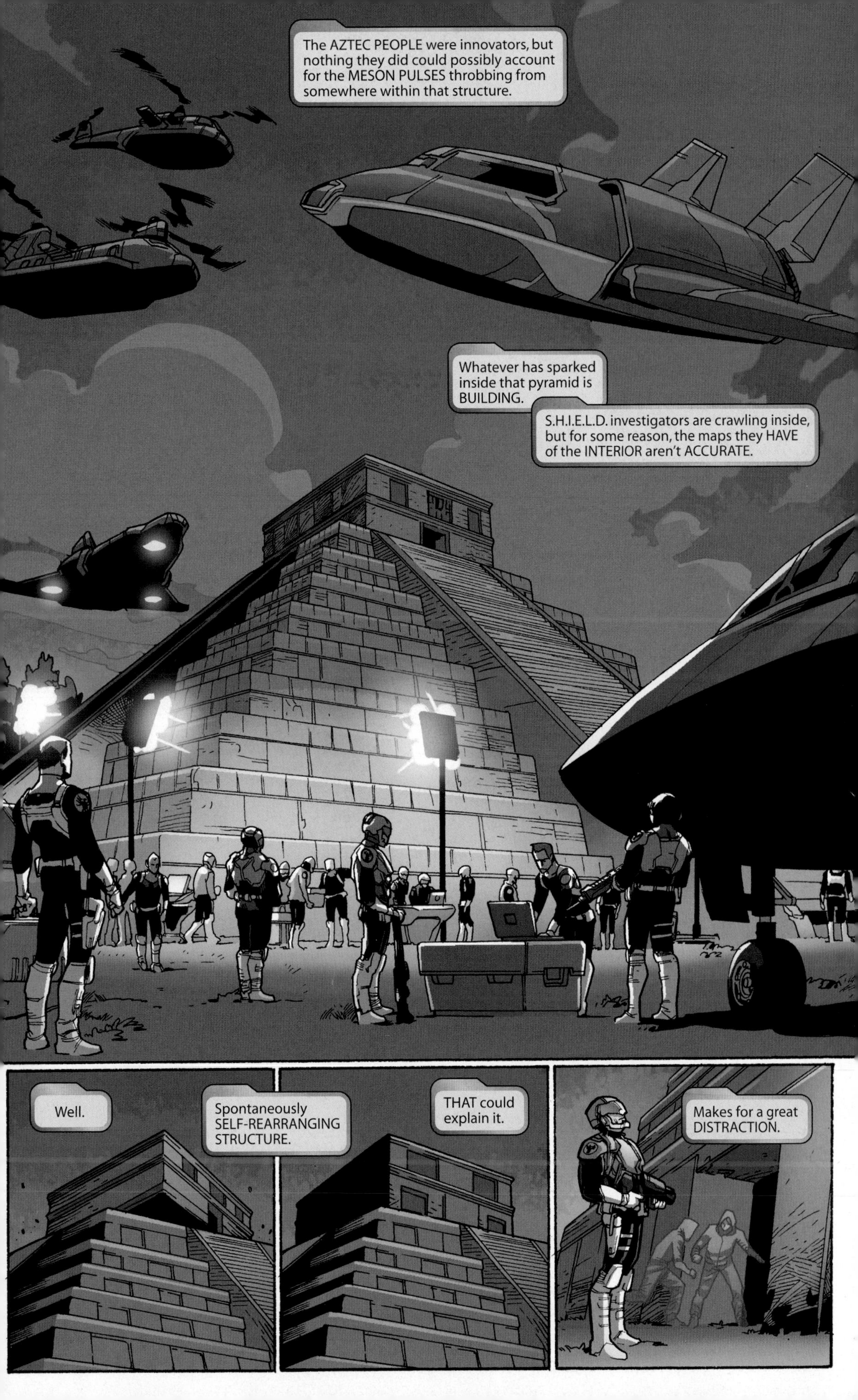
The AZTEC PEOPLE were innovators, but nothing they did could possibly account for the MESON PULSES throbbing from somewhere within that structure.
Whatever has sparked inside that pyramid is BUILDING.
S.H.I.E.L.D. investigators are crawling inside, but for some reason, the maps they HAVE of the INTERIOR aren't ACCURATE.
Well.
Spontaneously SELF-REARRANGING STRUCTURE.
THAT could explain it.
Makes for a great DISTRACTION.

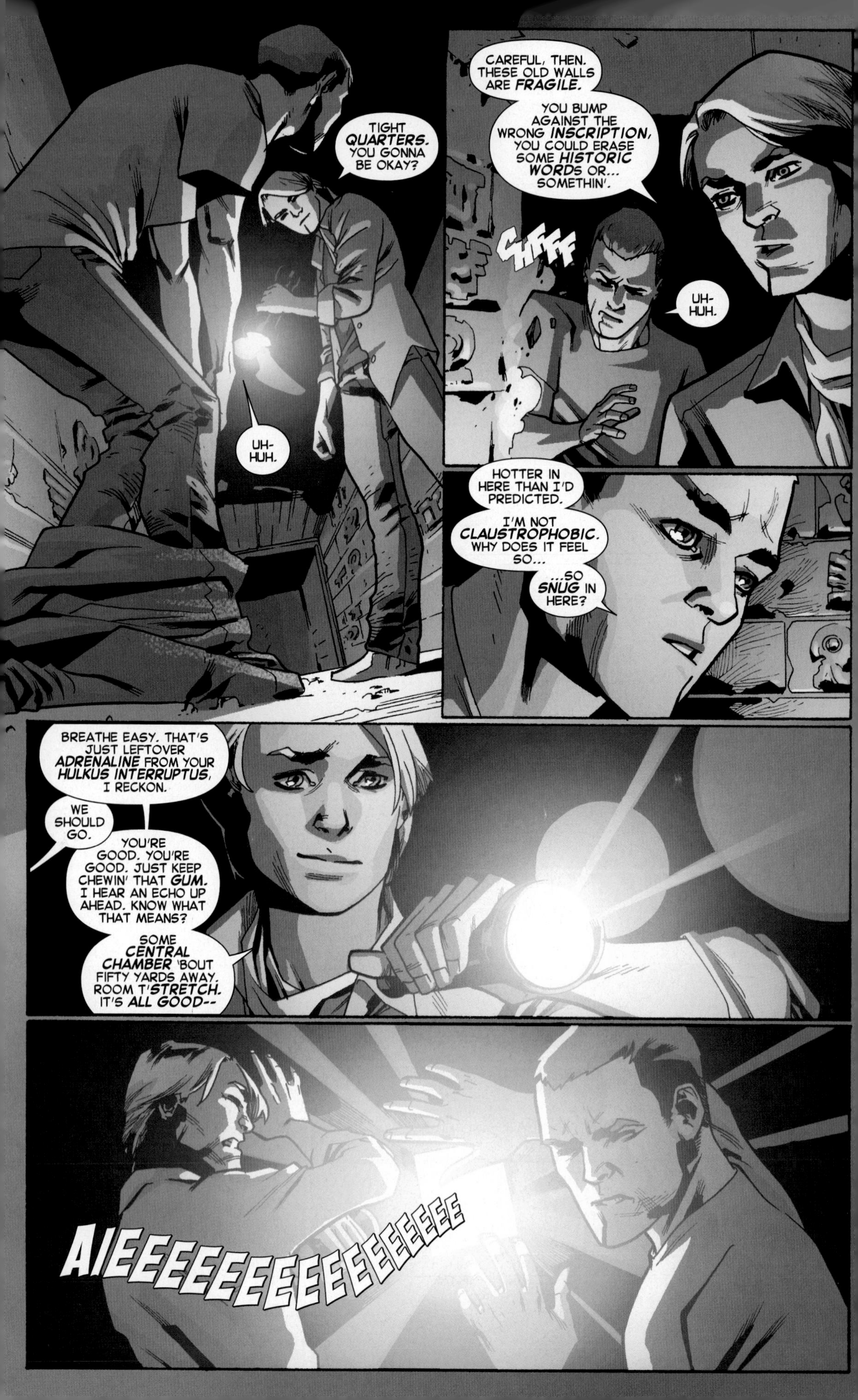
TIGHT QUARTERS. YOU GONNA BE OKAY?
UH-HUH.
CAREFUL, THEN. THESE OLD WALLS ARE FRAGILE.
YOU BUMP AGAINST THE WRONG INSCRIPTION, YOU COULD ERASE SOME HISTORIC WORDS OR... SOMETHIN'.
CHFFF
UH-HUH.
HOTTER IN HERE THAN I'D PREDICTED.
I'M NOT CLAUSTROPHOBIC. WHY DOES IT FEEL SO...
...SO SNUG IN HERE?
BREATHE EASY. THAT'S JUST LEFTOVER ADRENALINE FROM YOUR HULKUS INTERRUPTUS, I RECKON.
WE SHOULD GO.
YOU'RE GOOD. YOU'RE GOOD. JUST KEEP CHEWIN' THAT GUM. I HEAR AN ECHO UP AHEAD. KNOW WHAT THAT MEANS?
SOME CENTRAL CHAMBER 'BOUT FIFTY YARDS AWAY. ROOM T'STRETCH. IT'S ALL GOOD--
AIEEEEEEEEEEEEEEEE

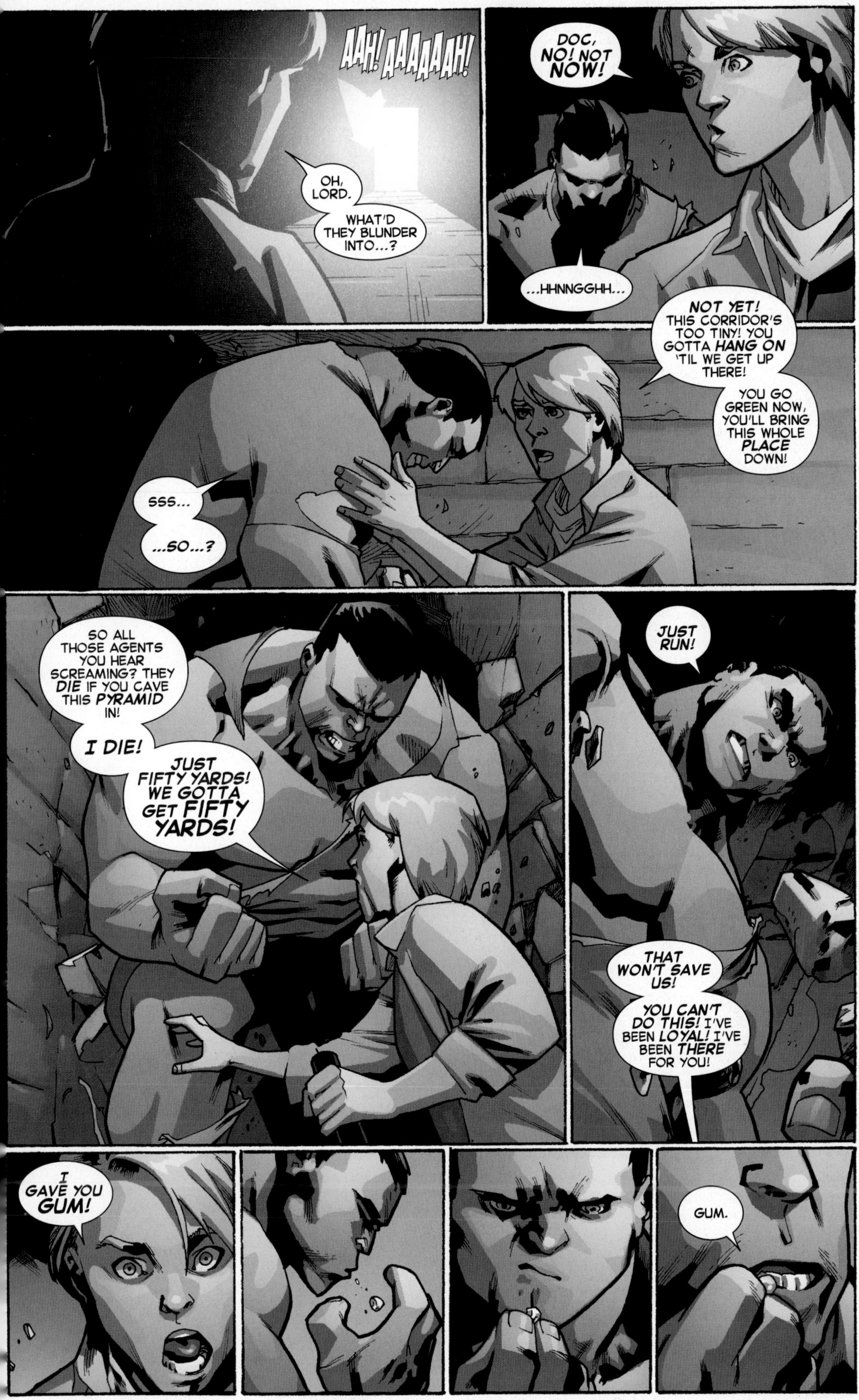
AAH! AAAAAAH!
OH, LORD.
WHAT'D THEY BLUNDER INTO...?
DOC, NO! NOT NOW!
...HHNNGGHH...
NOT YET! THIS CORRIDOR'S TOO TINY! YOU GOTTA HANG ON 'TIL WE GET UP THERE!
YOU GO GREEN NOW, YOU'LL BRING THIS WHOLE PLACE DOWN!
SSS...
...SO...?
SO ALL THOSE AGENTS YOU HEAR SCREAMING? THEY DIE IF YOU CAVE THIS PYRAMID IN!
I DIE!
JUST FIFTY YARDS! WE GOTTA GET FIFTY YARDS!
JUST RUN!
THAT WON'T SAVE US!
YOU CAN'T DO THIS! I'VE BEEN LOYAL! I'VE BEEN THERE FOR YOU!
I GAVE YOU GUM!
GUM.

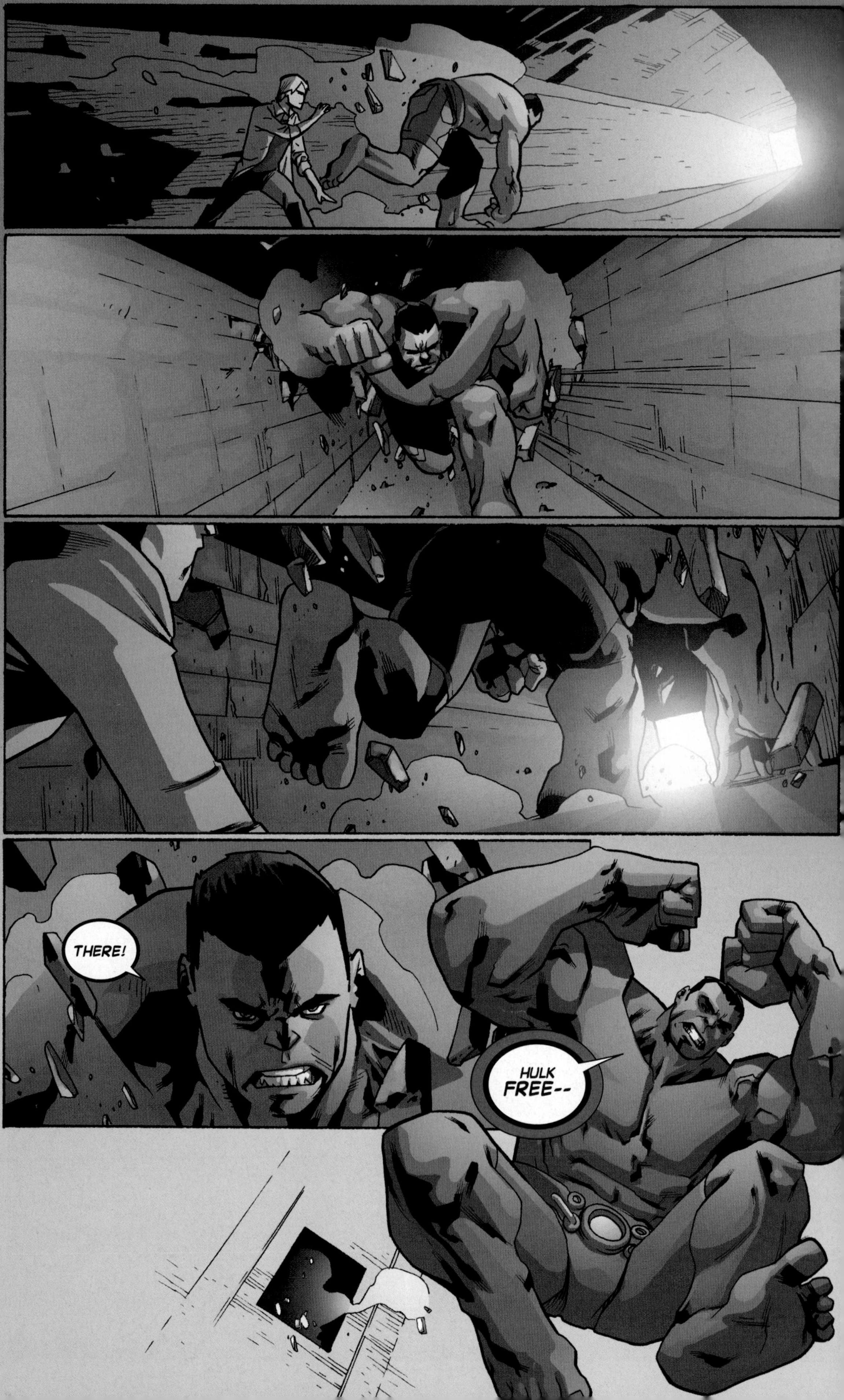
THERE!
HULK FREE--

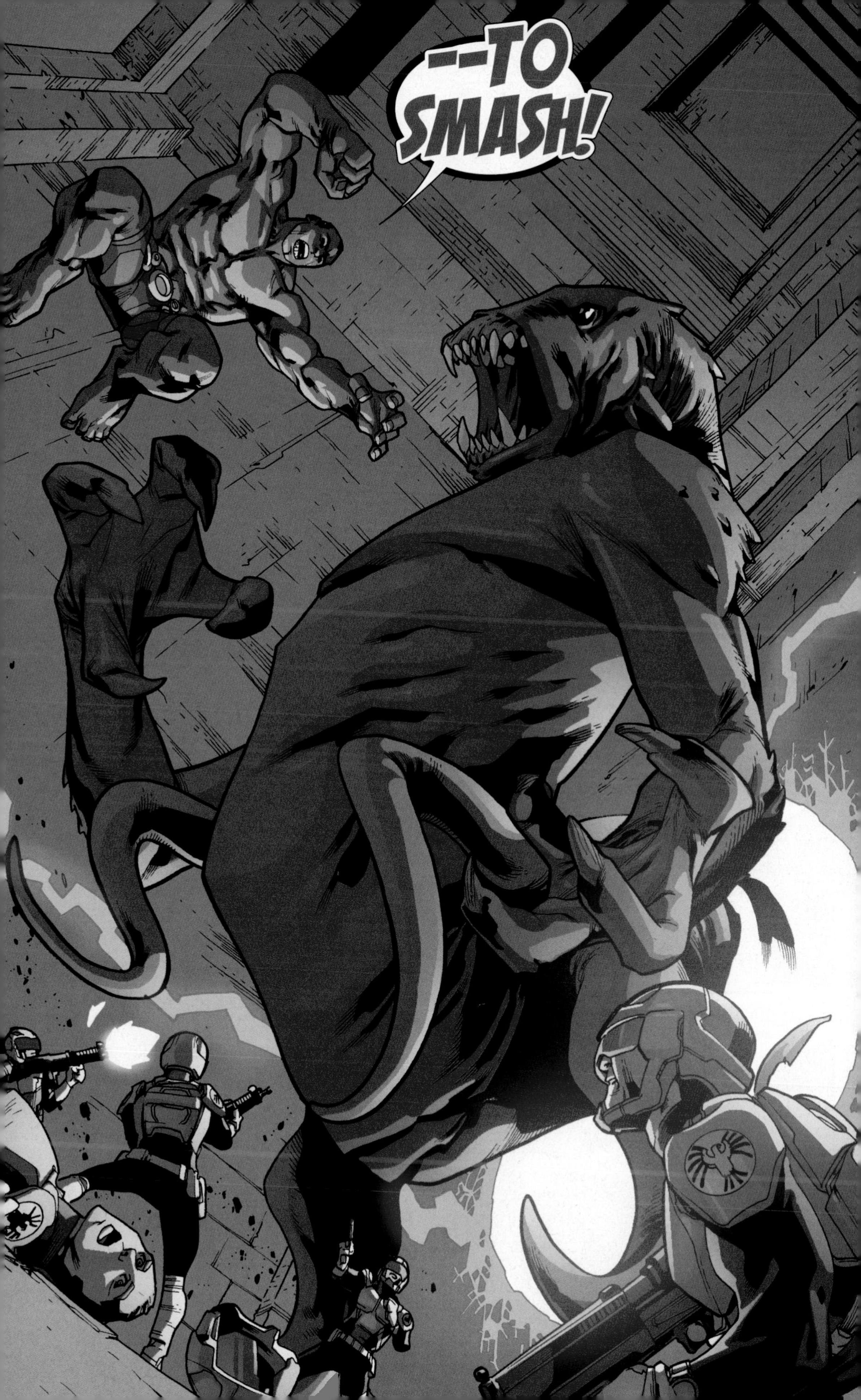
--TO SMASH!

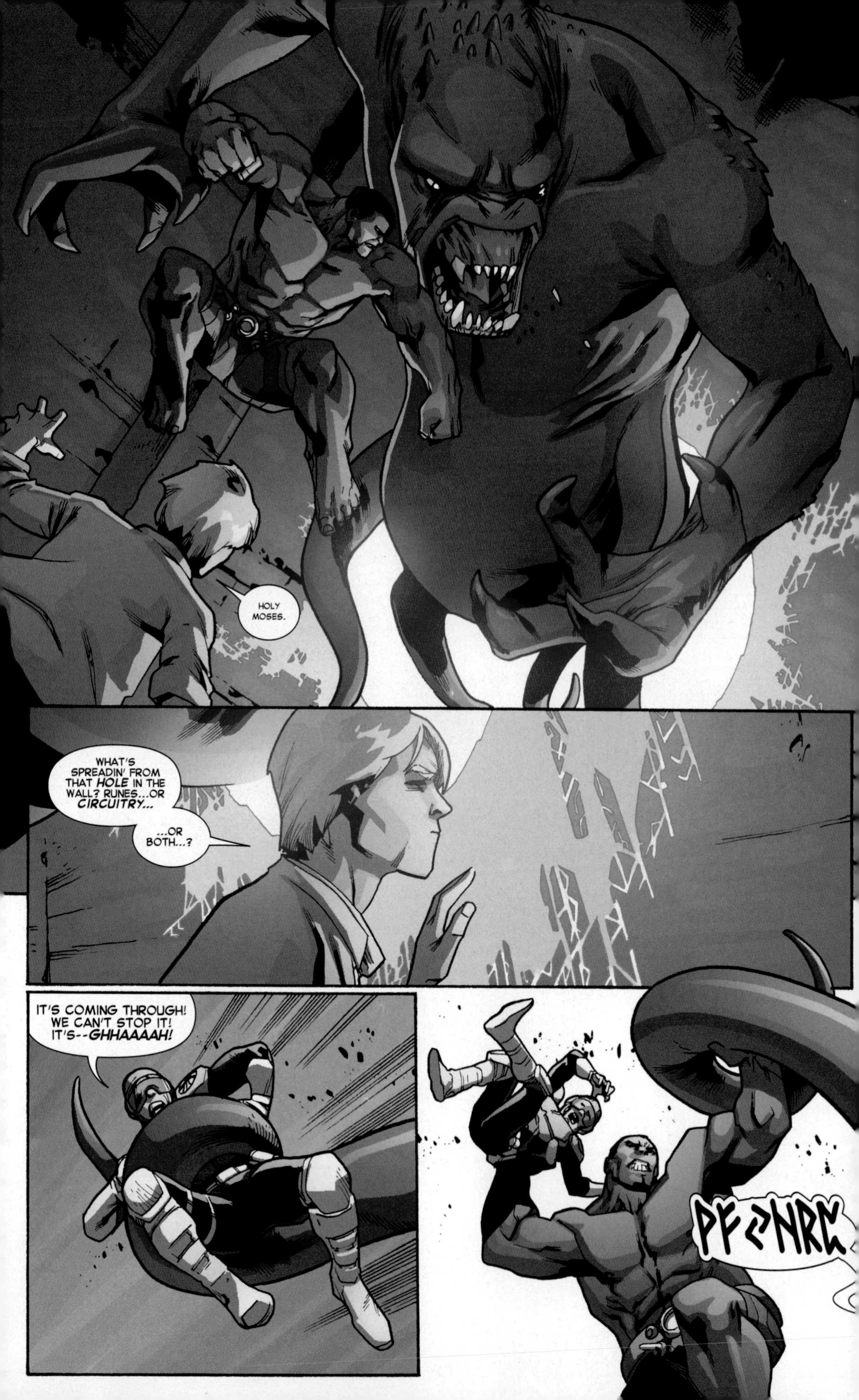
HOLY MOSES.
WHAT'S SPREADIN' FROM THAT HOLE IN THE WALL? RUNES...OR CIRCUITRY...
...OR BOTH...?
IT'S COMING THROUGH! WE CAN'T STOP IT! IT'S--GHHAAAAH!

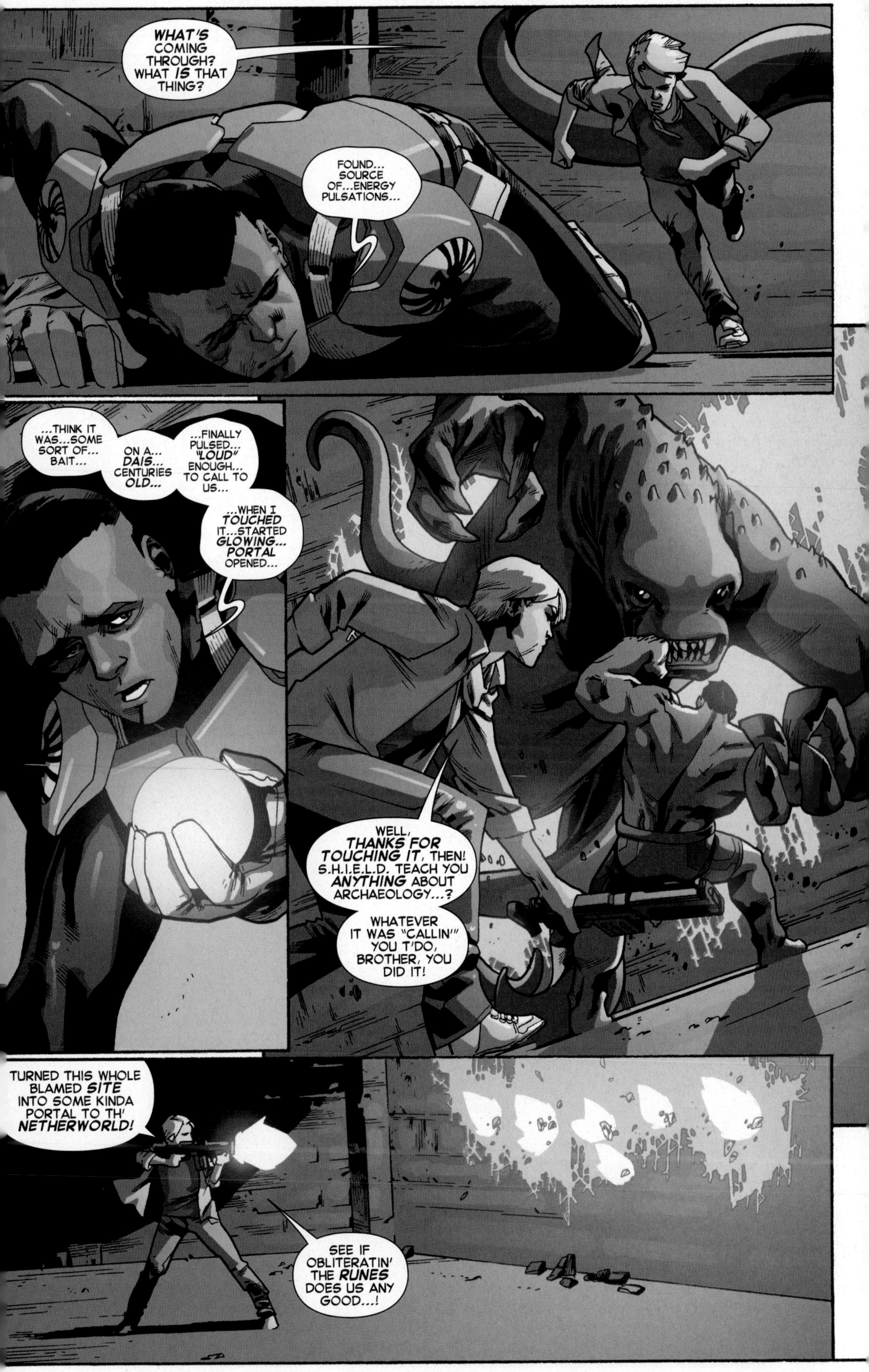
WHAT'S COMING THROUGH? WHAT IS THAT THING?
FOUND... SOURCE OF...ENERGY PULSATIONS...
...THINK IT WAS...SOME SORT OF... BAIT...
ON A... DAIS... CENTURIES OLD...
...FINALLY PULSED... "LOUD" ENOUGH... TO CALL TO US...
...WHEN I TOUCHED IT...STARTED GLOWING... PORTAL OPENED...
WELL, THANKS FOR TOUCHING IT, THEN! S.H.I.E.L.D. TEACH YOU ANYTHING ABOUT ARCHAEOLOGY...?
WHATEVER IT WAS "CALLIN'" YOU T'DO, BROTHER, YOU DID IT!
TURNED THIS WHOLE BLAMED SITE INTO SOME KINDA PORTAL TO TH' NETHERWORLD!
SEE IF OBLITERATIN' THE RUNES DOES US ANY GOOD...!

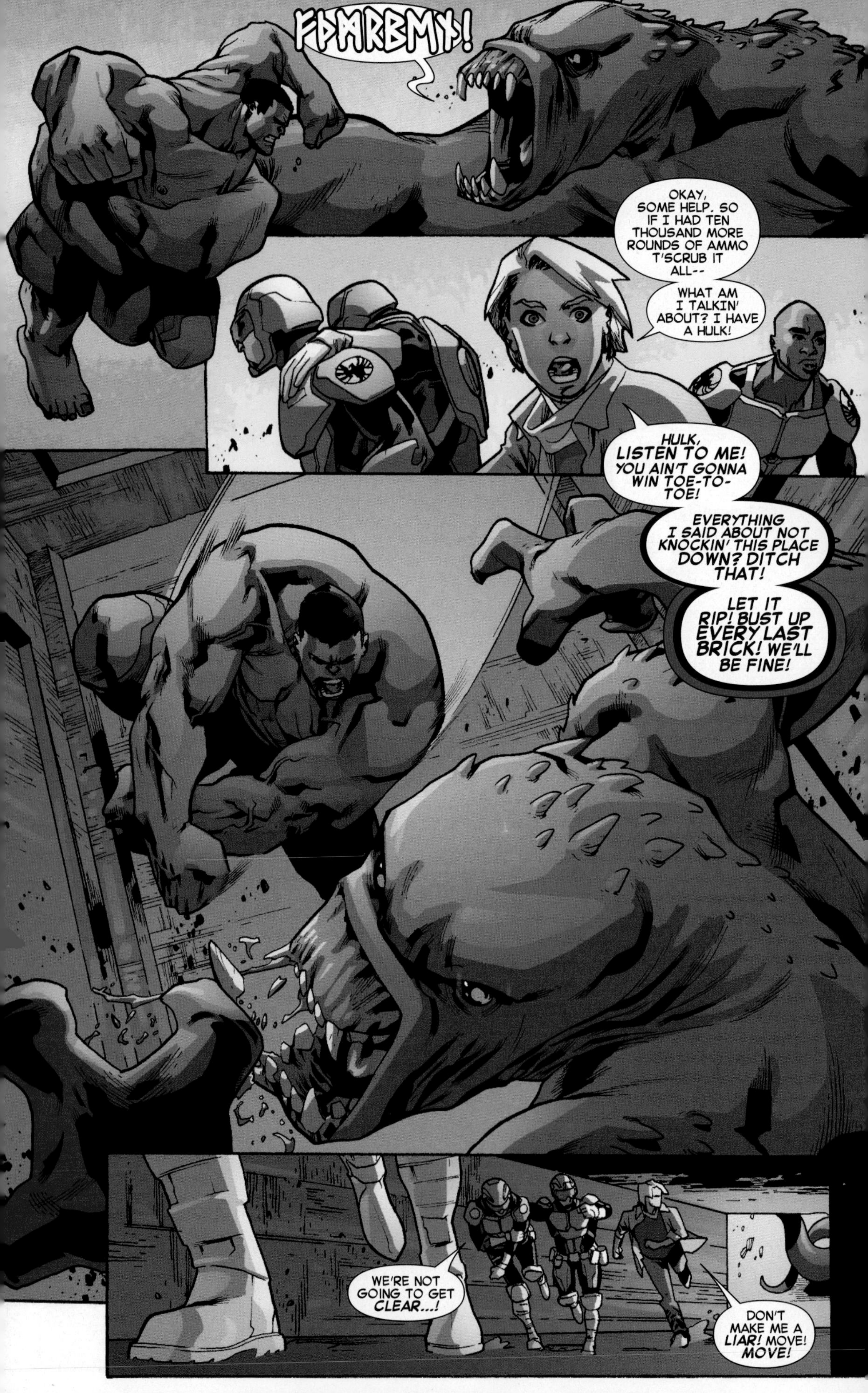

OKAY, SOME HELP. SO IF I HAD TEN THOUSAND MORE ROUNDS OF AMMO T'SCRUB IT ALL--
WHAT AM I TALKIN' ABOUT? I HAVE A HULK!
HULK, LISTEN TO ME! YOU AIN'T GONNA WIN TOE-TO-TOE!
EVERYTHING I SAID ABOUT NOT KNOCKIN' THIS PLACE DOWN? DITCH THAT!
LET IT RIP! BUST UP EVERY LAST BRICK! WE'LL BE FINE!
WE'RE NOT GOING TO GET CLEAR...!
DON'T MAKE ME A LIAR! MOVE! MOVE!

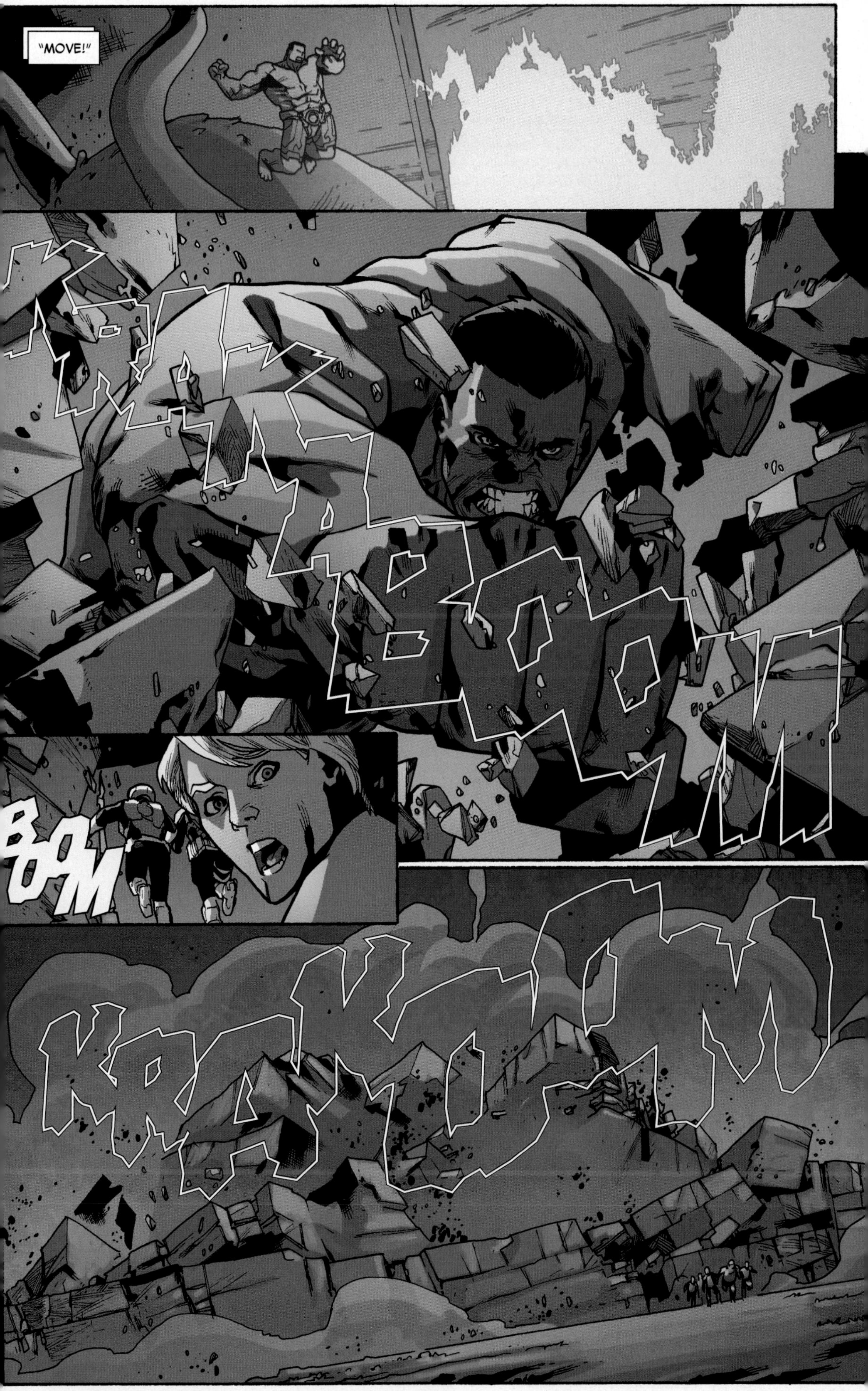
"MOVE!"
KA-BOOM
BOOM
KRAKOOOM

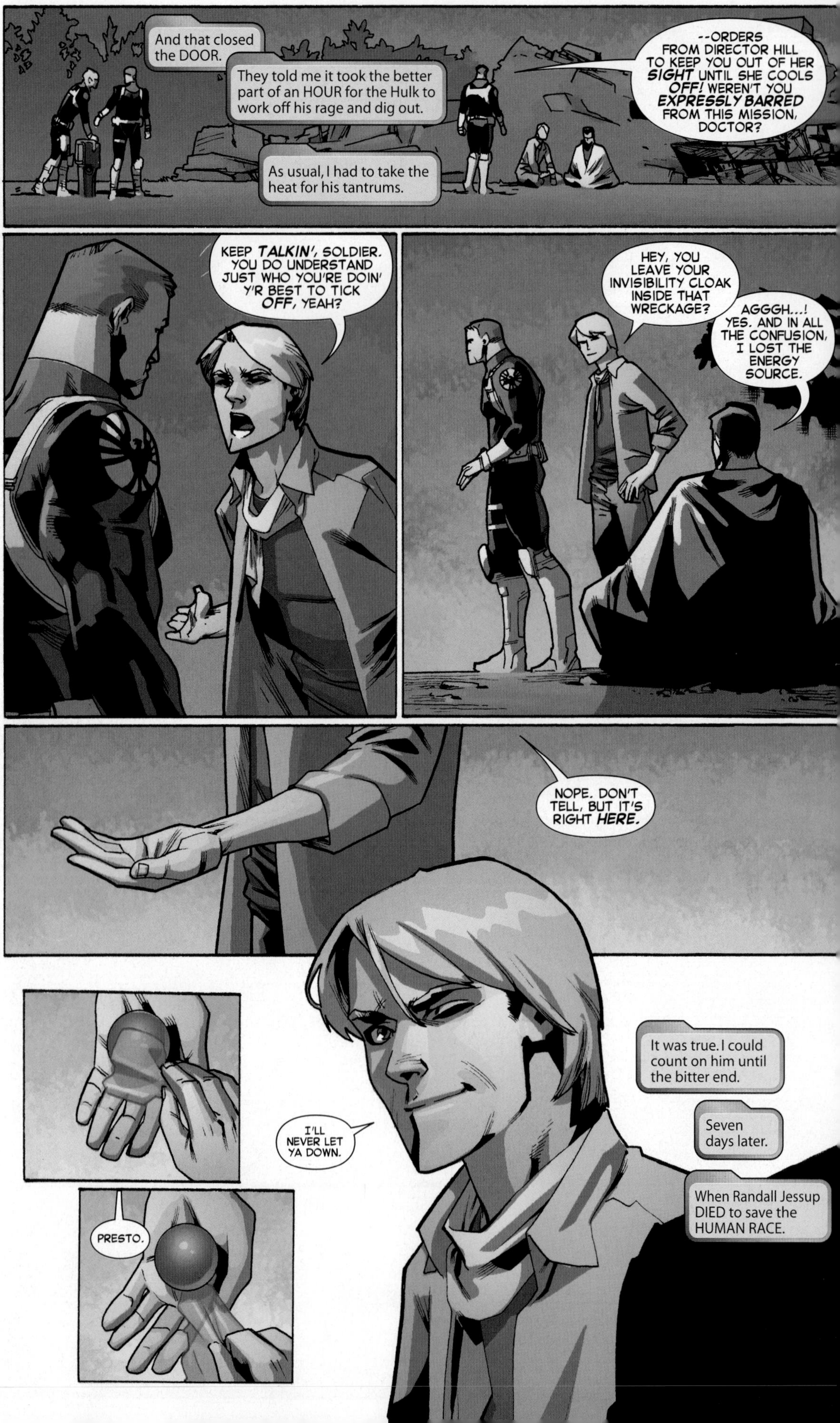

And that closed the DOOR.
They told me it took the better part of an HOUR for the Hulk to work off his rage and dig out.
As usual, I had to take the heat for his tantrums.
--ORDERS FROM DIRECTOR HILL TO KEEP YOU OUT OF HER SIGHT UNTIL SHE COOLS OFF! WEREN'T YOU EXPRESSLY BARRED FROM THIS MISSION, DOCTOR?
KEEP TALKIN', SOLDIER. YOU DO UNDERSTAND JUST WHO YOU'RE DOIN' Y'R BEST TO TICK OFF, YEAH?
HEY, YOU LEAVE YOUR INVISIBILITY CLOAK INSIDE THAT WRECKAGE?
AGGGH...! YES. AND IN ALL THE CONFUSION, I LOST THE ENERGY SOURCE.
NOPE. DON'T TELL, BUT IT'S RIGHT HERE.
PRESTO.
I'LL NEVER LET YA DOWN.
It was true. I could count on him until the bitter end.
Seven days later.
When Randall Jessup DIED to save the HUMAN RACE.

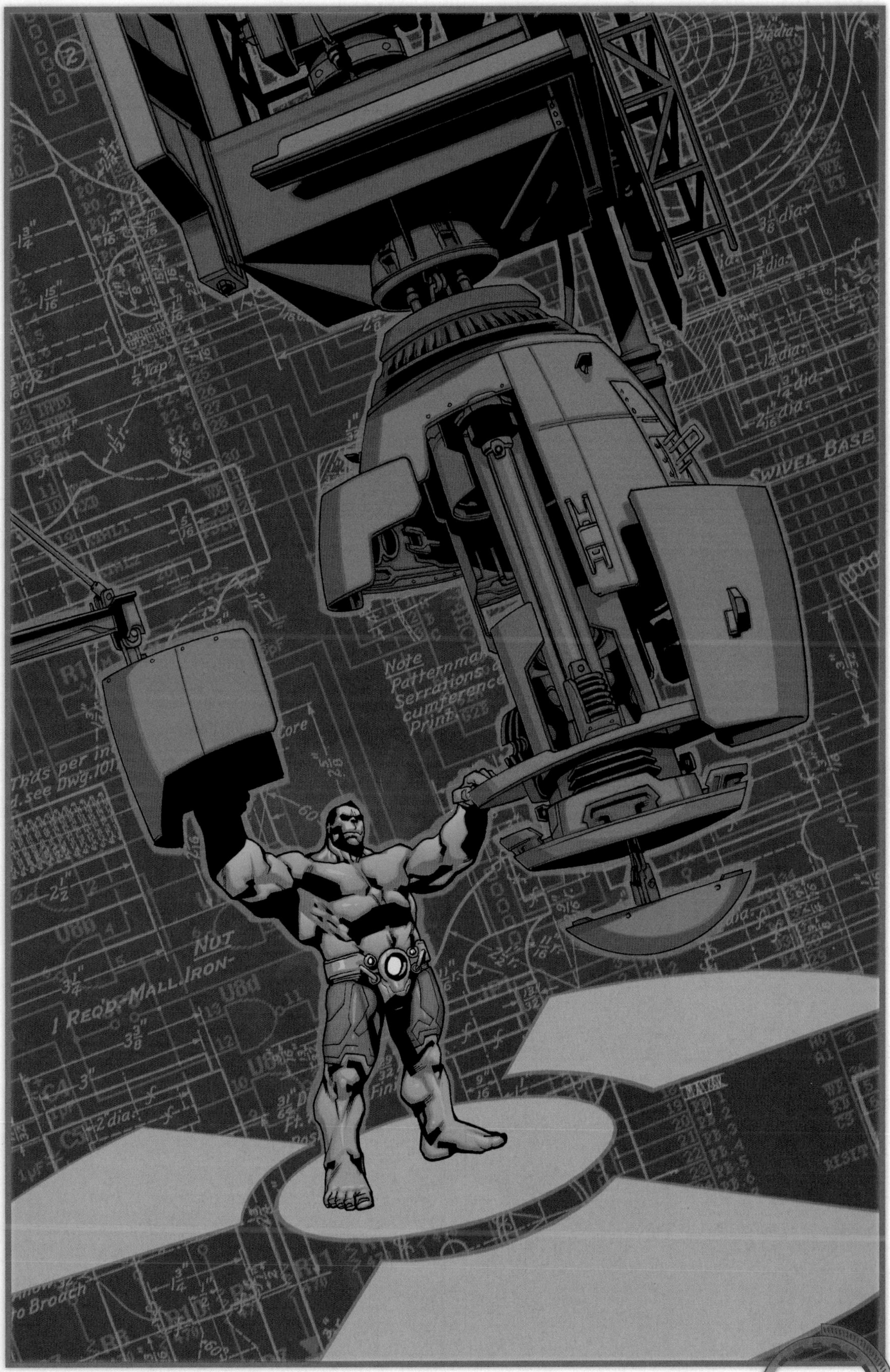
SWIVEL BASE
NUT
1 REQ'D.-MALL.IRON-

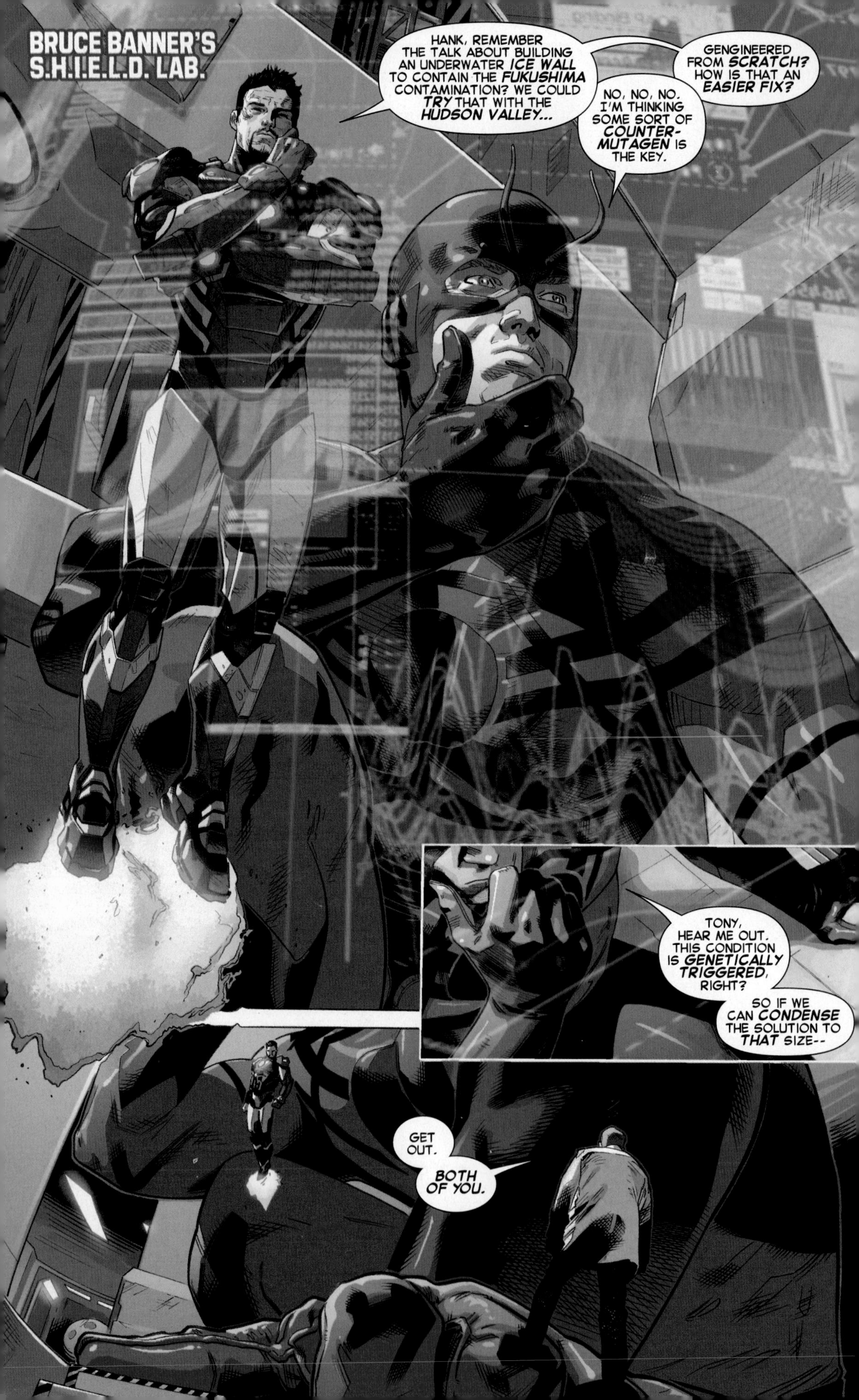
BRUCE BANNER'S S.H.I.E.L.D. LAB.
HANK, REMEMBER THE TALK ABOUT BUILDING AN UNDERWATER ICE WALL TO CONTAIN THE FUKUSHIMA CONTAMINATION? WE COULD TRY THAT WITH THE HUDSON VALLEY...
GENGINEERED FROM SCRATCH? HOW IS THAT AN EASIER FIX?
NO, NO, NO. I'M THINKING SOME SORT OF COUNTER-MUTAGEN IS THE KEY.
TONY, HEAR ME OUT. THIS CONDITION IS GENETICALLY TRIGGERED, RIGHT?
SO IF WE CAN CONDENSE THE SOLUTION TO THAT SIZE--
GET OUT.
BOTH OF YOU.

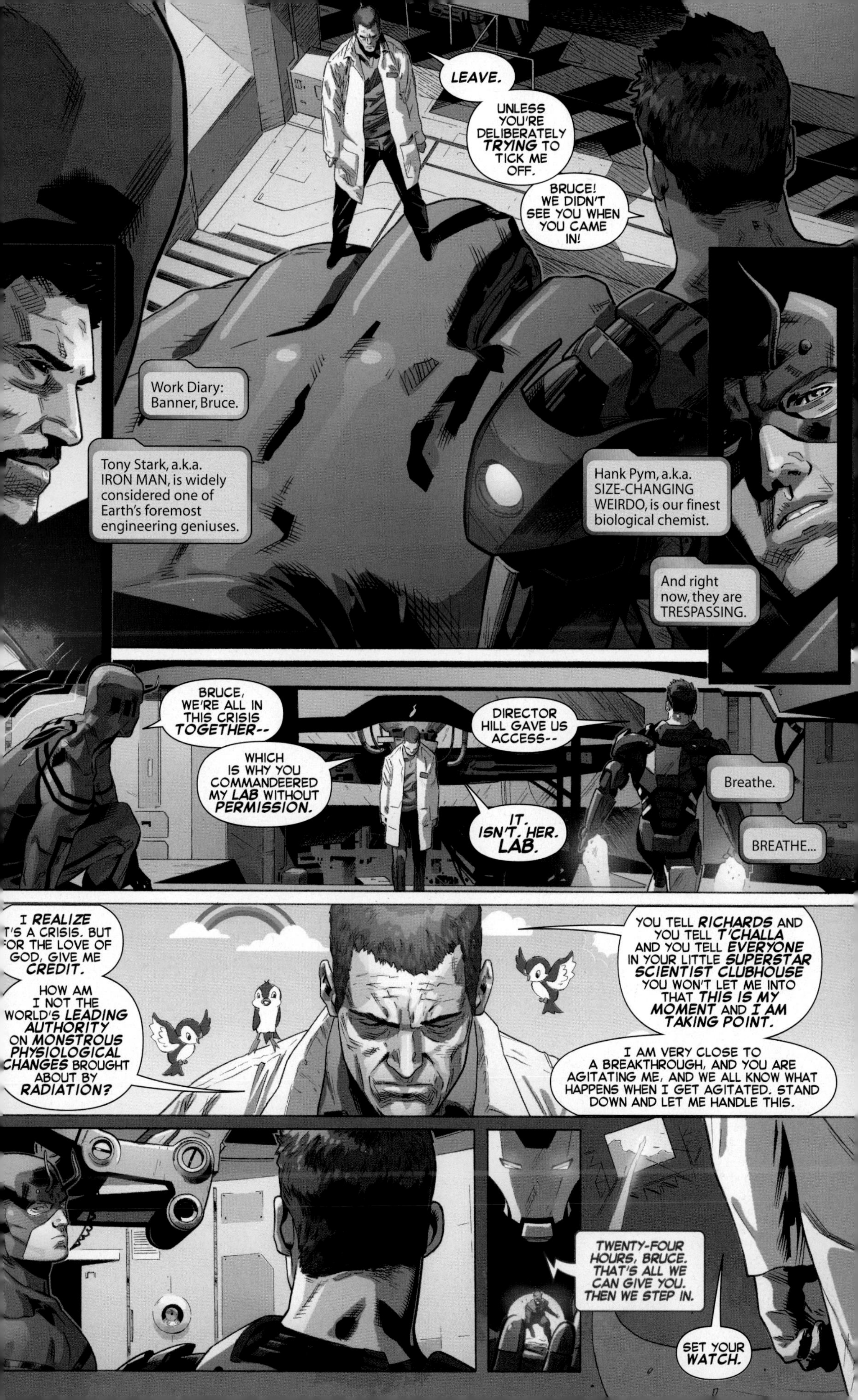
LEAVE.
UNLESS YOU'RE DELIBERATELY TRYING TO TICK ME OFF.
BRUCE! WE DIDN'T SEE YOU WHEN YOU CAME IN!
Work Diary: Banner, Bruce.
Tony Stark, a.k.a. IRON MAN, is widely considered one of Earth's foremost engineering geniuses.
Hank Pym, a.k.a. SIZE-CHANGING WEIRDO, is our finest biological chemist.
And right now, they are TRESPASSING.
BRUCE, WE'RE ALL IN THIS CRISIS TOGETHER--
DIRECTOR HILL GAVE US ACCESS--
WHICH IS WHY YOU COMMANDEERED MY LAB WITHOUT PERMISSION.
IT. ISN'T. HER. LAB.
Breathe.
BREATHE...
I REALIZE IT'S A CRISIS. BUT FOR THE LOVE OF GOD, GIVE ME CREDIT.
HOW AM I NOT THE WORLD'S LEADING AUTHORITY ON MONSTROUS PHYSIOLOGICAL CHANGES BROUGHT ABOUT BY RADIATION?
YOU TELL RICHARDS AND YOU TELL T'CHALLA AND YOU TELL EVERYONE IN YOUR LITTLE SUPERSTAR SCIENTIST CLUBHOUSE YOU WON'T LET ME INTO THAT THIS IS MY MOMENT AND I AM TAKING POINT.
I AM VERY CLOSE TO A BREAKTHROUGH, AND YOU ARE AGITATING ME, AND WE ALL KNOW WHAT HAPPENS WHEN I GET AGITATED. STAND DOWN AND LET ME HANDLE THIS.
TWENTY-FOUR HOURS, BRUCE. THAT'S ALL WE CAN GIVE YOU. THEN WE STEP IN.
SET YOUR WATCH.

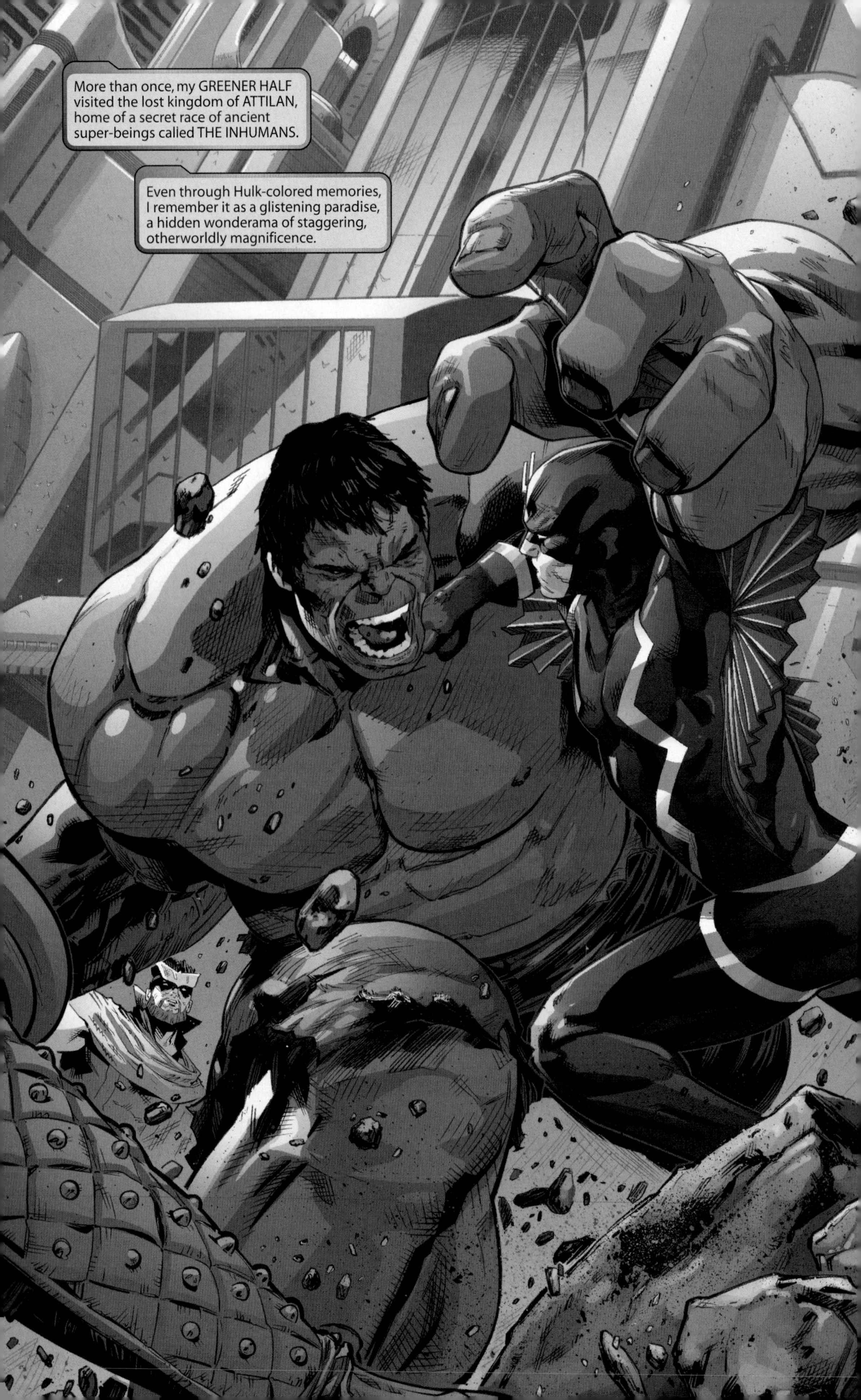
More than once, my GREENER HALF visited the lost kingdom of ATTILAN, home of a secret race of ancient super-beings called THE INHUMANS.
Even through Hulk-colored memories, I remember it as a glistening paradise, a hidden wonderama of staggering, otherworldly magnificence.

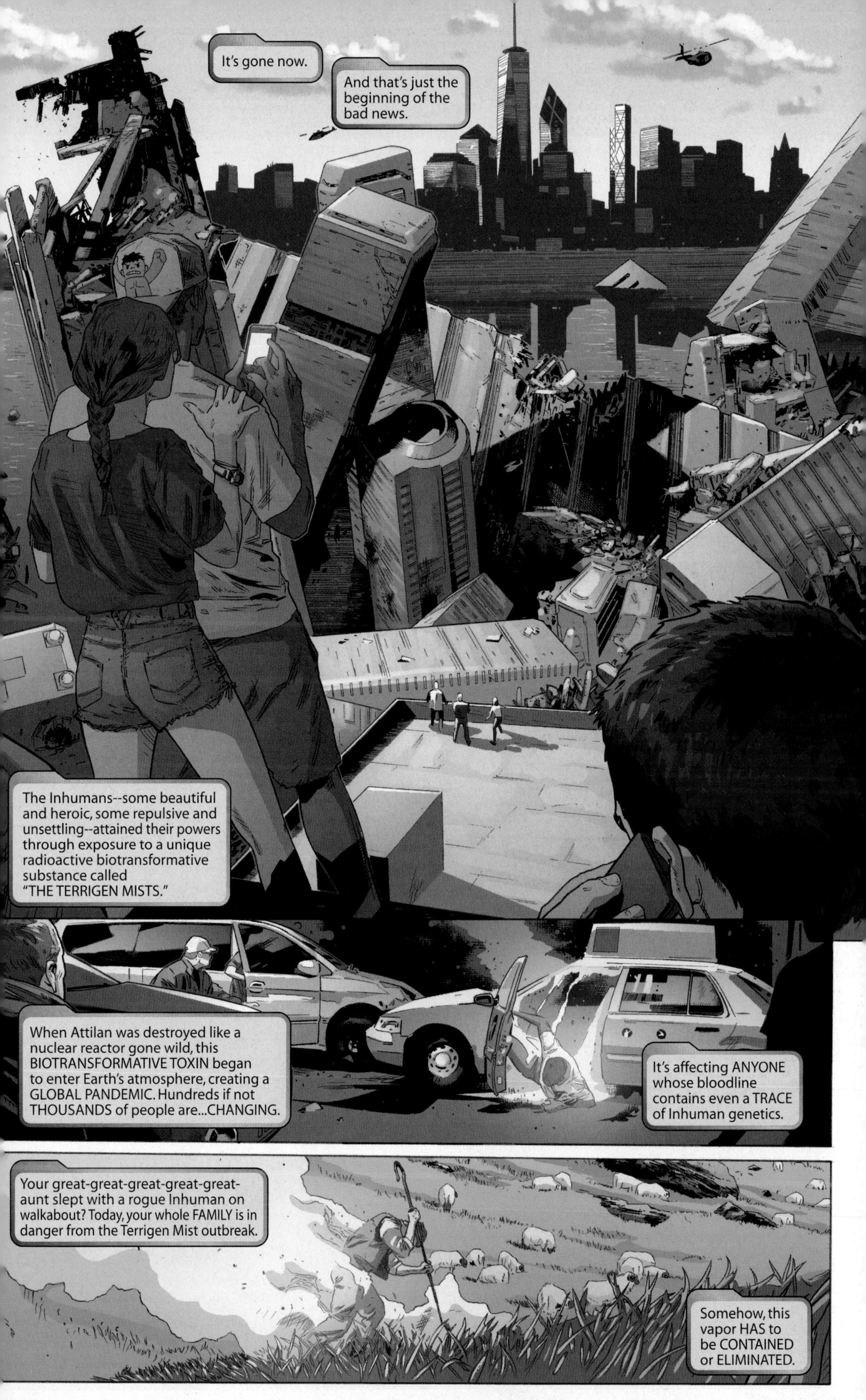
It's gone now.
And that's just the beginning of the bad news.
The Inhumans--some beautiful and heroic, some repulsive and unsettling--attained their powers through exposure to a unique radioactive biotransformative substance called "THE TERRIGEN MISTS."
When Attilan was destroyed like a nuclear reactor gone wild, this BIOTRANSFORMATIVE TOXIN began to enter Earth's atmosphere, creating a GLOBAL PANDEMIC. Hundreds if not THOUSANDS of people are...CHANGING.
It's affecting ANYONE whose bloodline contains even a TRACE of Inhuman genetics.
Your great-great-great-great-great-aunt slept with a rogue Inhuman on walkabout? Today, your whole FAMILY is in danger from the Terrigen Mist outbreak.
Somehow, this vapor HAS to be CONTAINED or ELIMINATED.

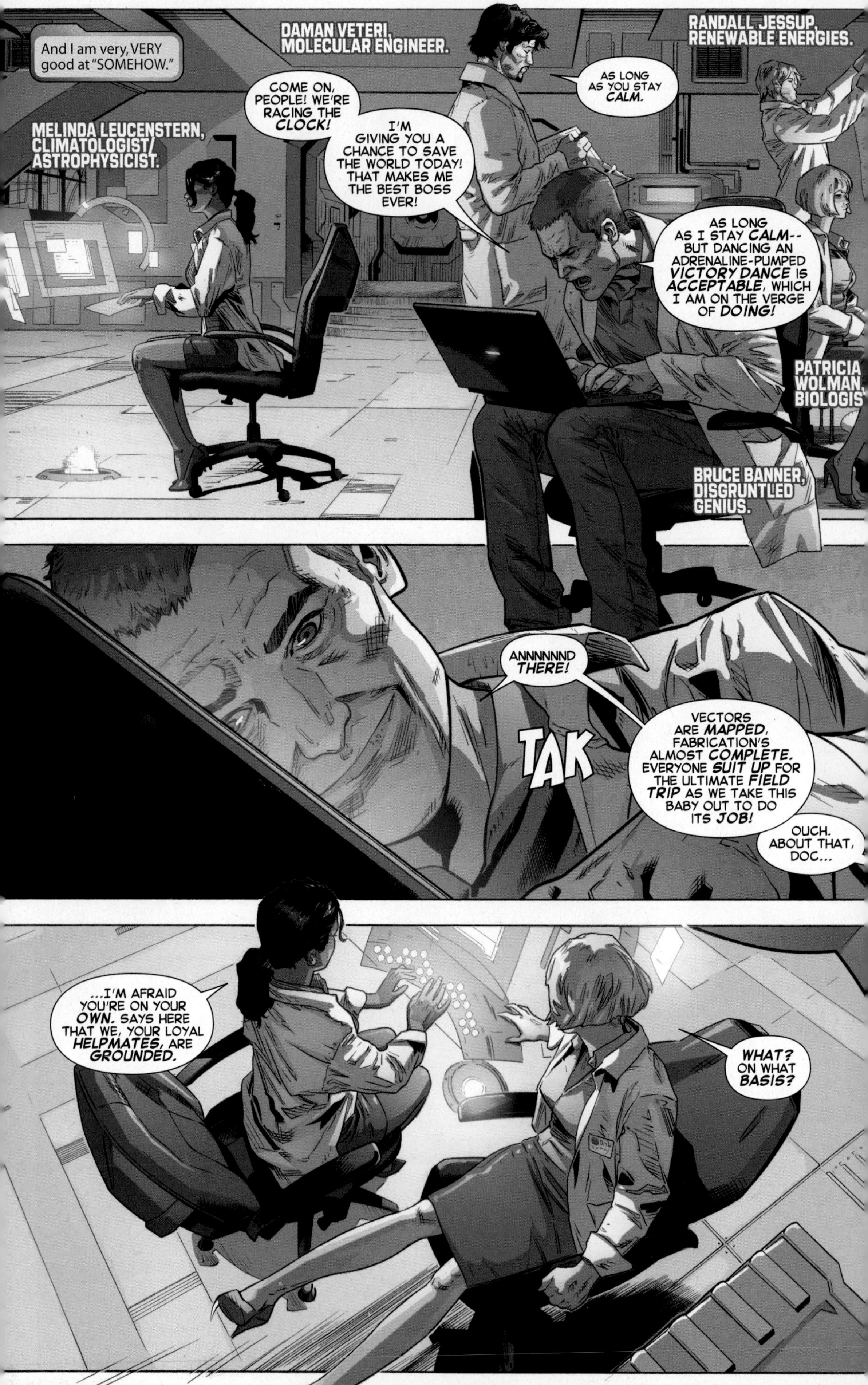
And I am very, VERY good at "SOMEHOW."
DAMAN VETERI, MOLECULAR ENGINEER.
RANDALL JESSUP, RENEWABLE ENERGIES.
MELINDA LEUCENSTERN, CLIMATOLOGIST/ ASTROPHYSICIST.
COME ON, PEOPLE! WE'RE RACING THE CLOCK!
I'M GIVING YOU A CHANCE TO SAVE THE WORLD TODAY! THAT MAKES ME THE BEST BOSS EVER!
AS LONG AS YOU STAY CALM.
AS LONG AS I STAY CALM-- BUT DANCING AN ADRENALINE-PUMPED VICTORY DANCE IS ACCEPTABLE, WHICH I AM ON THE VERGE OF DOING!
PATRICIA WOLMAN, BIOLOGIS
BRUCE BANNER, DISGRUNTLED GENIUS.
ANNNNNND THERE!
TAK
VECTORS ARE MAPPED, FABRICATION'S ALMOST COMPLETE. EVERYONE SUIT UP FOR THE ULTIMATE FIELD TRIP AS WE TAKE THIS BABY OUT TO DO ITS JOB!
OUCH. ABOUT THAT, DOC...
...I'M AFRAID YOU'RE ON YOUR OWN. SAYS HERE THAT WE, YOUR LOYAL HELPMATES, ARE GROUNDED.
WHAT? ON WHAT BASIS?

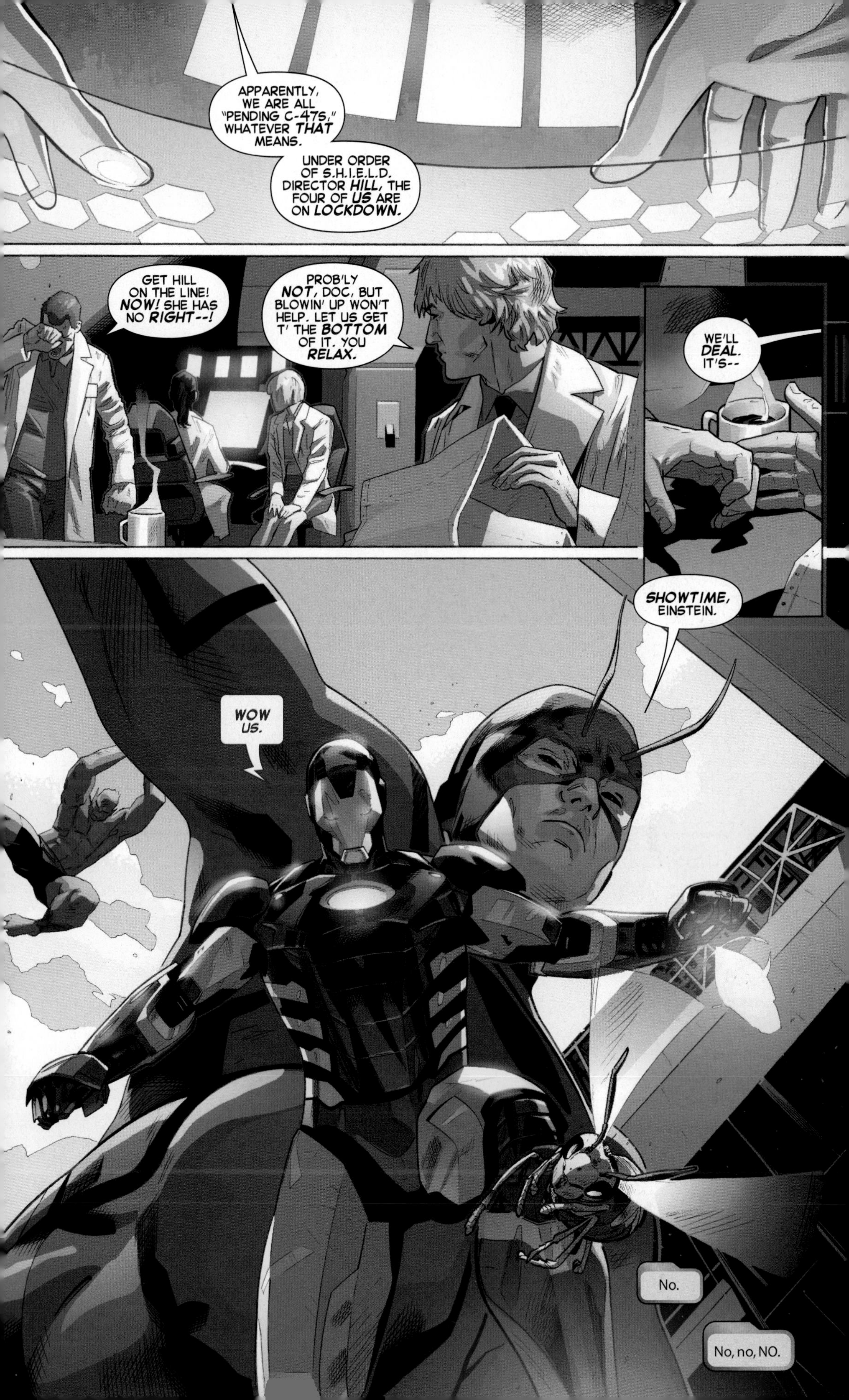
APPARENTLY, WE ARE ALL "PENDING C-47S," WHATEVER THAT MEANS.
UNDER ORDER OF S.H.I.E.L.D. DIRECTOR HILL, THE FOUR OF US ARE ON LOCKDOWN.
GET HILL ON THE LINE! NOW! SHE HAS NO RIGHT--!
PROB'LY NOT, DOC, BUT BLOWIN' UP WON'T HELP. LET US GET T' THE BOTTOM OF IT. YOU RELAX.
WE'LL DEAL. IT'S--
SHOWTIME, EINSTEIN.
WOW US.
No.
No, no, NO.

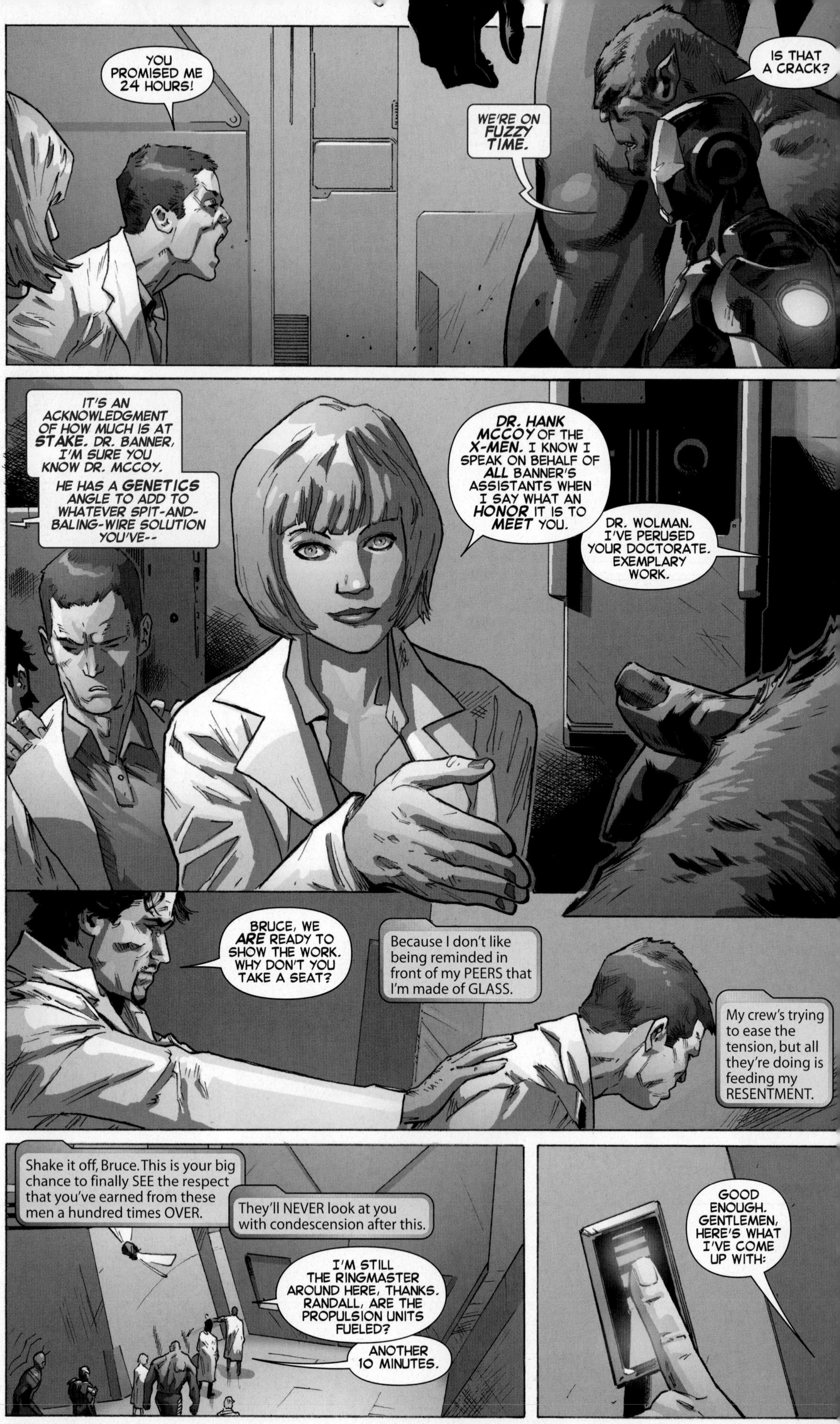
YOU PROMISED ME 24 HOURS!
WE'RE ON FUZZY TIME.
IS THAT A CRACK?
IT'S AN ACKNOWLEDGMENT OF HOW MUCH IS AT STAKE. DR. BANNER, I'M SURE YOU KNOW DR. MCCOY.
HE HAS A GENETICS ANGLE TO ADD TO WHATEVER SPIT-AND-BALING-WIRE SOLUTION YOU'VE--
DR. HANK MCCOY OF THE X-MEN. I KNOW I SPEAK ON BEHALF OF ALL BANNER'S ASSISTANTS WHEN I SAY WHAT AN HONOR IT IS TO MEET YOU.
DR. WOLMAN. I'VE PERUSED YOUR DOCTORATE. EXEMPLARY WORK.
BRUCE, WE ARE READY TO SHOW THE WORK. WHY DON'T YOU TAKE A SEAT?
Because I don't like being reminded in front of my PEERS that I'm made of GLASS.
My crew's trying to ease the tension, but all they're doing is feeding my RESENTMENT.
Shake it off, Bruce. This is your big chance to finally SEE the respect that you've earned from these men a hundred times OVER.
They'll NEVER look at you with condescension after this.
I'M STILL THE RINGMASTER AROUND HERE, THANKS. RANDALL, ARE THE PROPULSION UNITS FUELED?
ANOTHER 10 MINUTES.
GOOD ENOUGH. GENTLEMEN, HERE'S WHAT I'VE COME UP WITH:

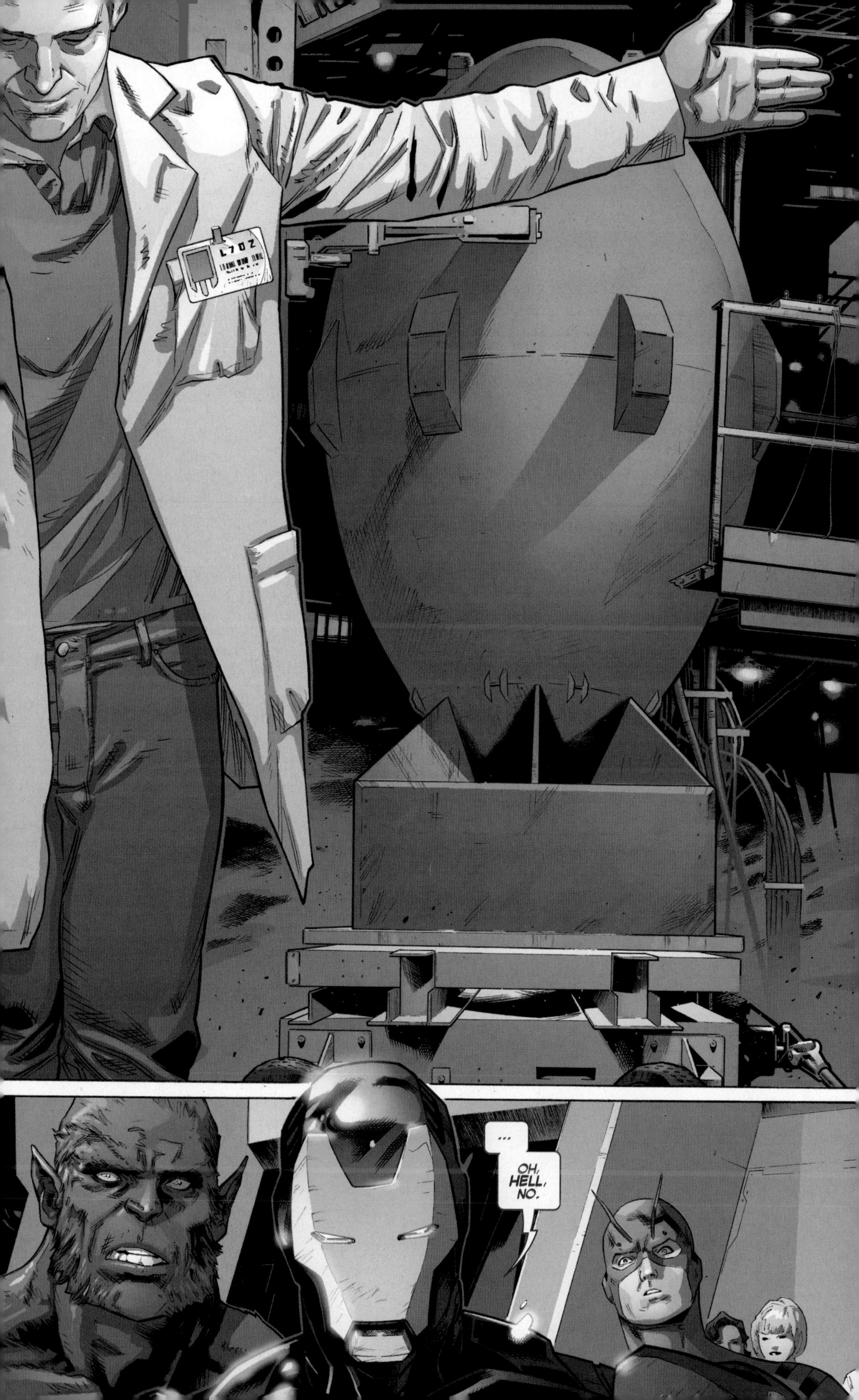
...
OH, HELL, NO.

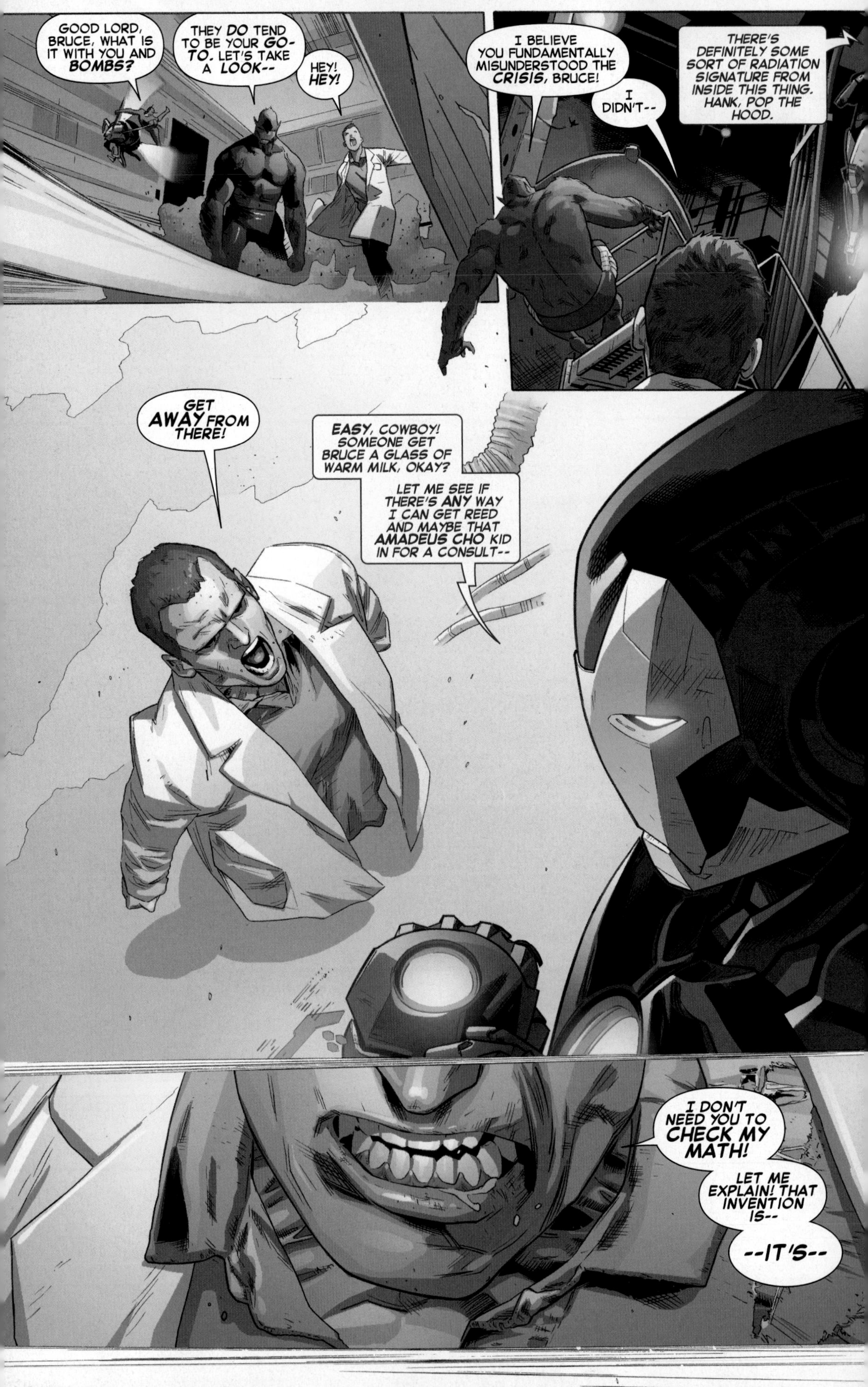
GOOD LORD, BRUCE, WHAT IS IT WITH YOU AND BOMBS?
THEY DO TEND TO BE YOUR GO-TO. LET'S TAKE A LOOK--
HEY! HEY!
I BELIEVE YOU FUNDAMENTALLY MISUNDERSTOOD THE CRISIS, BRUCE!
I DIDN'T--
THERE'S DEFINITELY SOME SORT OF RADIATION SIGNATURE FROM INSIDE THIS THING. HANK, POP THE HOOD.
GET AWAY FROM THERE!
EASY, COWBOY! SOMEONE GET BRUCE A GLASS OF WARM MILK, OKAY?
LET ME SEE IF THERE'S ANY WAY I CAN GET REED AND MAYBE THAT AMADEUS CHO KID IN FOR A CONSULT--
I DON'T NEED YOU TO CHECK MY MATH!
LET ME EXPLAIN! THAT INVENTION IS--
--IT'S--

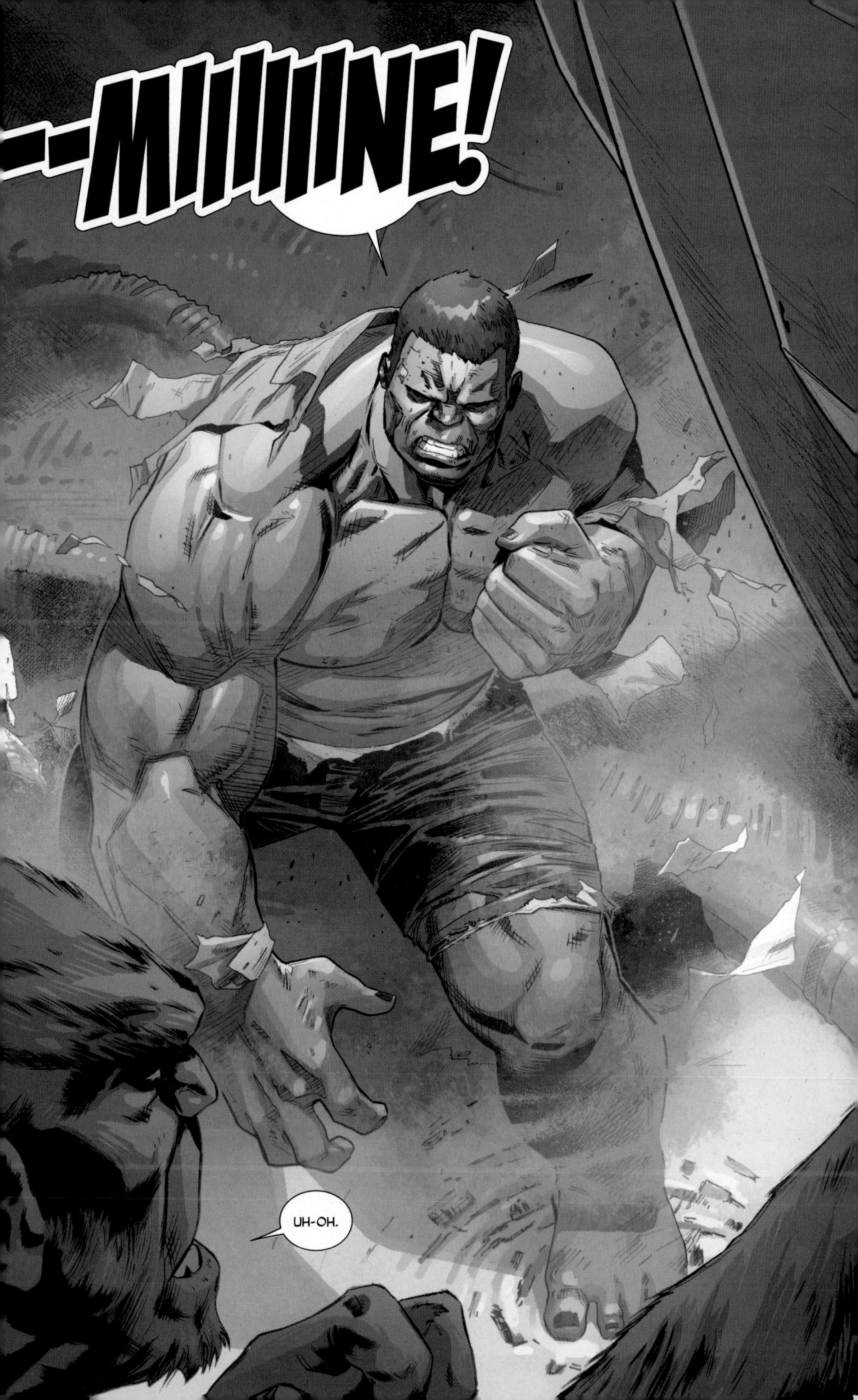
--MIIIIINE!
UH-OH.

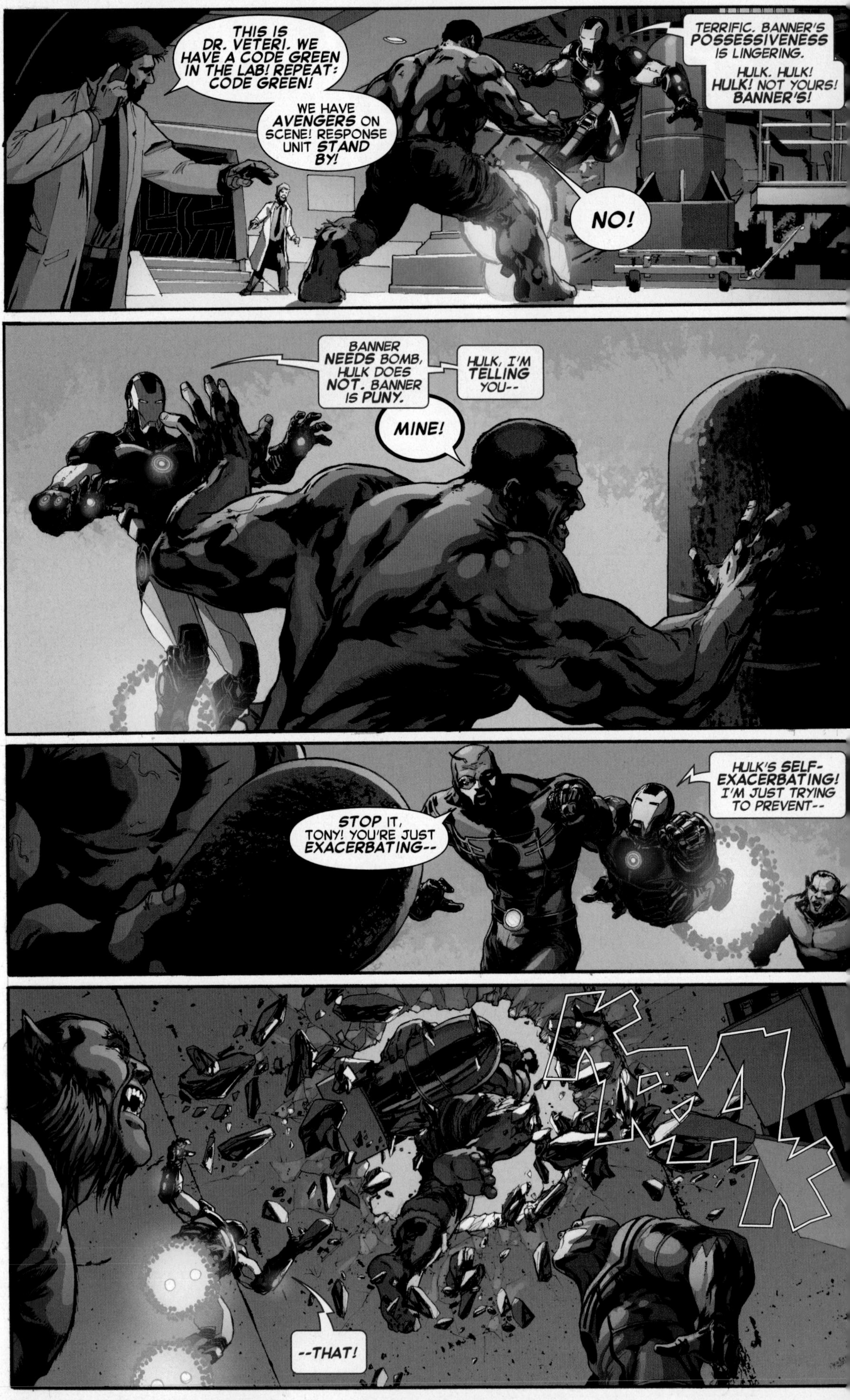
THIS IS DR. VETERI. WE HAVE A CODE GREEN IN THE LAB! REPEAT: CODE GREEN!
WE HAVE AVENGERS ON SCENE! RESPONSE UNIT STAND BY!
TERRIFIC. BANNER'S POSSESSIVENESS IS LINGERING.
HULK. HULK! HULK! NOT YOURS! BANNER'S!
NO!
BANNER NEEDS BOMB, HULK DOES NOT. BANNER IS PUNY.
HULK, I'M TELLING YOU--
MINE!
STOP IT, TONY! YOU'RE JUST EXACERBATING--
HULK'S SELF-EXACERBATING! I'M JUST TRYING TO PREVENT--
--THAT!

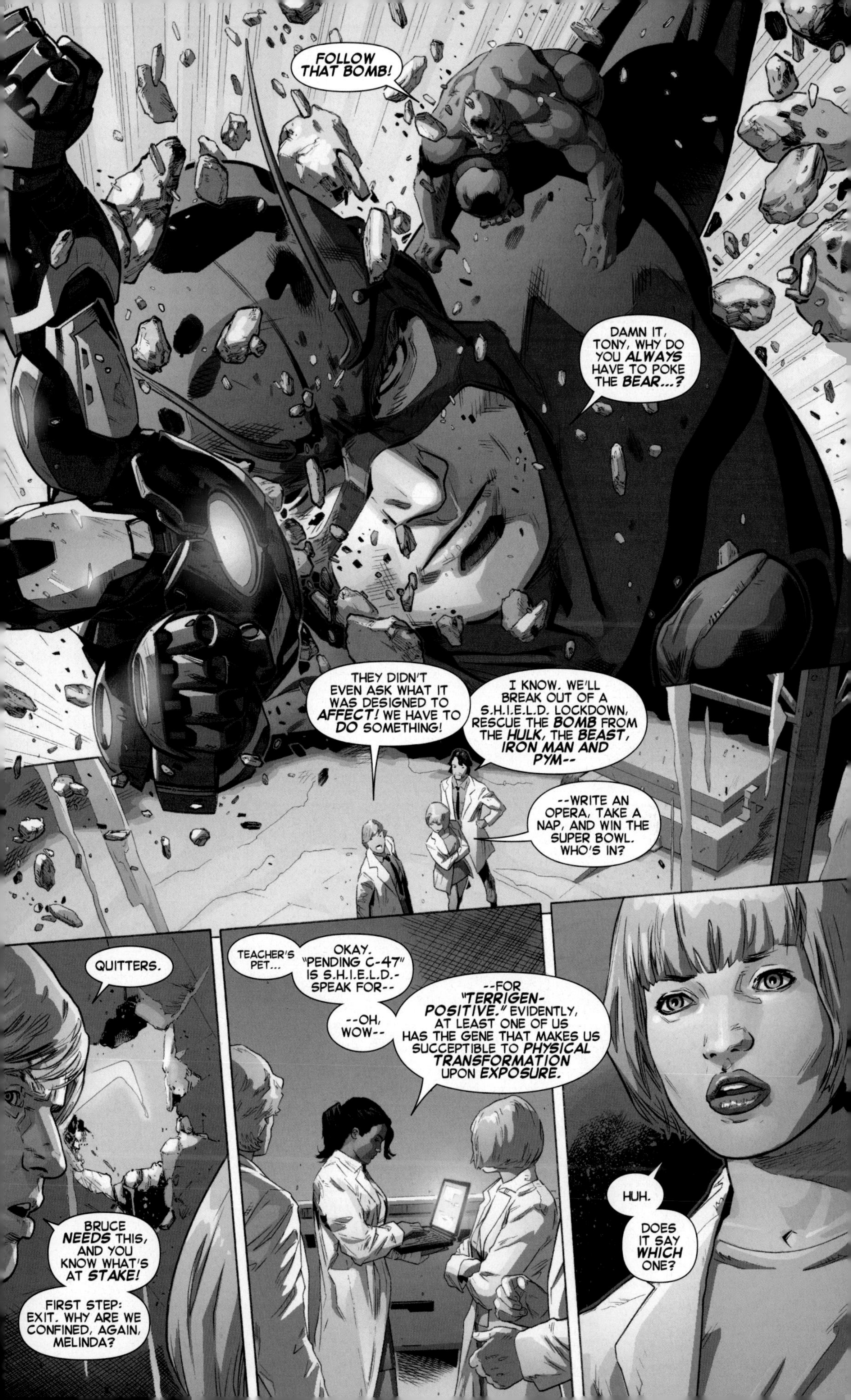
FOLLOW THAT BOMB!
DAMN IT, TONY, WHY DO YOU ALWAYS HAVE TO POKE THE BEAR...?
THEY DIDN'T EVEN ASK WHAT IT WAS DESIGNED TO AFFECT! WE HAVE TO DO SOMETHING!
I KNOW. WE'LL BREAK OUT OF A S.H.I.E.L.D. LOCKDOWN, RESCUE THE BOMB FROM THE HULK, THE BEAST, IRON MAN AND PYM--
--WRITE AN OPERA, TAKE A NAP, AND WIN THE SUPER BOWL. WHO'S IN?
QUITTERS.
BRUCE NEEDS THIS, AND YOU KNOW WHAT'S AT STAKE!
FIRST STEP: EXIT. WHY ARE WE CONFINED, AGAIN, MELINDA?
TEACHER'S PET...
OKAY. "PENDING C-47" IS S.H.I.E.L.D.-SPEAK FOR--
--OH, WOW--
--FOR "TERRIGEN-POSITIVE." EVIDENTLY, AT LEAST ONE OF US HAS THE GENE THAT MAKES US SUCCEPTIBLE TO PHYSICAL TRANSFORMATION UPON EXPOSURE.
HUH.
DOES IT SAY WHICH ONE?

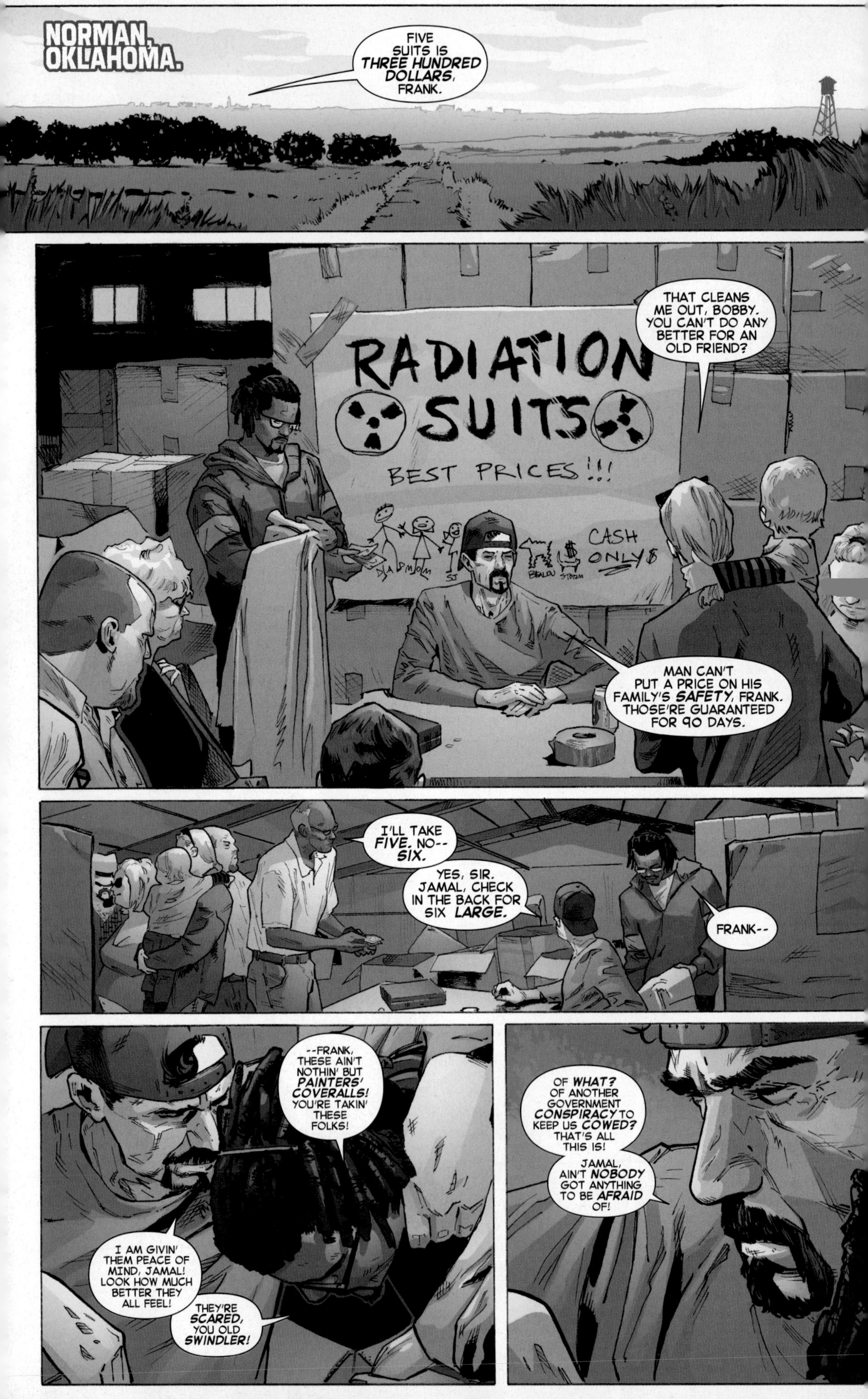
NORMAN, OKLAHOMA.
FIVE SUITS IS THREE HUNDRED DOLLARS, FRANK.
RADIATION SUITS
BEST PRICES!!!
CASH ONLY
THAT CLEANS ME OUT, BOBBY. YOU CAN'T DO ANY BETTER FOR AN OLD FRIEND?
MAN CAN'T PUT A PRICE ON HIS FAMILY'S SAFETY, FRANK. THOSE'RE GUARANTEED FOR 90 DAYS.
I'LL TAKE FIVE. NO-- SIX.
YES, SIR. JAMAL, CHECK IN THE BACK FOR SIX LARGE.
FRANK--
--FRANK, THESE AIN'T NOTHIN' BUT PAINTERS' COVERALLS! YOU'RE TAKIN' THESE FOLKS!
I AM GIVIN' THEM PEACE OF MIND, JAMAL! LOOK HOW MUCH BETTER THEY ALL FEEL!
THEY'RE SCARED, YOU OLD SWINDLER!
OF WHAT? OF ANOTHER GOVERNMENT CONSPIRACY TO KEEP US COWED? THAT'S ALL THIS IS!
JAMAL, AIN'T NOBODY GOT ANYTHING TO BE AFRAID OF!

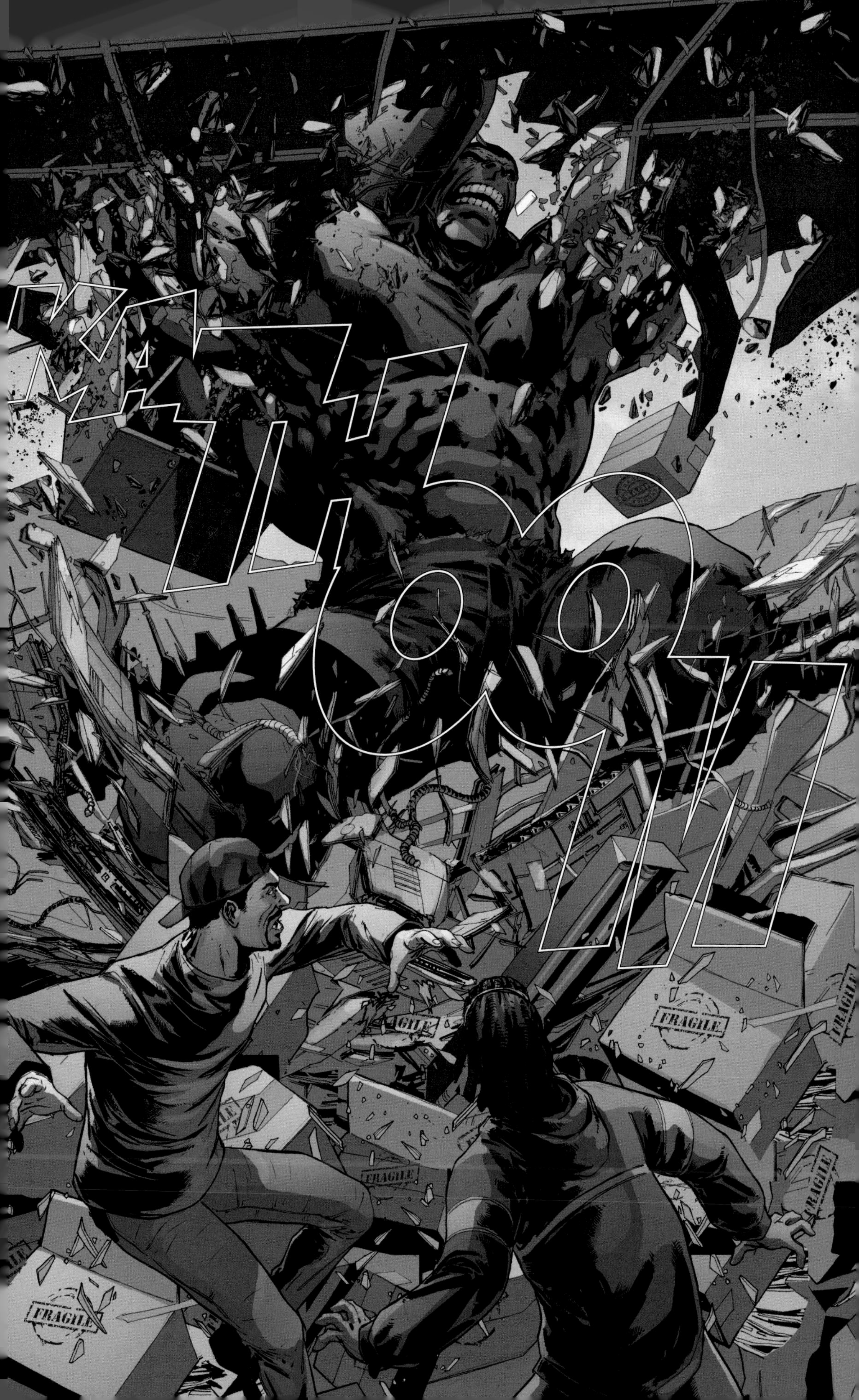
FRAGILE
FRAGILE
FRAGILE
FRAGILE
FRAGILE

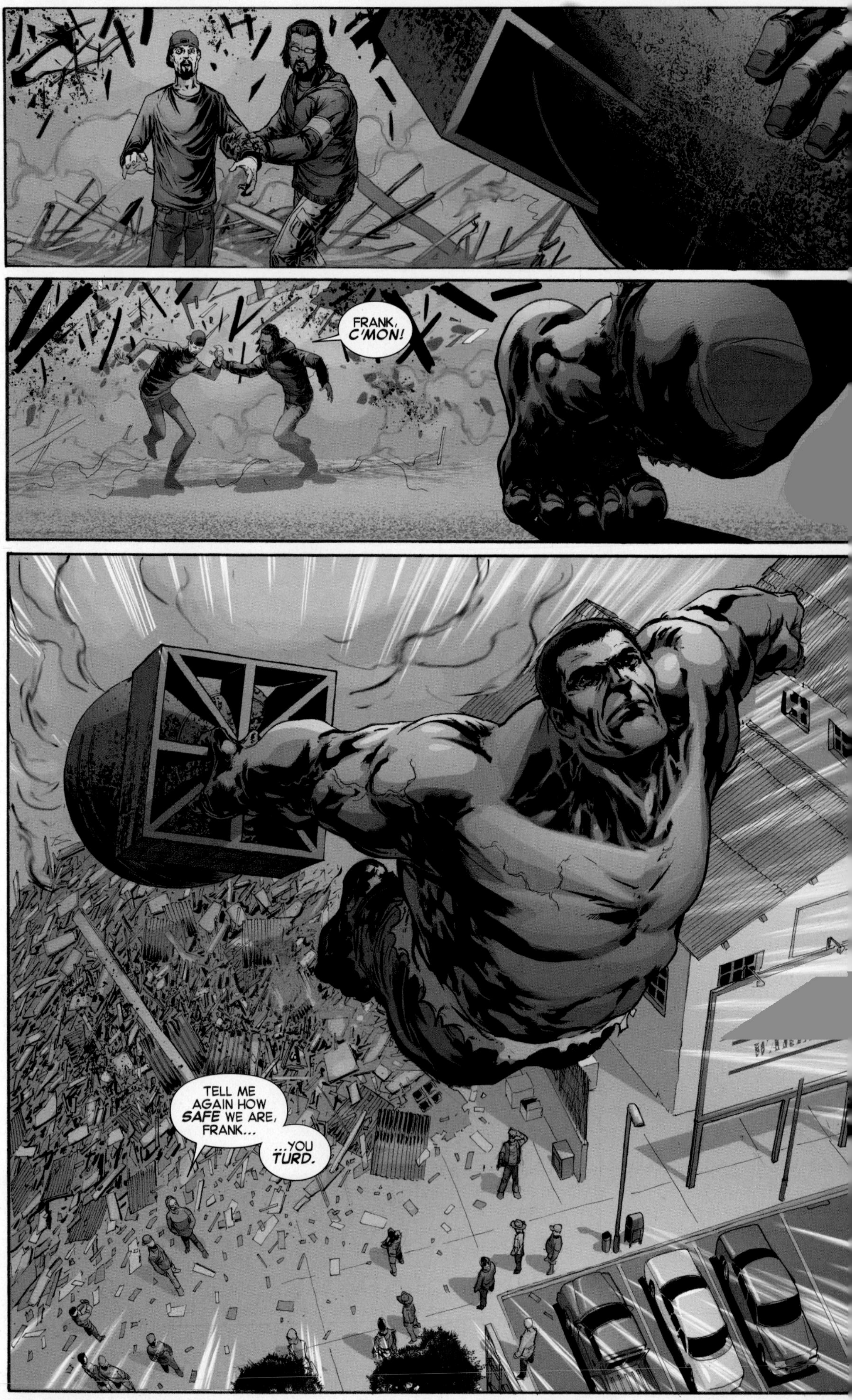
FRANK, C'MON!
TELL ME AGAIN HOW SAFE WE ARE, FRANK...
...YOU TURD.

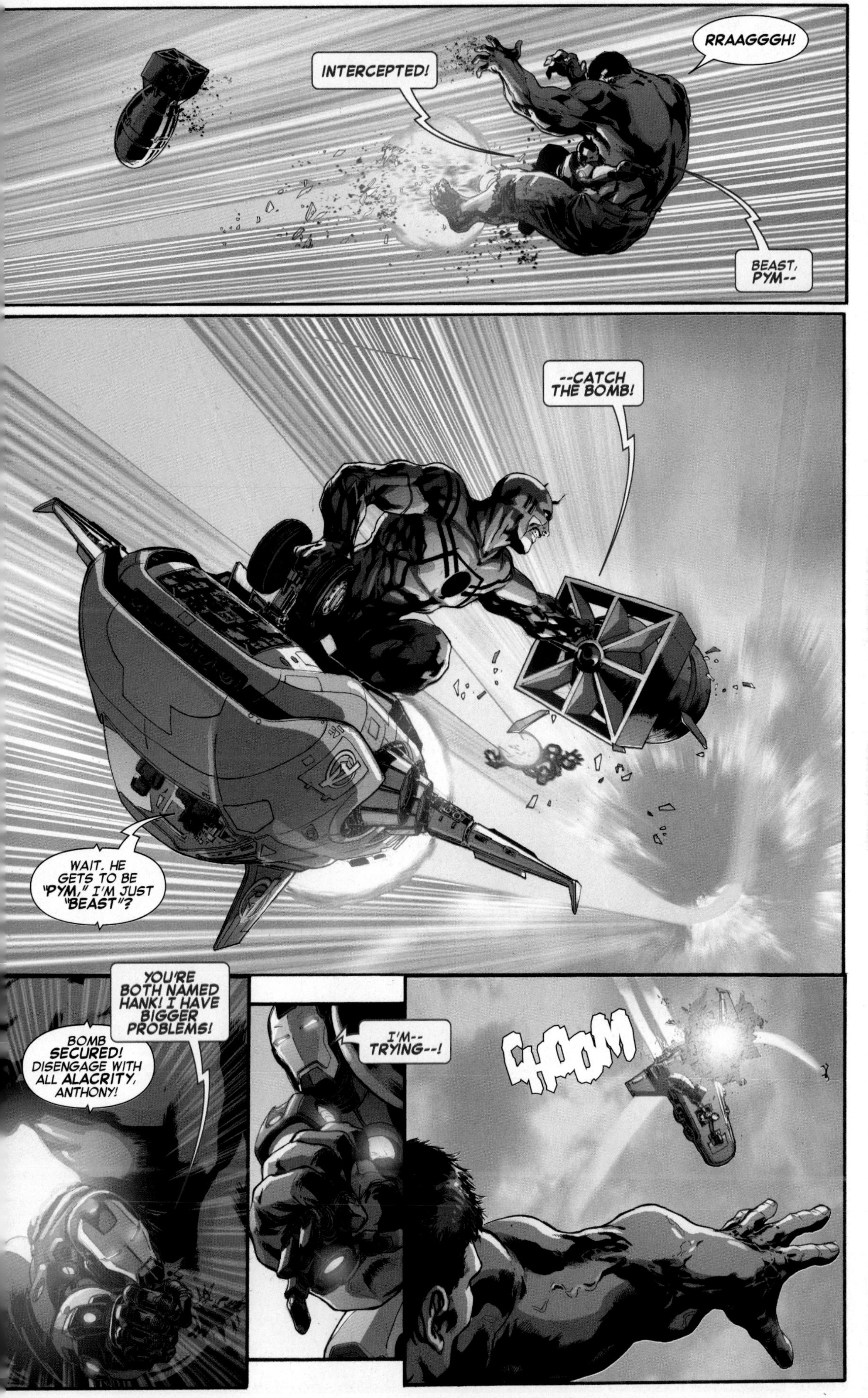
INTERCEPTED!
RRAAGGGH!
BEAST, PYM--
--CATCH THE BOMB!
WAIT. HE GETS TO BE "PYM," I'M JUST "BEAST"?
YOU'RE BOTH NAMED HANK! I HAVE BIGGER PROBLEMS!
BOMB SECURED! DISENGAGE WITH ALL ALACRITY, ANTHONY!
I'M-- TRYING--!
CHOOM

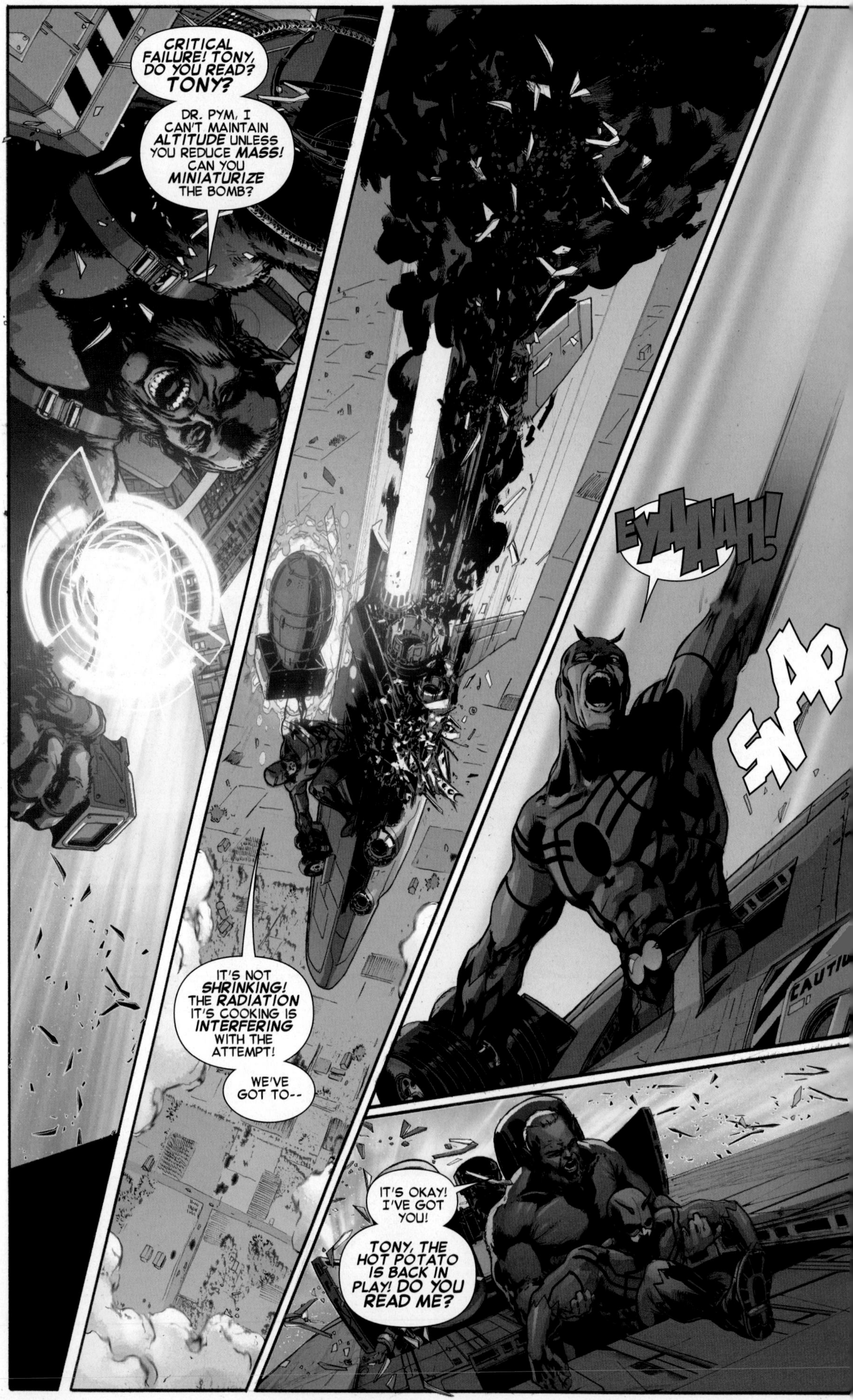
CRITICAL FAILURE! TONY, DO YOU READ? TONY?
DR. PYM, I CAN'T MAINTAIN ALTITUDE UNLESS YOU REDUCE MASS! CAN YOU MINIATURIZE THE BOMB?
IT'S NOT SHRINKING! THE RADIATION IT'S COOKING IS INTERFERING WITH THE ATTEMPT!
WE'VE GOT TO--
EYAAAH!
SNAP
CAUTI
IT'S OKAY! I'VE GOT YOU!
TONY, THE HOT POTATO IS BACK IN PLAY! DO YOU READ ME?

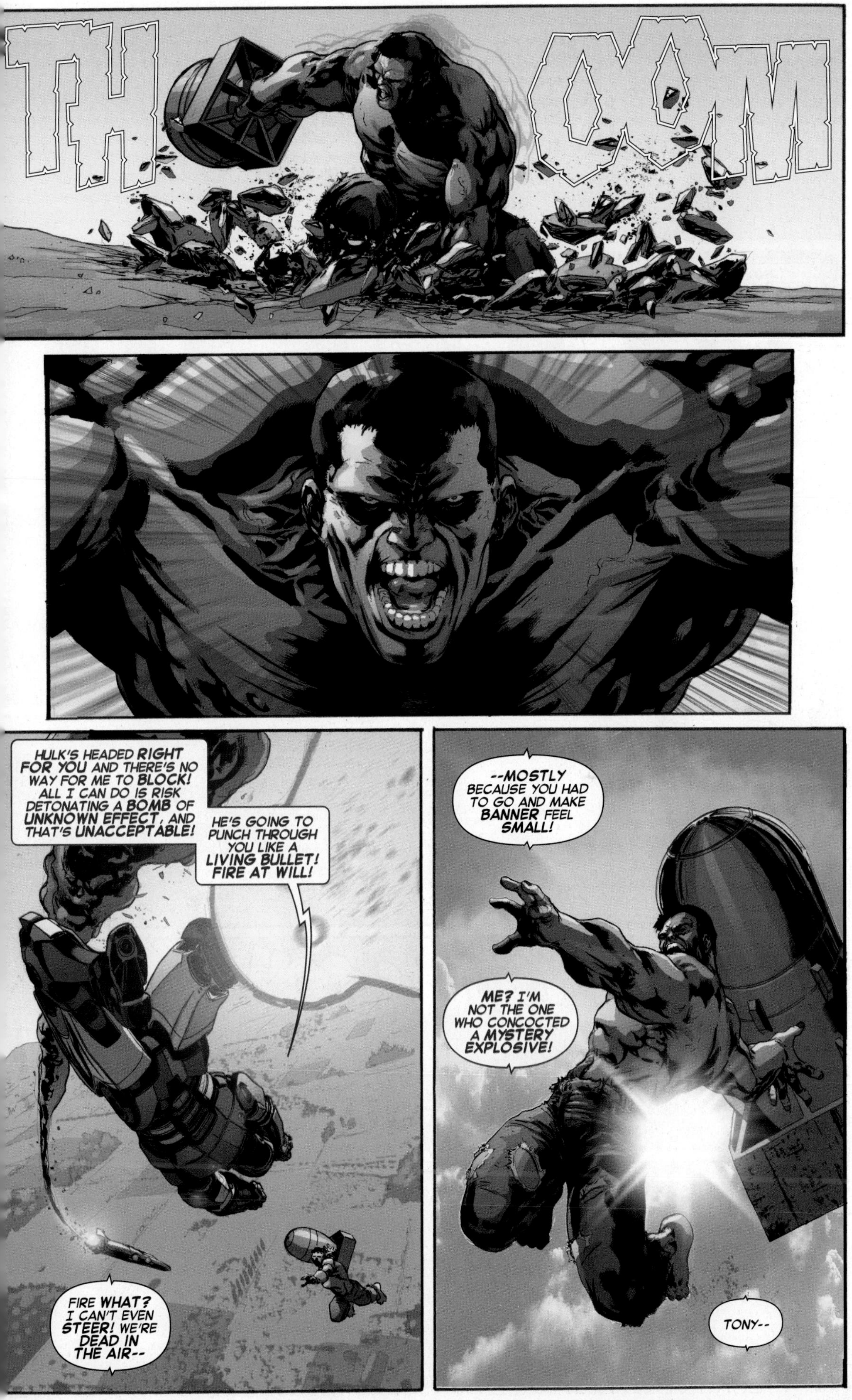
THOOM
HULK'S HEADED RIGHT FOR YOU AND THERE'S NO WAY FOR ME TO BLOCK! ALL I CAN DO IS RISK DETONATING A BOMB OF UNKNOWN EFFECT, AND THAT'S UNACCEPTABLE!
HE'S GOING TO PUNCH THROUGH YOU LIKE A LIVING BULLET! FIRE AT WILL!
FIRE WHAT? I CAN'T EVEN STEER! WE'RE DEAD IN THE AIR--
--MOSTLY BECAUSE YOU HAD TO GO AND MAKE BANNER FEEL SMALL!
ME? I'M NOT THE ONE WHO CONCOCTED A MYSTERY EXPLOSIVE!
TONY--

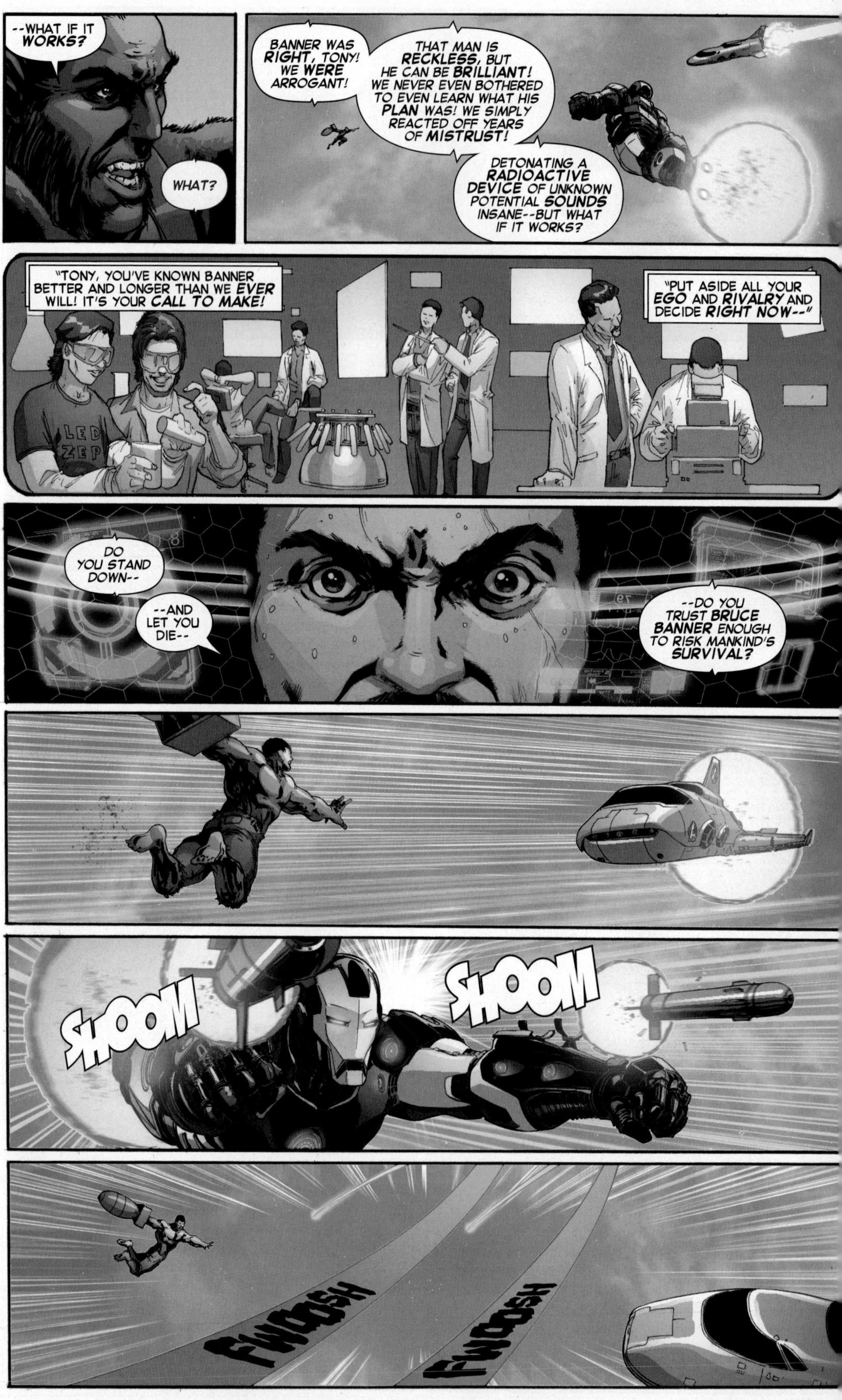
--WHAT IF IT WORKS?
WHAT?
BANNER WAS RIGHT, TONY! WE WERE ARROGANT!
THAT MAN IS RECKLESS, BUT HE CAN BE BRILLIANT! WE NEVER EVEN BOTHERED TO EVEN LEARN WHAT HIS PLAN WAS! WE SIMPLY REACTED OFF YEARS OF MISTRUST!
DETONATING A RADIOACTIVE DEVICE OF UNKNOWN POTENTIAL SOUNDS INSANE--BUT WHAT IF IT WORKS?
"TONY, YOU'VE KNOWN BANNER BETTER AND LONGER THAN WE EVER WILL! IT'S YOUR CALL TO MAKE!
"PUT ASIDE ALL YOUR EGO AND RIVALRY AND DECIDE RIGHT NOW--"
LED ZEP
DO YOU STAND DOWN--
--AND LET YOU DIE--
--DO YOU TRUST BRUCE BANNER ENOUGH TO RISK MANKIND'S SURVIVAL?
SHOOM
SHOOM
FWOOSH
FWOOSH

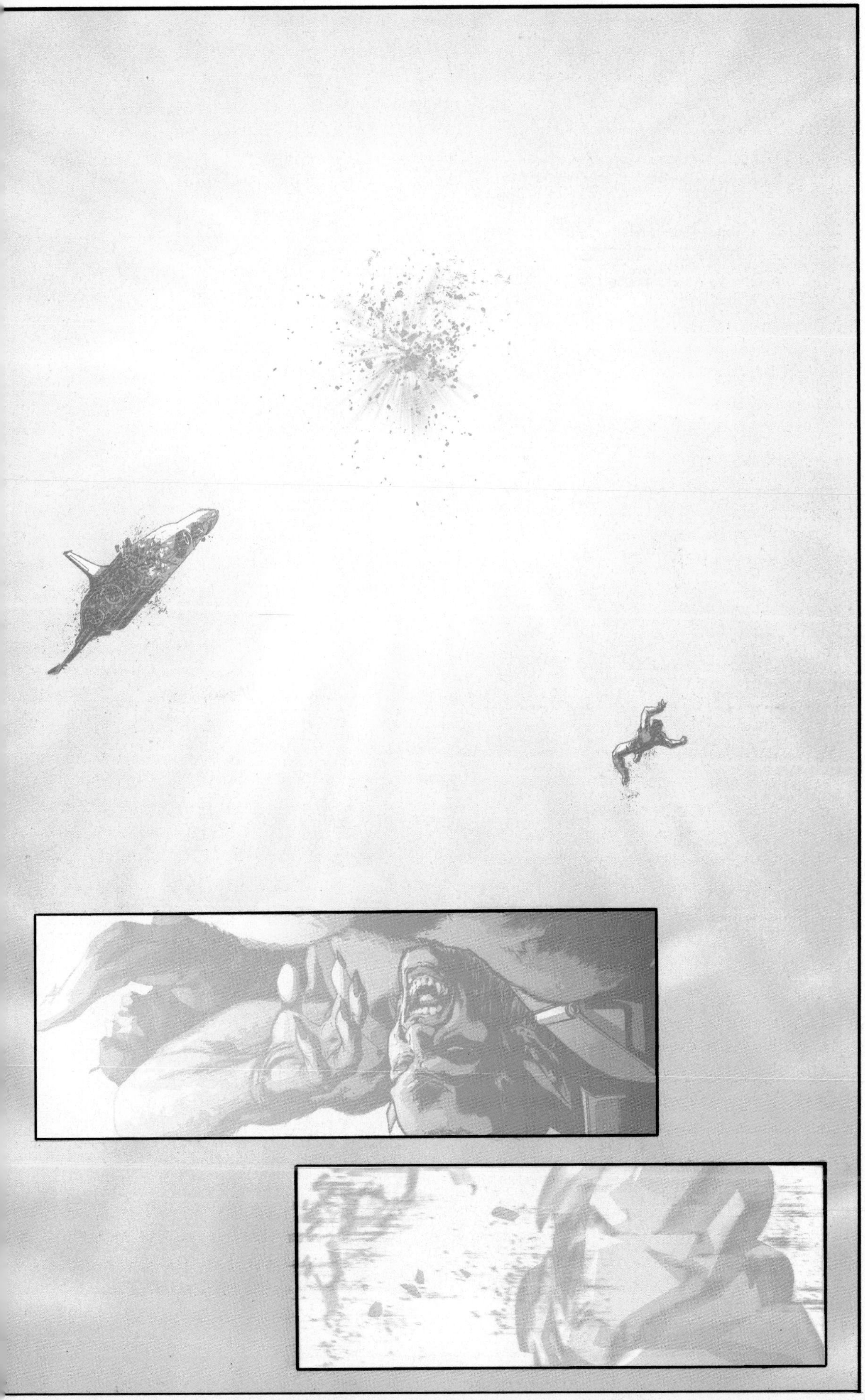

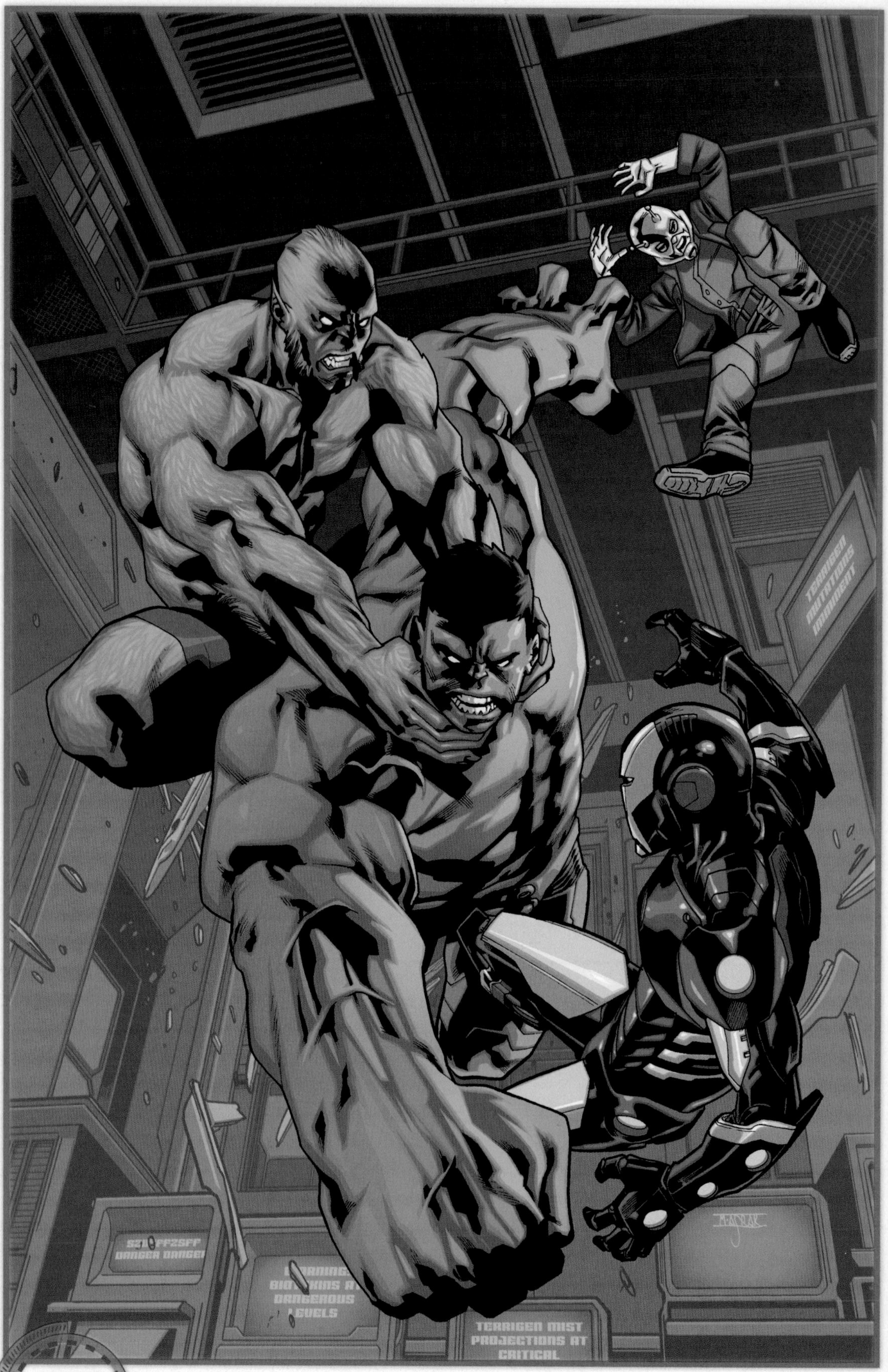
TERRIGEN MUTATIONS IMMINENT
TERRIGEN MIST PROJECTIONS AT CRITICAL

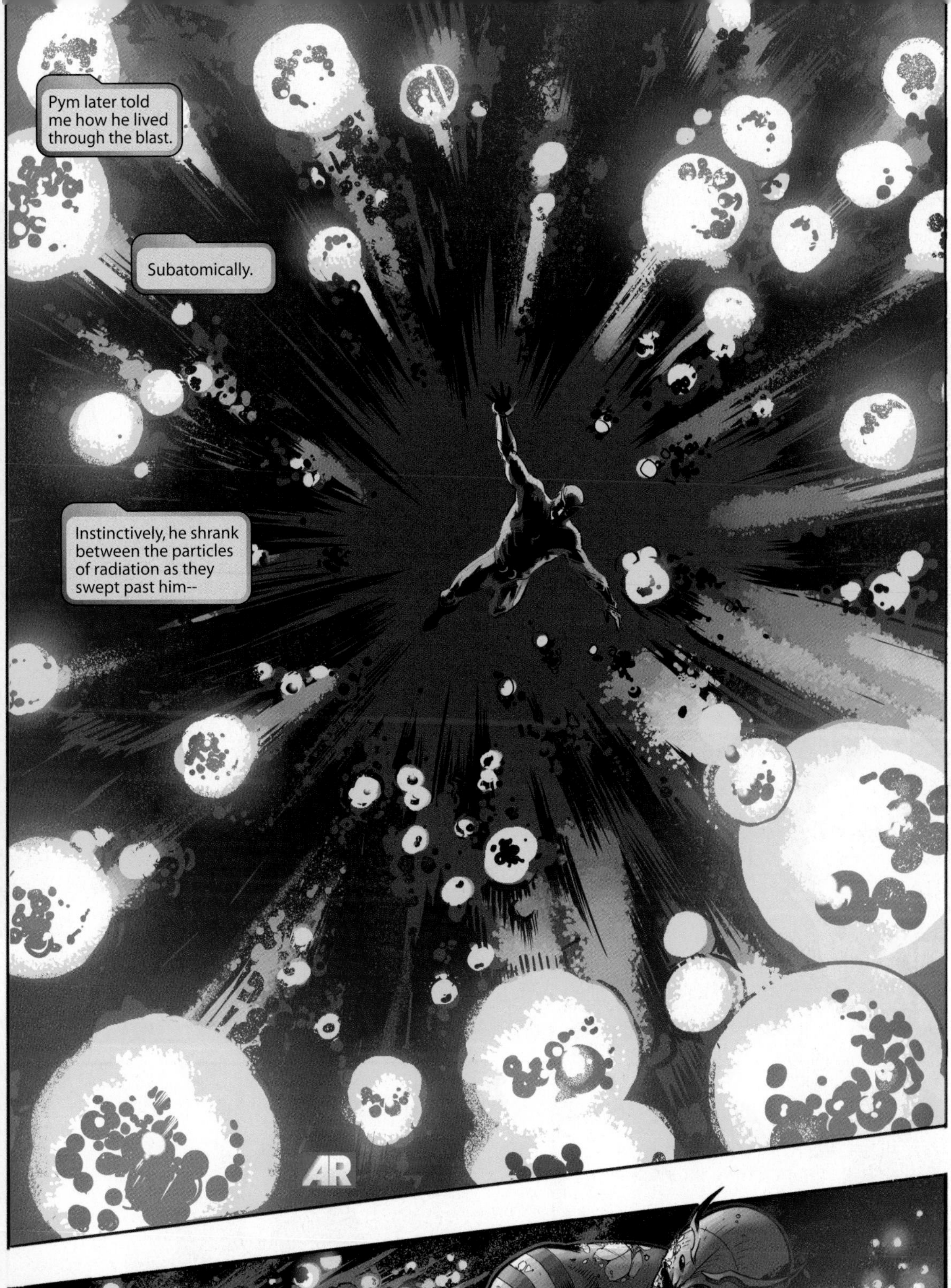
Pym later told me how he lived through the blast.
Subatomically.
Instinctively, he shrank between the particles of radiation as they swept past him--
AR
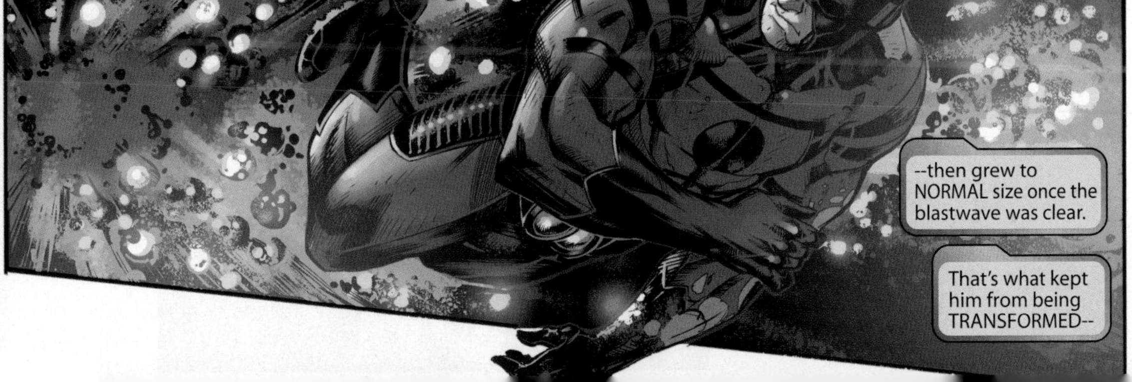
--then grew to NORMAL size once the blastwave was clear.
That's what kept him from being TRANSFORMED--

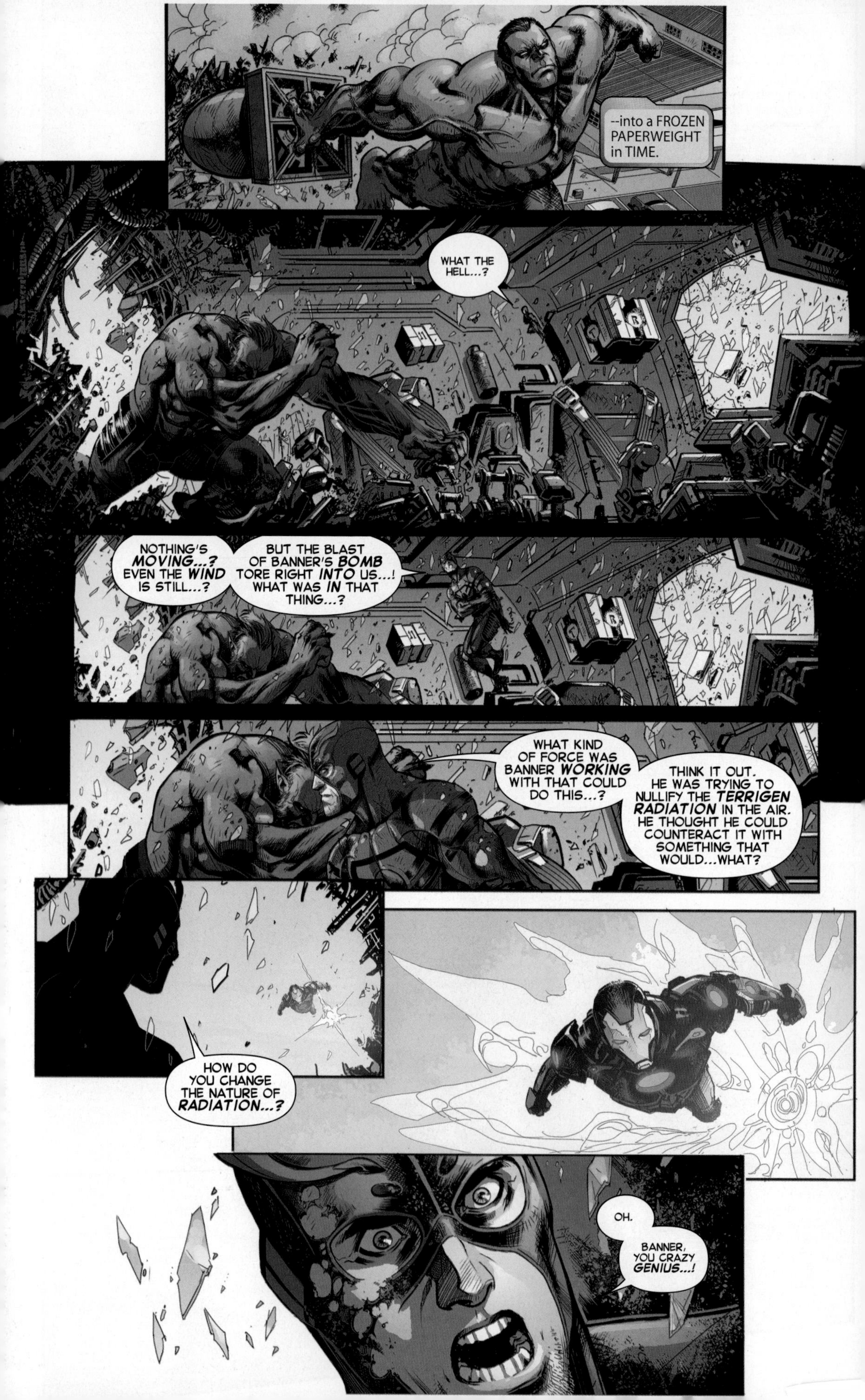
--into a FROZEN PAPERWEIGHT in TIME.
WHAT THE HELL...?
NOTHING'S MOVING...? EVEN THE WIND IS STILL...?
BUT THE BLAST OF BANNER'S BOMB TORE RIGHT INTO US...! WHAT WAS IN THAT THING...?
WHAT KIND OF FORCE WAS BANNER WORKING WITH THAT COULD DO THIS...?
THINK IT OUT. HE WAS TRYING TO NULLIFY THE TERRIGEN RADIATION IN THE AIR. HE THOUGHT HE COULD COUNTERACT IT WITH SOMETHING THAT WOULD...WHAT?
HOW DO YOU CHANGE THE NATURE OF RADIATION...?
OH.
BANNER, YOU CRAZY GENIUS...!

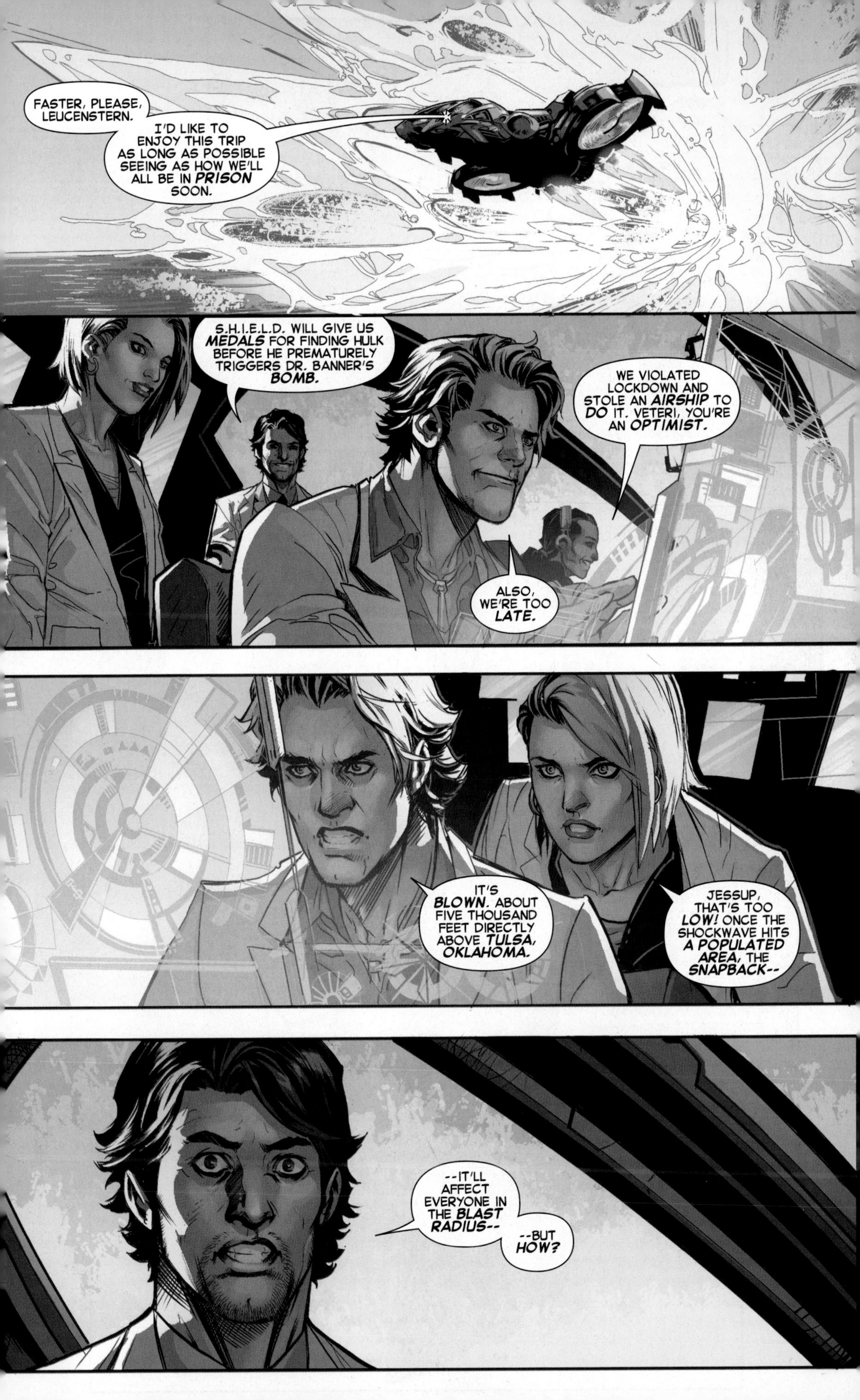
FASTER, PLEASE, LEUCENSTERN.
I'D LIKE TO ENJOY THIS TRIP AS LONG AS POSSIBLE SEEING AS HOW WE'LL ALL BE IN PRISON SOON.
S.H.I.E.L.D. WILL GIVE US MEDALS FOR FINDING HULK BEFORE HE PREMATURELY TRIGGERS DR. BANNER'S BOMB.
WE VIOLATED LOCKDOWN AND STOLE AN AIRSHIP TO DO IT. VETERI, YOU'RE AN OPTIMIST.
ALSO, WE'RE TOO LATE.
IT'S BLOWN. ABOUT FIVE THOUSAND FEET DIRECTLY ABOVE TULSA, OKLAHOMA.
JESSUP, THAT'S TOO LOW! ONCE THE SHOCKWAVE HITS A POPULATED AREA, THE SNAPBACK--
--IT'LL AFFECT EVERYONE IN THE BLAST RADIUS--
--BUT HOW?

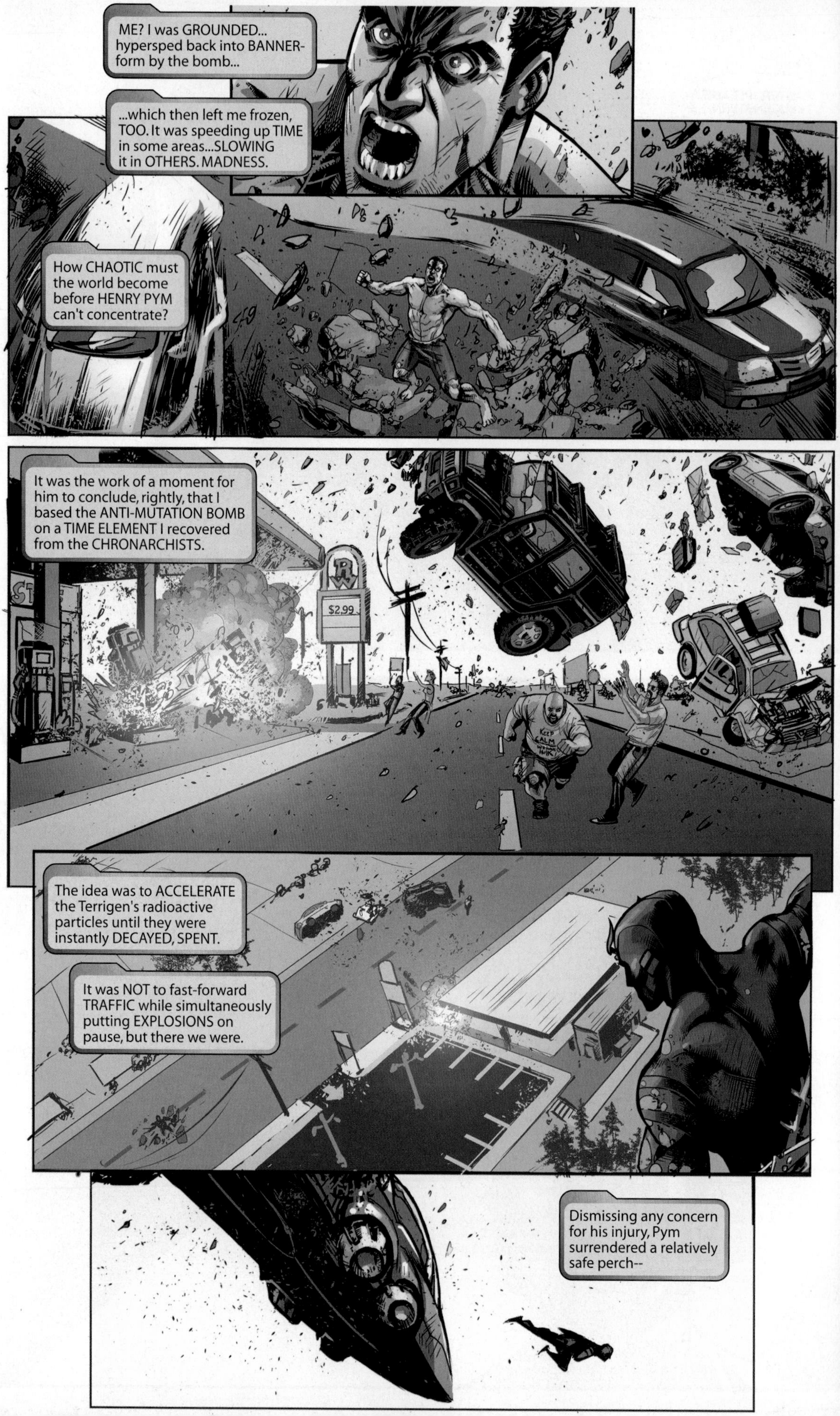

ME? I was GROUNDED... hypersped back into BANNER-form by the bomb...
...which then left me frozen, TOO. It was speeding up TIME in some areas...SLOWING it in OTHERS. MADNESS.
How CHAOTIC must the world become before HENRY PYM can't concentrate?
It was the work of a moment for him to conclude, rightly, that I based the ANTI-MUTATION BOMB on a TIME ELEMENT I recovered from the CHRONARCHISTS.
$2.99
The idea was to ACCELERATE the Terrigen's radioactive particles until they were instantly DECAYED, SPENT.
It was NOT to fast-forward TRAFFIC while simultaneously putting EXPLOSIONS on pause, but there we were.
Dismissing any concern for his injury, Pym surrendered a relatively safe perch--

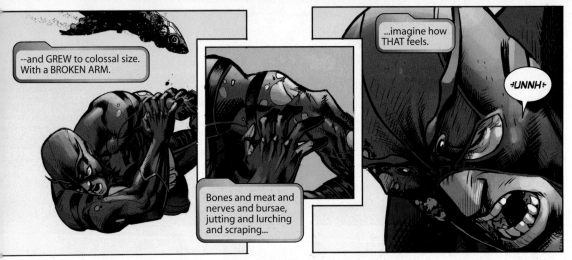

--and GREW to colossal size. With a BROKEN ARM.

Bones and meat and nerves and bursae, jutting and lurching and scraping...

...imagine how THAT feels.

‡UNNH‡

OW. C'MON, HANK, TOUGH IT *OUT*...

YOU! THIS WAY!

AAAH!

NO! DON'T *MOVE!* YOU *CAN'T!* STAY PAUSED! I NEED MORE *TIME*--!

STOP WHINING, HANK.

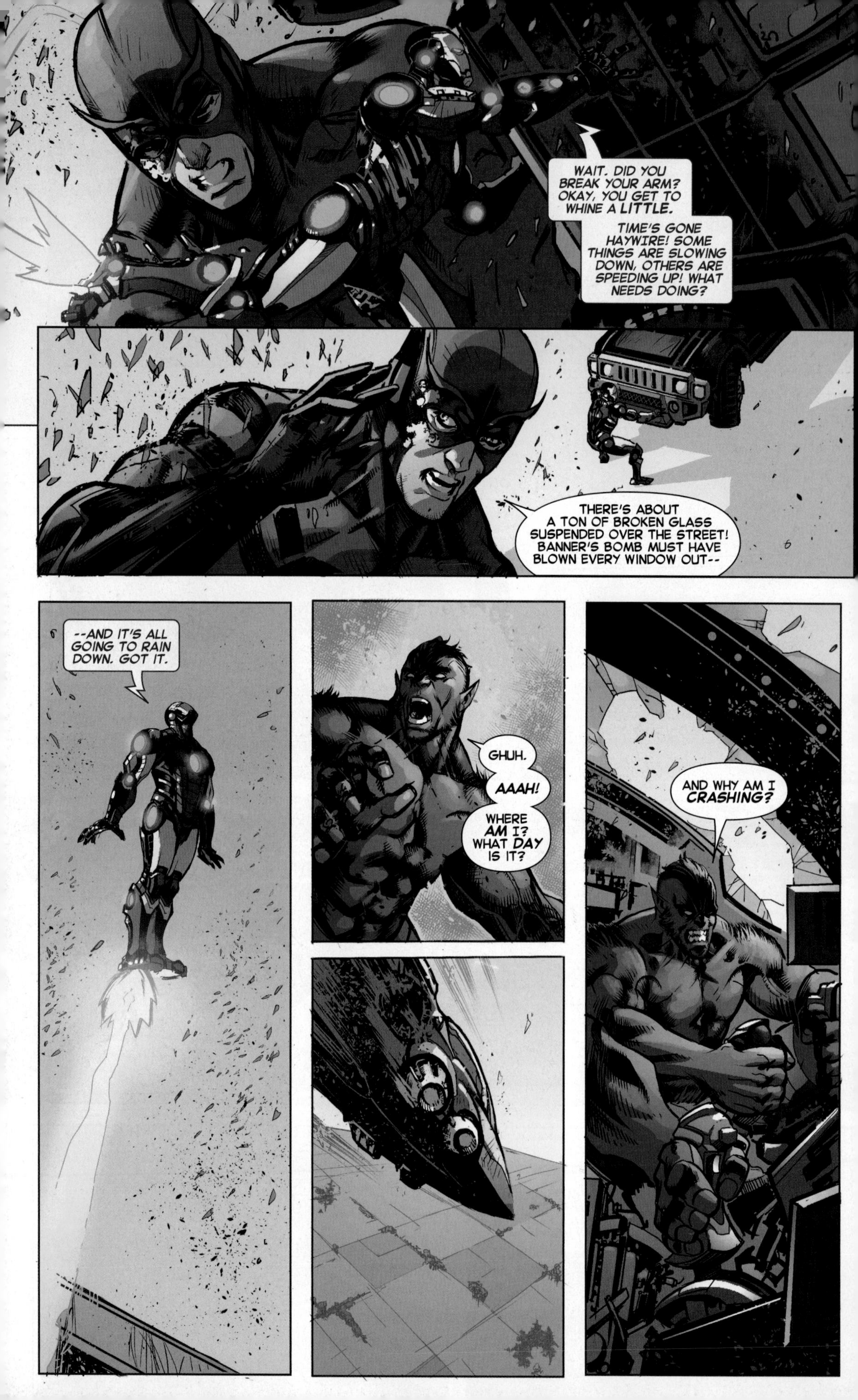

WAIT. DID YOU BREAK YOUR ARM? OKAY, YOU GET TO WHINE A LITTLE.
TIME'S GONE HAYWIRE! SOME THINGS ARE SLOWING DOWN, OTHERS ARE SPEEDING UP! WHAT NEEDS DOING?
THERE'S ABOUT A TON OF BROKEN GLASS SUSPENDED OVER THE STREET! BANNER'S BOMB MUST HAVE BLOWN EVERY WINDOW OUT--
--AND IT'S ALL GOING TO RAIN DOWN. GOT IT.
GHUH.
AAAH!
WHERE AM I? WHAT DAY IS IT?
AND WHY AM I CRASHING?

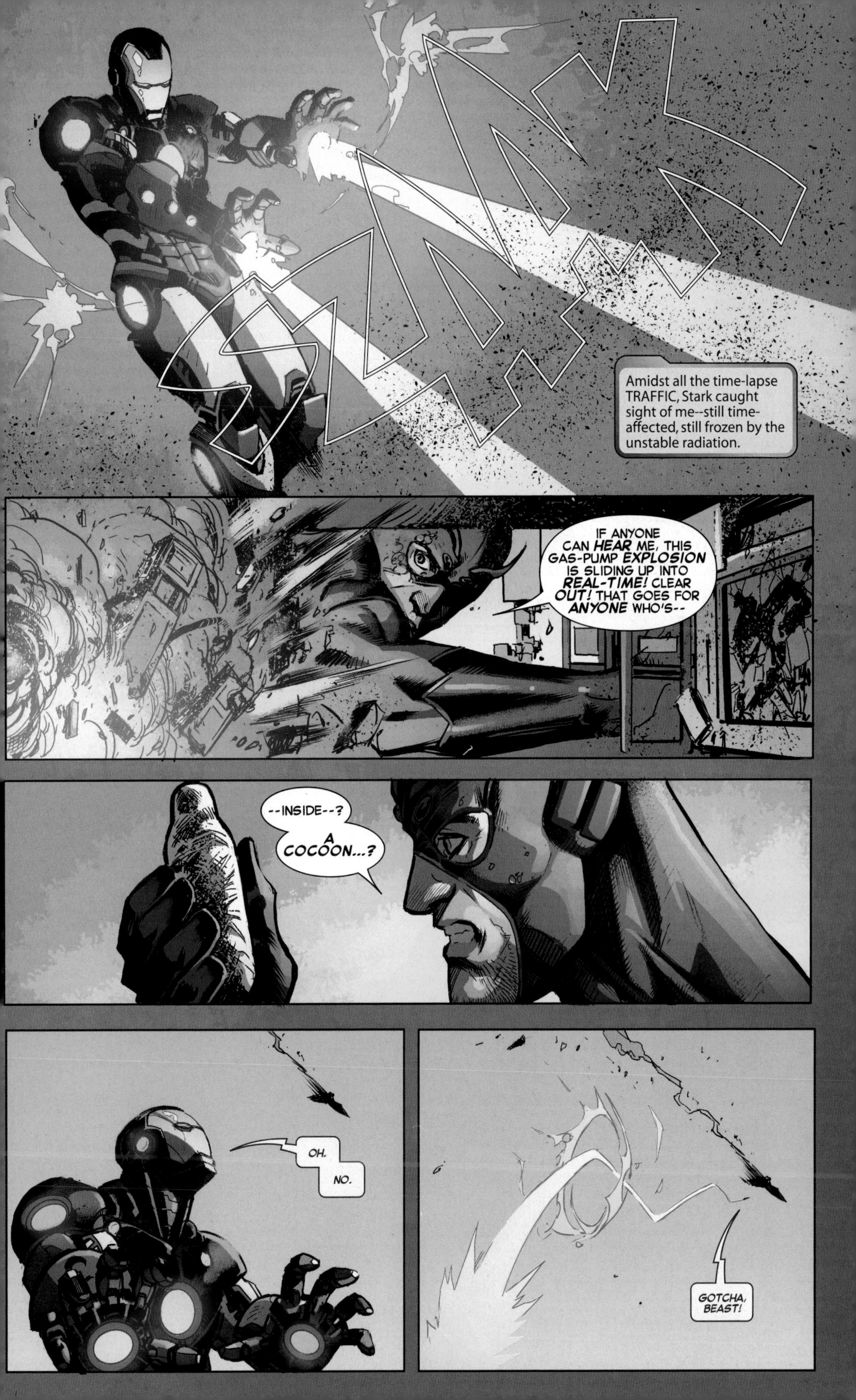
Amidst all the time-lapse TRAFFIC, Stark caught sight of me--still time-affected, still frozen by the unstable radiation.
IF ANYONE CAN HEAR ME, THIS GAS-PUMP EXPLOSION IS SLIDING UP INTO REAL-TIME! CLEAR OUT! THAT GOES FOR ANYONE WHO'S--
--INSIDE--?
A COCOON...?
OH.
NO.
GOTCHA, BEAST!

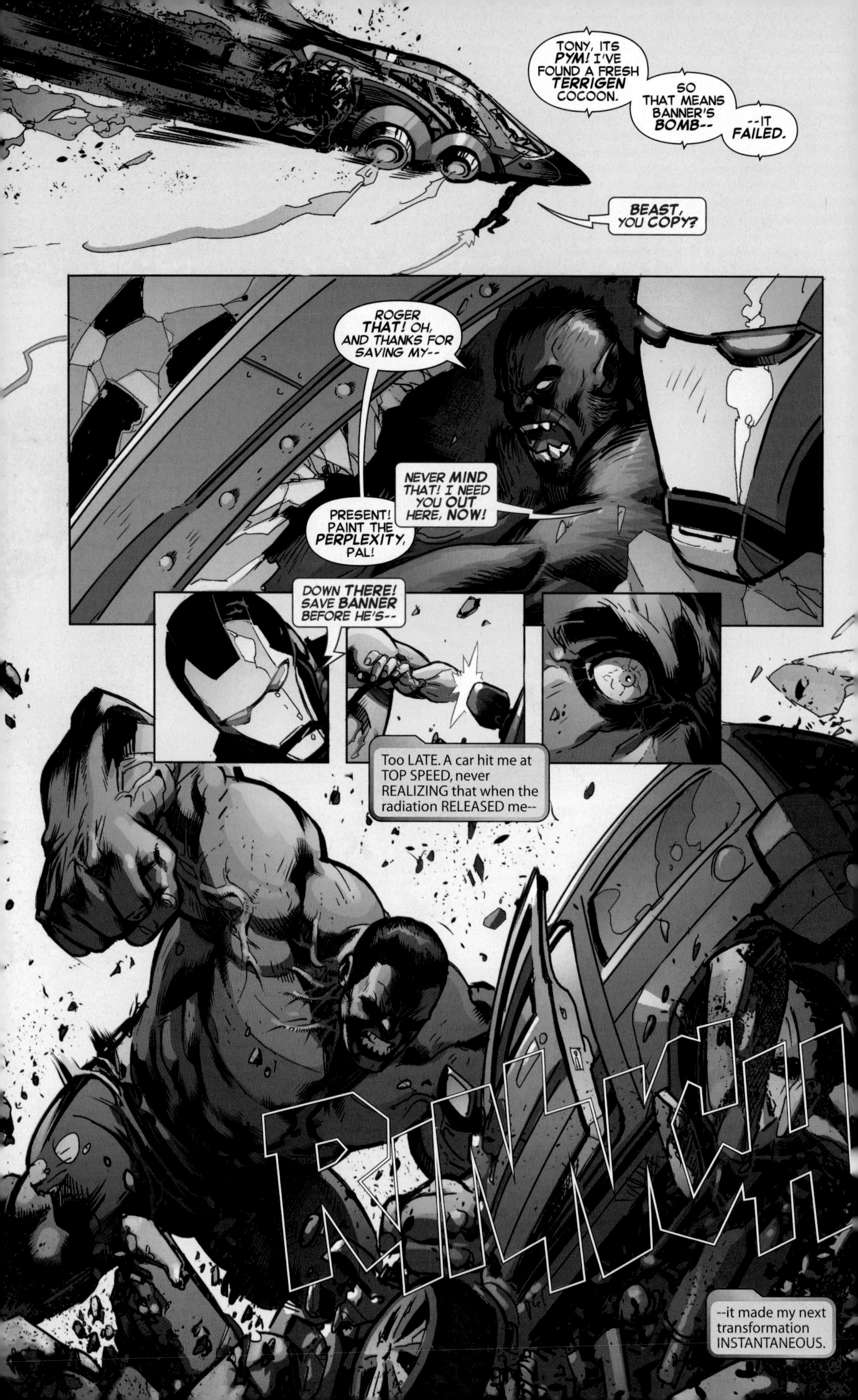
TONY, ITS PYM! I'VE FOUND A FRESH TERRIGEN COCOON.
SO THAT MEANS BANNER'S BOMB--
--IT FAILED.
BEAST, YOU COPY?
ROGER THAT! OH, AND THANKS FOR SAVING MY--
PRESENT! PAINT THE PERPLEXITY, PAL!
NEVER MIND THAT! I NEED YOU OUT HERE, NOW!
DOWN THERE! SAVE BANNER BEFORE HE'S--
Too LATE. A car hit me at TOP SPEED, never REALIZING that when the radiation RELEASED me--
RNKKH
--it made my next transformation INSTANTANEOUS.

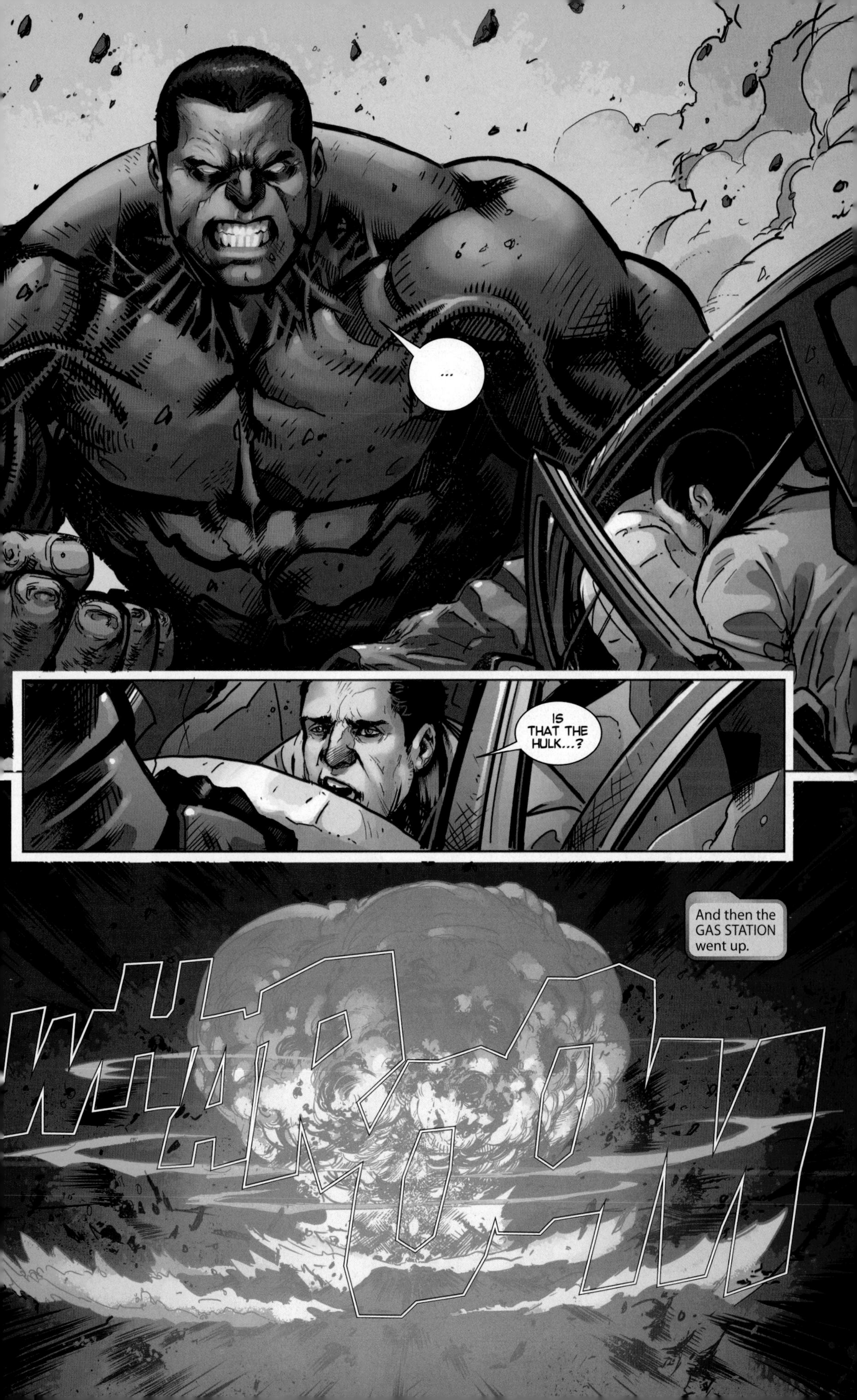
...
IS THAT THE HULK...?
And then the GAS STATION went up.

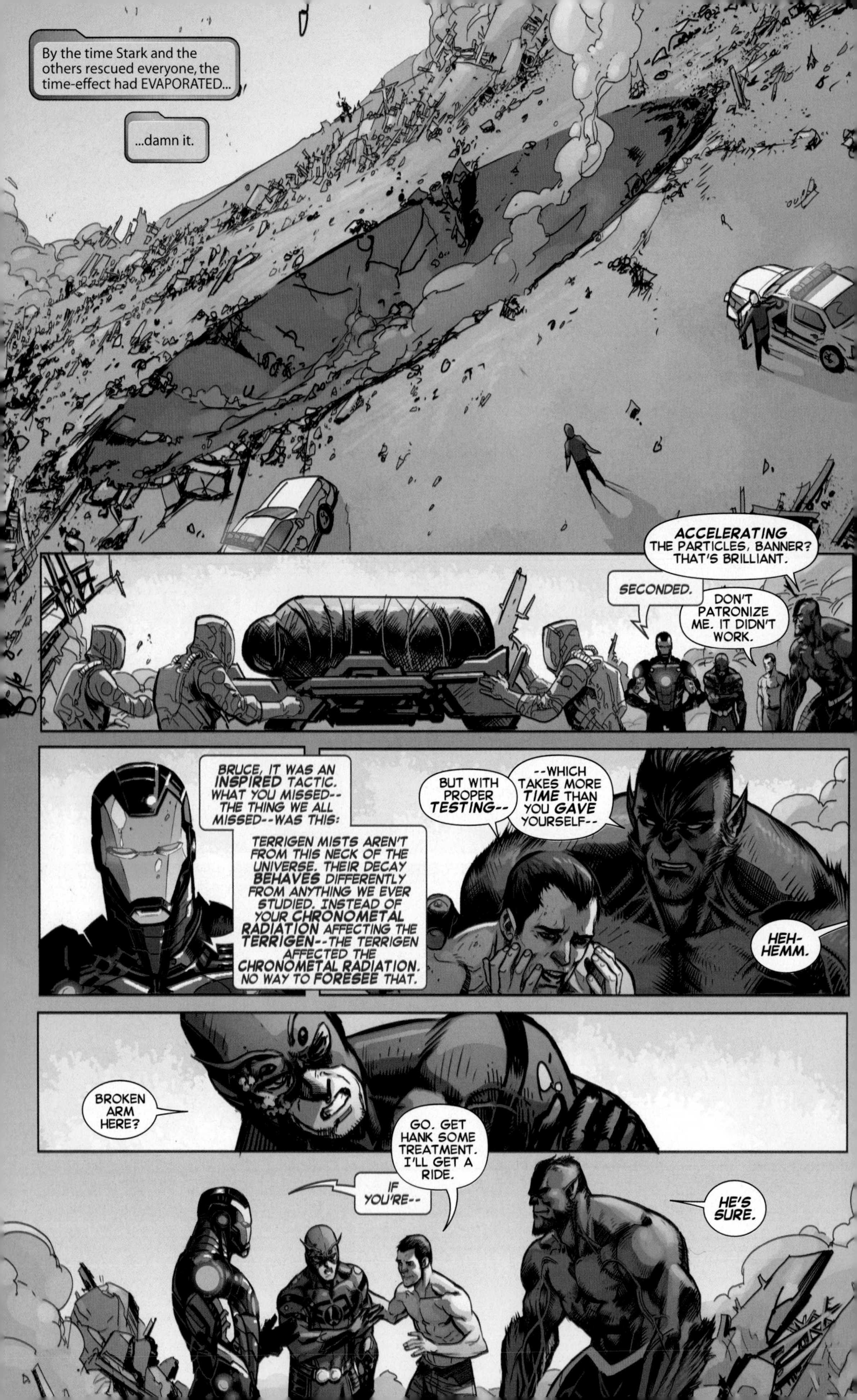

By the time Stark and the others rescued everyone, the time-effect had EVAPORATED...
...damn it.
ACCELERATING THE PARTICLES, BANNER? THAT'S BRILLIANT.
SECONDED.
DON'T PATRONIZE ME. IT DIDN'T WORK.
BRUCE, IT WAS AN INSPIRED TACTIC. WHAT YOU MISSED--THE THING WE ALL MISSED--WAS THIS:
TERRIGEN MISTS AREN'T FROM THIS NECK OF THE UNIVERSE. THEIR DECAY BEHAVES DIFFERENTLY FROM ANYTHING WE EVER STUDIED. INSTEAD OF YOUR CHRONOMETAL RADIATION AFFECTING THE TERRIGEN--THE TERRIGEN AFFECTED THE CHRONOMETAL RADIATION. NO WAY TO FORESEE THAT.
BUT WITH PROPER TESTING--
--WHICH TAKES MORE TIME THAN YOU GAVE YOURSELF--
HEH-HEMM.
BROKEN ARM HERE?
GO. GET HANK SOME TREATMENT. I'LL GET A RIDE.
IF YOU'RE--
HE'S SURE.

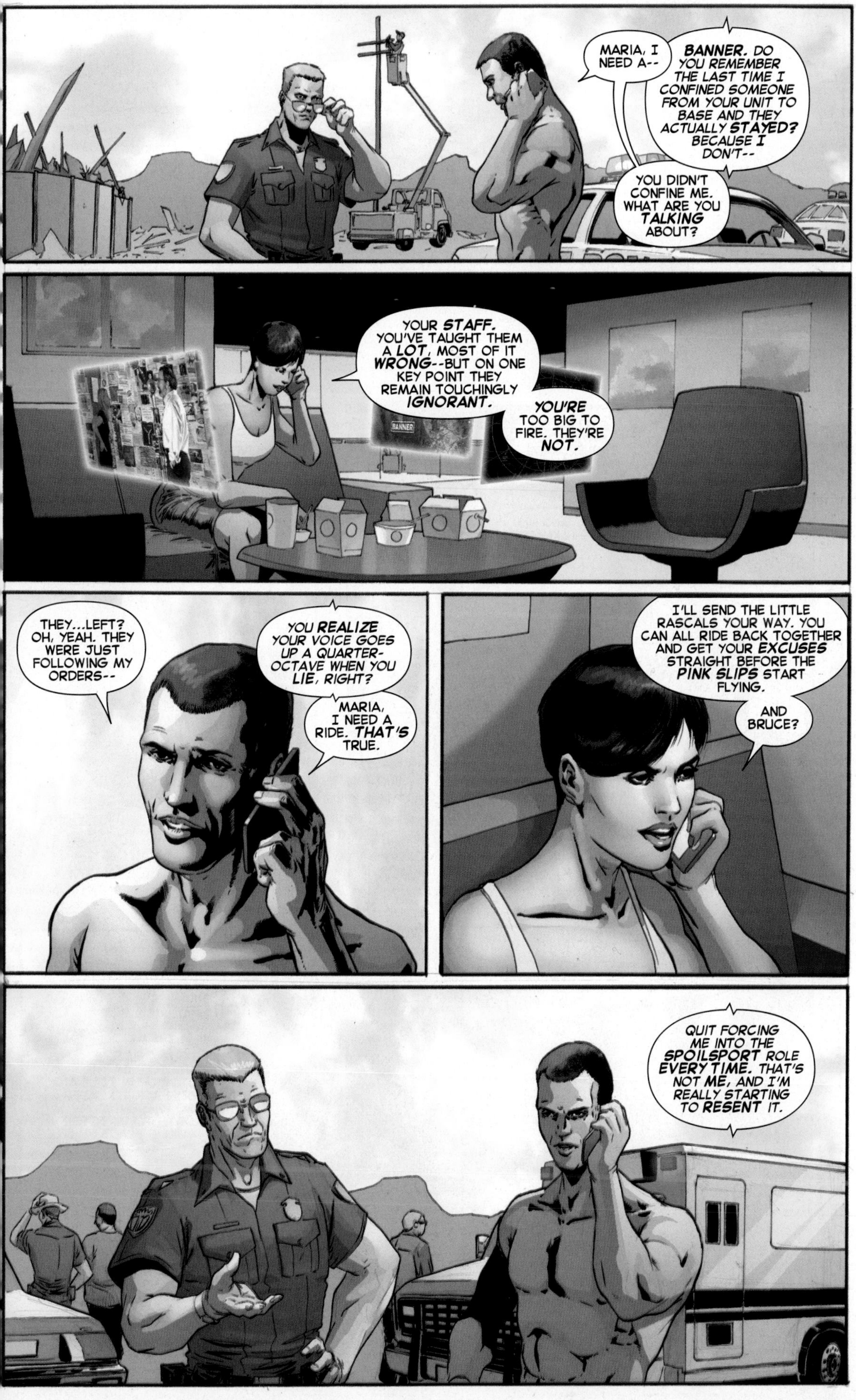

MARIA, I NEED A--
BANNER. DO YOU REMEMBER THE LAST TIME I CONFINED SOMEONE FROM YOUR UNIT TO BASE AND THEY ACTUALLY STAYED? BECAUSE I DON'T--
YOU DIDN'T CONFINE ME. WHAT ARE YOU TALKING ABOUT?
YOUR STAFF. YOU'VE TAUGHT THEM A LOT, MOST OF IT WRONG--BUT ON ONE KEY POINT THEY REMAIN TOUCHINGLY IGNORANT.
YOU'RE TOO BIG TO FIRE. THEY'RE NOT.
BANNER
THEY...LEFT? OH, YEAH. THEY WERE JUST FOLLOWING MY ORDERS--
YOU REALIZE YOUR VOICE GOES UP A QUARTER-OCTAVE WHEN YOU LIE, RIGHT?
MARIA, I NEED A RIDE. THAT'S TRUE.
I'LL SEND THE LITTLE RASCALS YOUR WAY. YOU CAN ALL RIDE BACK TOGETHER AND GET YOUR EXCUSES STRAIGHT BEFORE THE PINK SLIPS START FLYING.
AND BRUCE?
QUIT FORCING ME INTO THE SPOILSPORT ROLE EVERY TIME. THAT'S NOT ME, AND I'M REALLY STARTING TO RESENT IT.

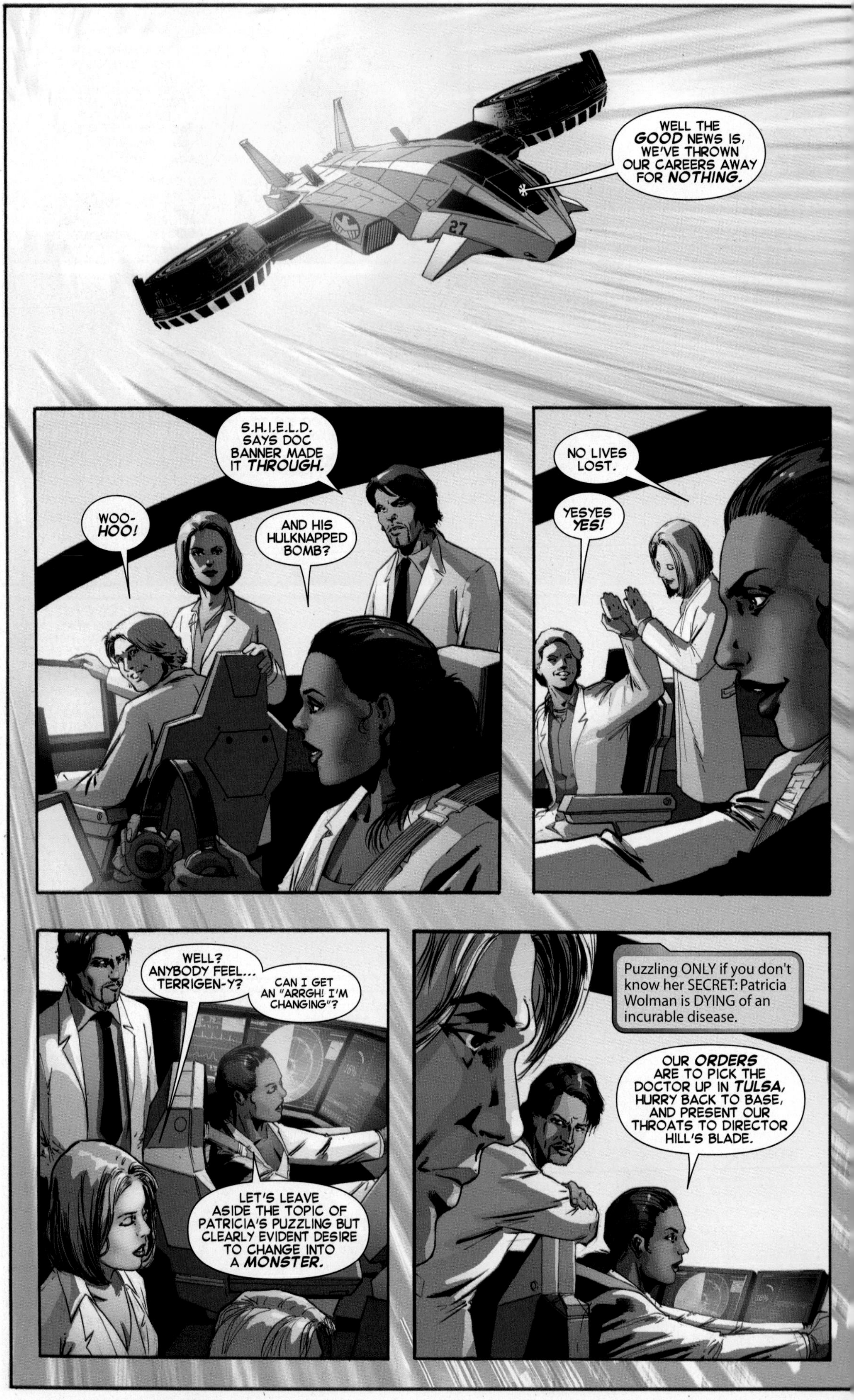
WELL THE GOOD NEWS IS, WE'VE THROWN OUR CAREERS AWAY FOR NOTHING.
27
S.H.I.E.L.D. SAYS DOC BANNER MADE IT THROUGH.
WOO-HOO!
AND HIS HULKNAPPED BOMB?
NO LIVES LOST.
YESYES YES!
WELL? ANYBODY FEEL... TERRIGEN-Y?
CAN I GET AN "ARRGH! I'M CHANGING"?
LET'S LEAVE ASIDE THE TOPIC OF PATRICIA'S PUZZLING BUT CLEARLY EVIDENT DESIRE TO CHANGE INTO A MONSTER.
Puzzling ONLY if you don't know her SECRET: Patricia Wolman is DYING of an incurable disease.
OUR ORDERS ARE TO PICK THE DOCTOR UP IN TULSA, HURRY BACK TO BASE, AND PRESENT OUR THROATS TO DIRECTOR HILL'S BLADE.

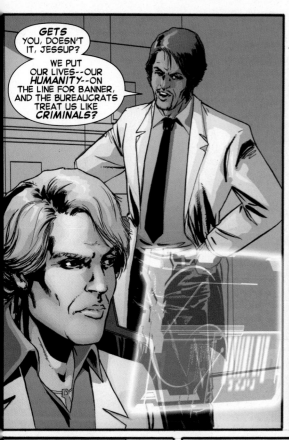

GETS YOU, DOESN'T IT, JESSUP?

WE PUT OUR LIVES--OUR *HUMANITY*--ON THE LINE FOR BANNER, AND THE BUREAUCRATS TREAT US LIKE *CRIMINALS*?

IT'LL WORK OUT, VETERI. HILL'S GOT TO CROSS HER T'S IS ALL.

CLASSIC JESSUP. KING OF NON-CONFRONTATION. YOU ALWAYS DO THIS.

SOMEONE TICKS YOU OFF, AND A CASUAL OBSERVER WOULD MISS IT. BUT THOSE OF US WHO *KNOW* YOU CAN SEE THE RAGE FLICKER ACROSS YOUR FACE.

THEN YOU STUFF IT DOWN AND SMILE, AND MAKE SOME LAME EXCUSE FOR WHOEVER OR WHATEVER *PROVOKED* YOU.

THINGS ARE STRESSFUL FOR ALL OF US, I *KNOW* THAT. WE WALK ON EGGSHELLS AROUND DR. BANNER 24-7, AND SOME OF THE WAYS WE *DEAL* AREN'T *IDEAL*--

HA! YOU'RE DOING IT *NOW!* EXCUSING *ME!* OH, YOU'RE A PIECE OF WORK, JESSUP.

I CAN *SEE* HOW YOU BECAME BANNER'S *PET*.

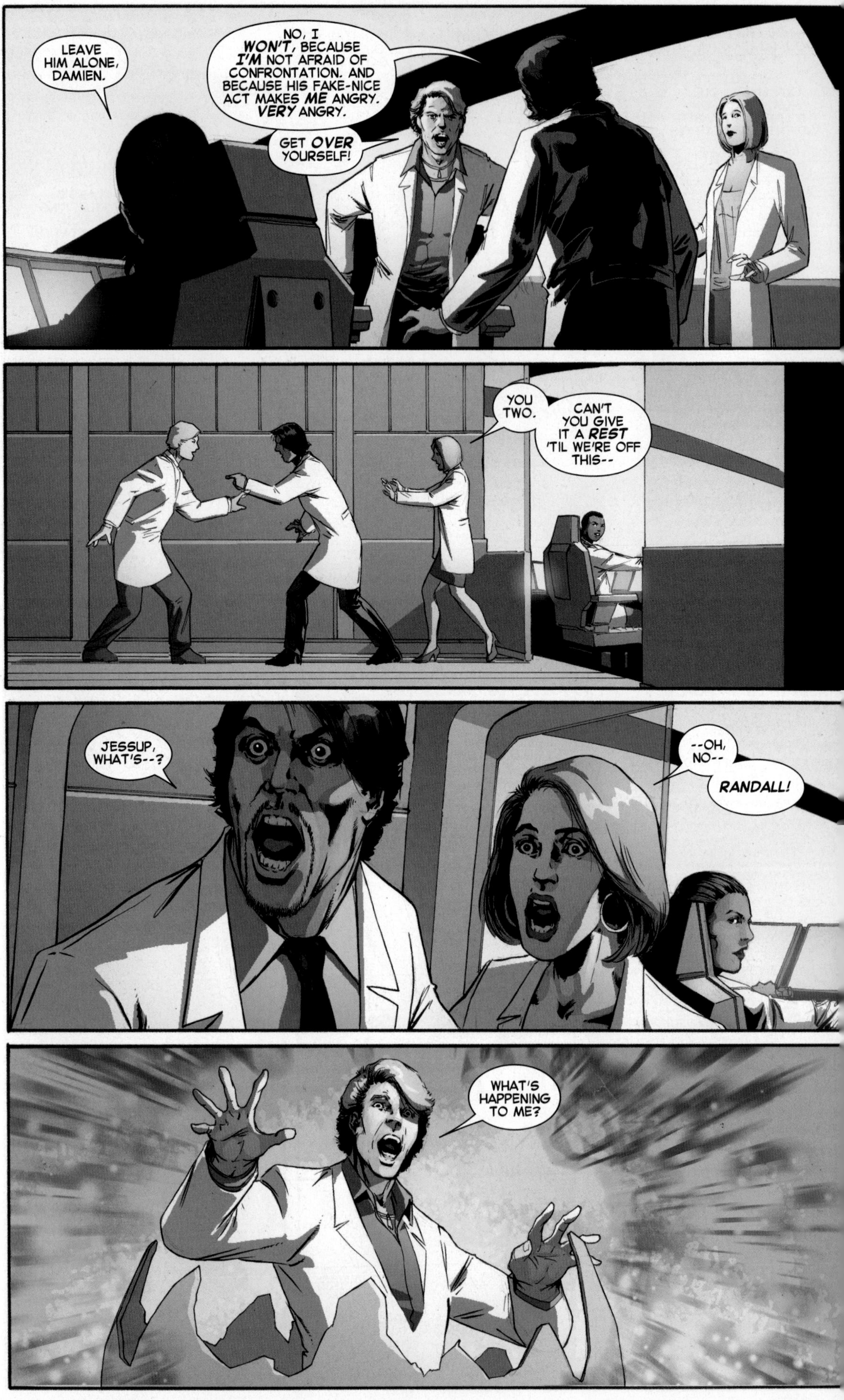
LEAVE HIM ALONE, DAMIEN.
NO, I WON'T, BECAUSE I'M NOT AFRAID OF CONFRONTATION. AND BECAUSE HIS FAKE-NICE ACT MAKES ME ANGRY. VERY ANGRY.
GET OVER YOURSELF!
YOU TWO.
CAN'T YOU GIVE IT A REST 'TIL WE'RE OFF THIS--
JESSUP, WHAT'S--?
--OH, NO--
RANDALL!
WHAT'S HAPPENING TO ME?

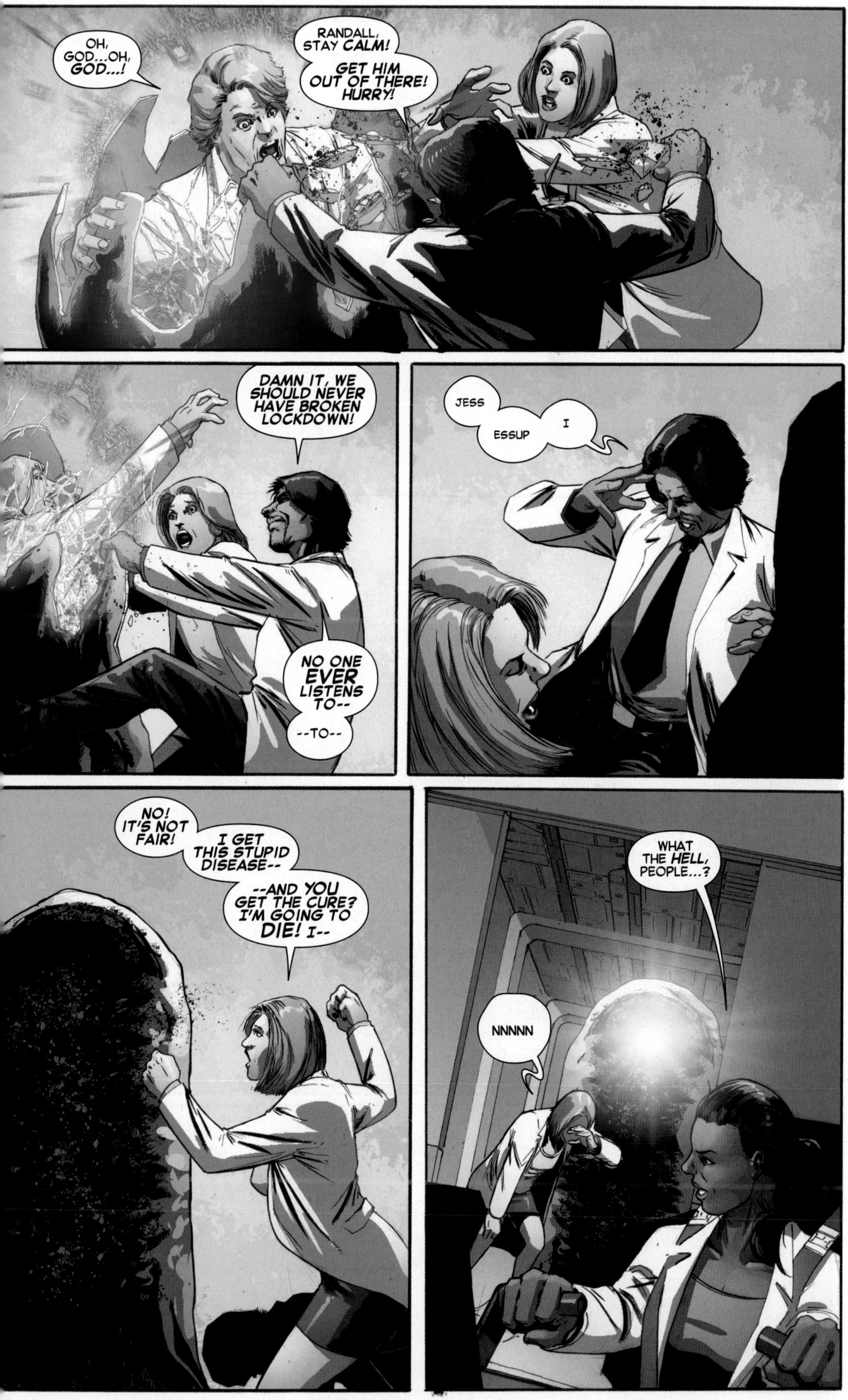
OH, GOD...OH, GOD...!
RANDALL, STAY CALM!
GET HIM OUT OF THERE! HURRY!
DAMN IT, WE SHOULD NEVER HAVE BROKEN LOCKDOWN!
NO ONE EVER LISTENS TO--
--TO--
JESS
ESSUP
I
NO! IT'S NOT FAIR!
I GET THIS STUPID DISEASE--
--AND YOU GET THE CURE? I'M GOING TO DIE! I--
WHAT THE HELL, PEOPLE...?
NNNNN

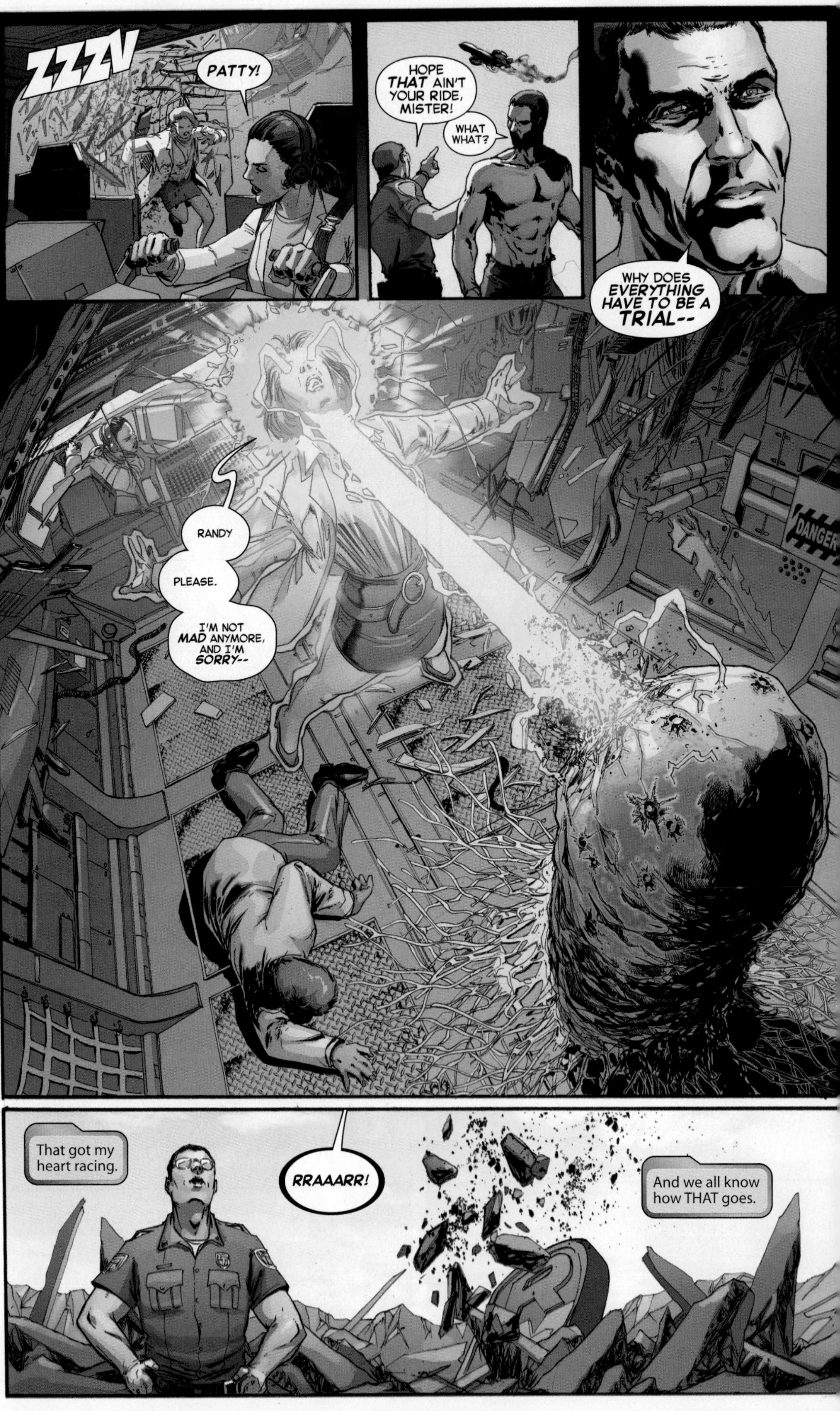
ZZZV
PATTY!
HOPE THAT AIN'T YOUR RIDE, MISTER!
WHAT WHAT?
WHY DOES EVERYTHING HAVE TO BE A TRIAL--
DANGER
RANDY
PLEASE.
I'M NOT MAD ANYMORE, AND I'M SORRY--
That got my heart racing.
RRAAARR!
And we all know how THAT goes.

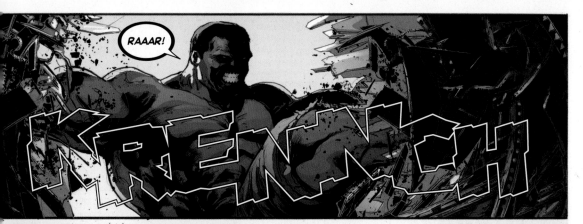

RAAAR!

KRENNCH

RANDY

Normally, SOLUTIONS are pretty STRAIGHTFORWARD. Hulk sees problem, Hulk HITS problem. But it helps to have SOME idea of what he's looking at.

DON'T BE MAD

That doesn't stop him from BLUSTERING and BULLYING--

NO CRASH PLANE!

--or ATTEMPTING to, anyway.

ZZZV

AAH!

The BEAMS, I would learn later, were as confusing to EVERYONE as they were to HULK. They didn't BURN, they didn't hurt FLESH...

...so what was their PURPOSE?

RAAAR!

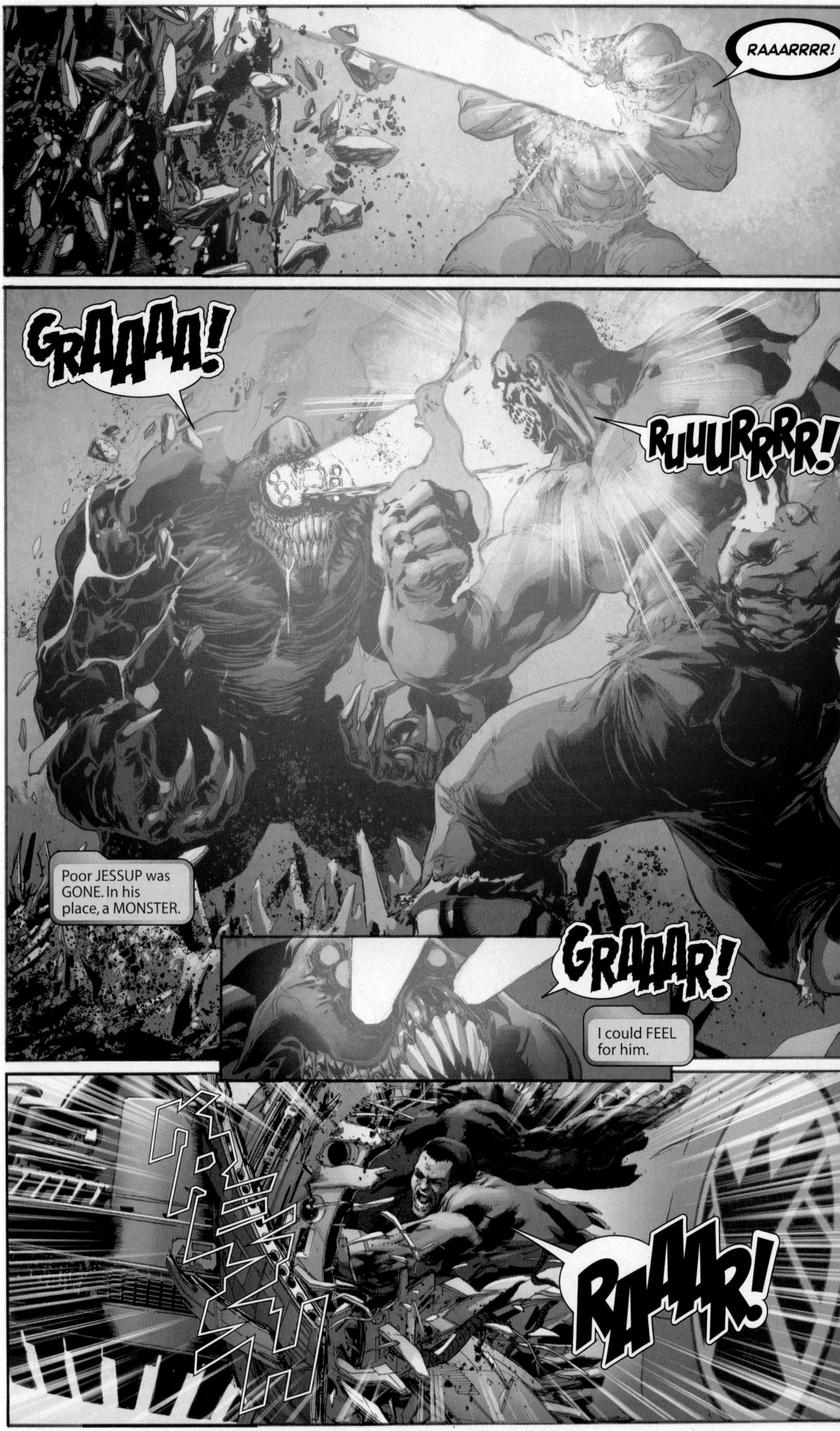
RAAARRRR!
GRAAAA!
RUUURRRR!
Poor JESSUP was GONE. In his place, a MONSTER.
GRAAAR!
I could FEEL for him.
RAAAR!

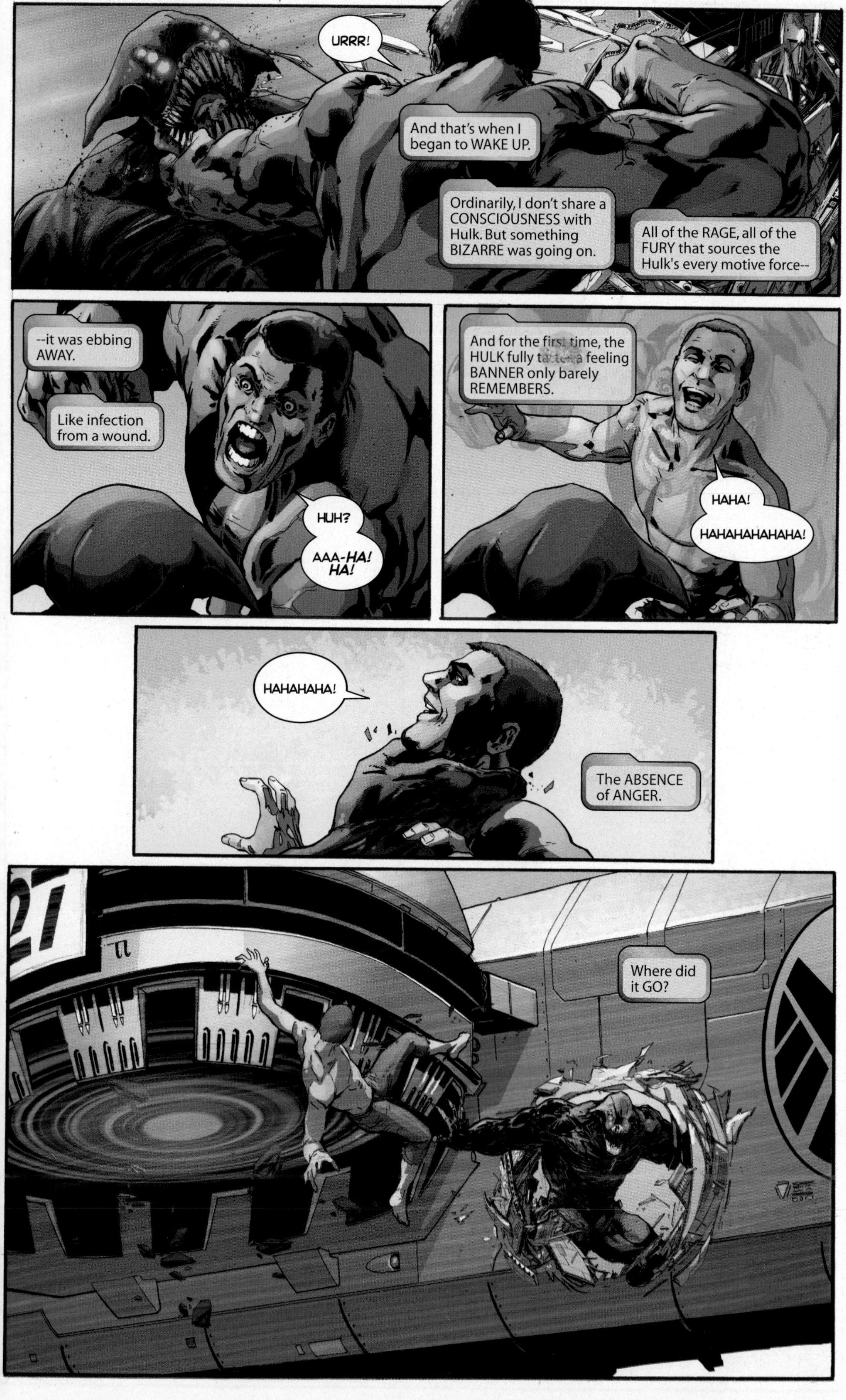
URRR!
And that's when I began to WAKE UP.
Ordinarily, I don't share a CONSCIOUSNESS with Hulk. But something BIZARRE was going on.
All of the RAGE, all of the FURY that sources the Hulk's every motive force--
--it was ebbing AWAY.
Like infection from a wound.
HUH?
AAA-HA! HA!
And for the first time, the HULK fully tastes a feeling BANNER only barely REMEMBERS.
HAHA!
HAHAHAHAHAHA!
HAHAHAHA!
The ABSENCE of ANGER.
Where did it GO?

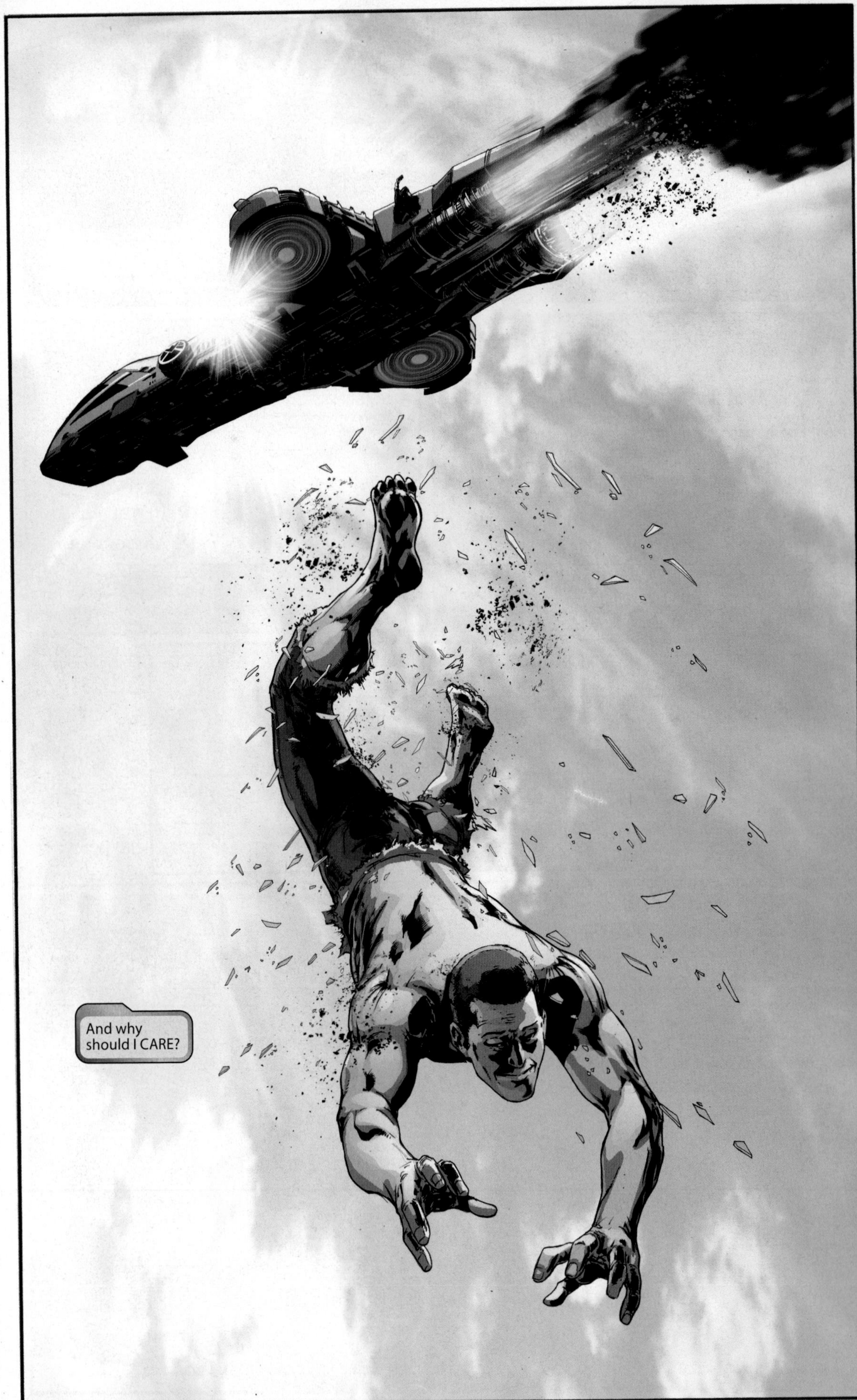
And why should I CARE?

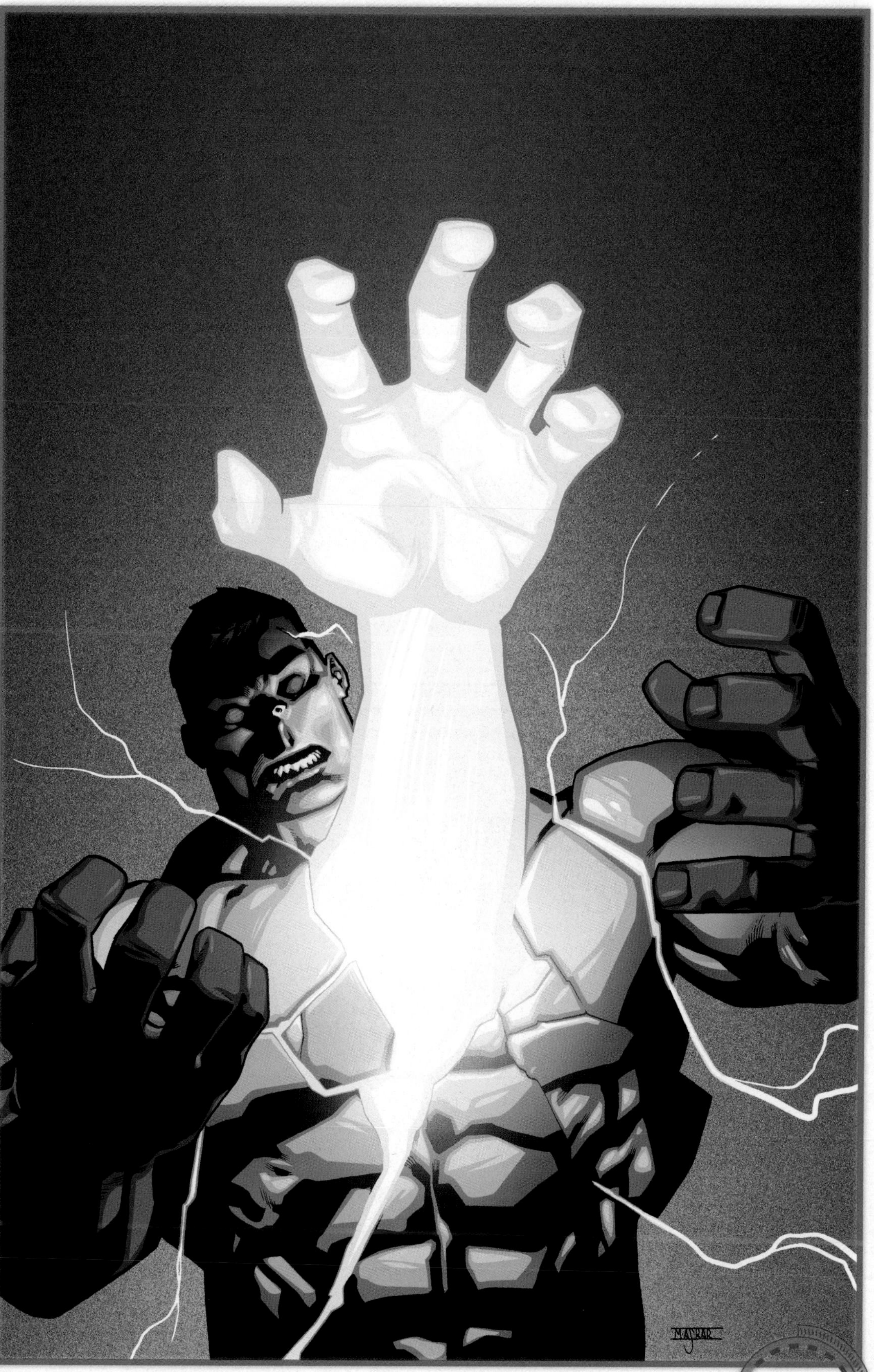

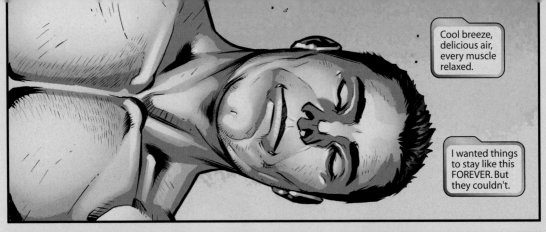

Cool breeze, delicious air, every muscle relaxed.

I wanted things to stay like this FOREVER. But they couldn't.

Obviously.

THIS body would NEVER survive the next 60 seconds, and the big GREEN one's suddenly UNAVAILABLE...

...because I can't stop feeling GREAT.

Despite the fall, my PULSE isn't racing fast enough to trigger the change--

--I can summon no ANXIETY to QUICKEN it, and for the very first time in recent memory--

--I can't get ANGRY to save my LIFE.

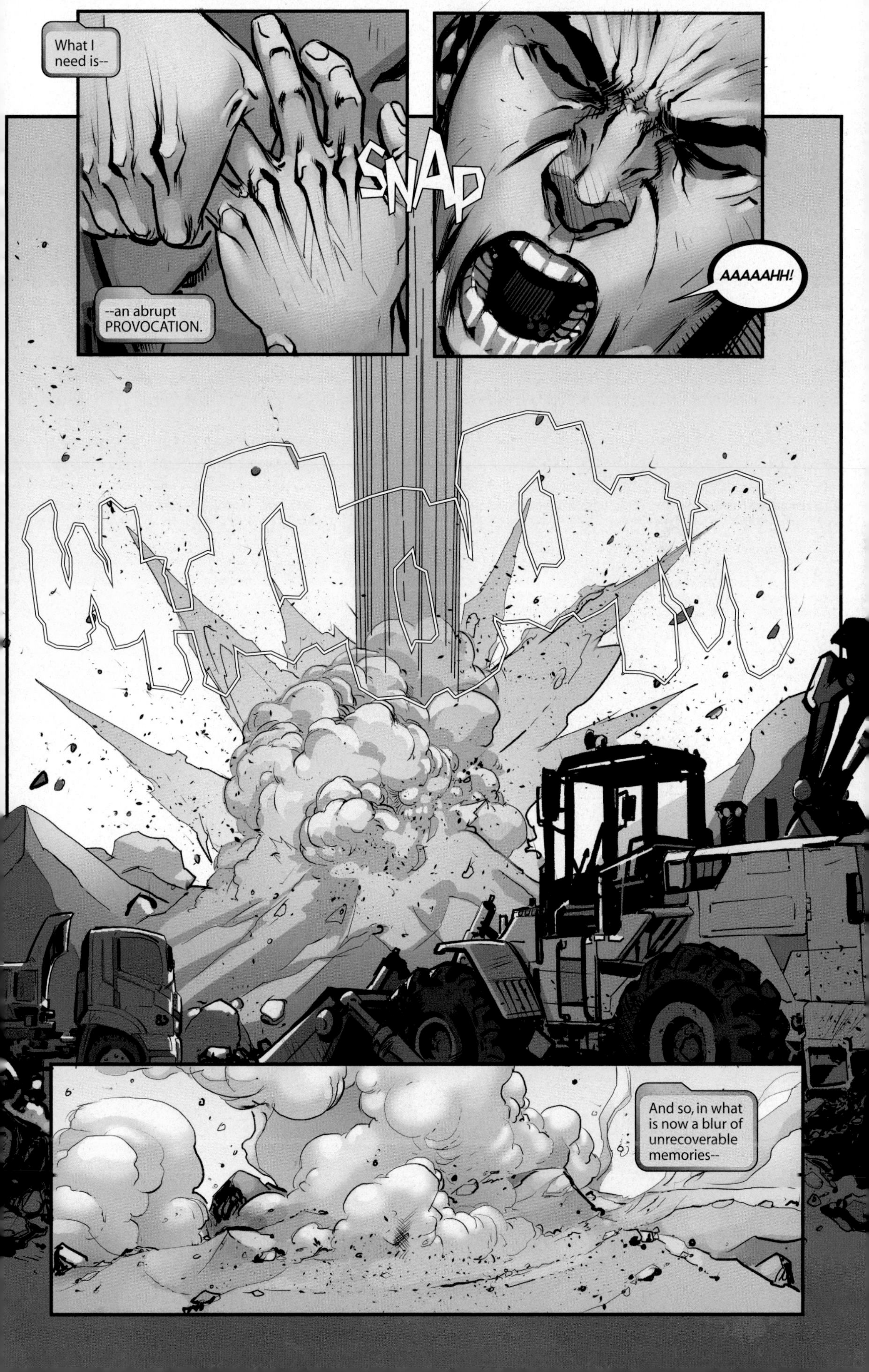
What I need is--
--an abrupt PROVOCATION.
SNAP
AAAAAHH!
And so, in what is now a blur of unrecoverable memories--

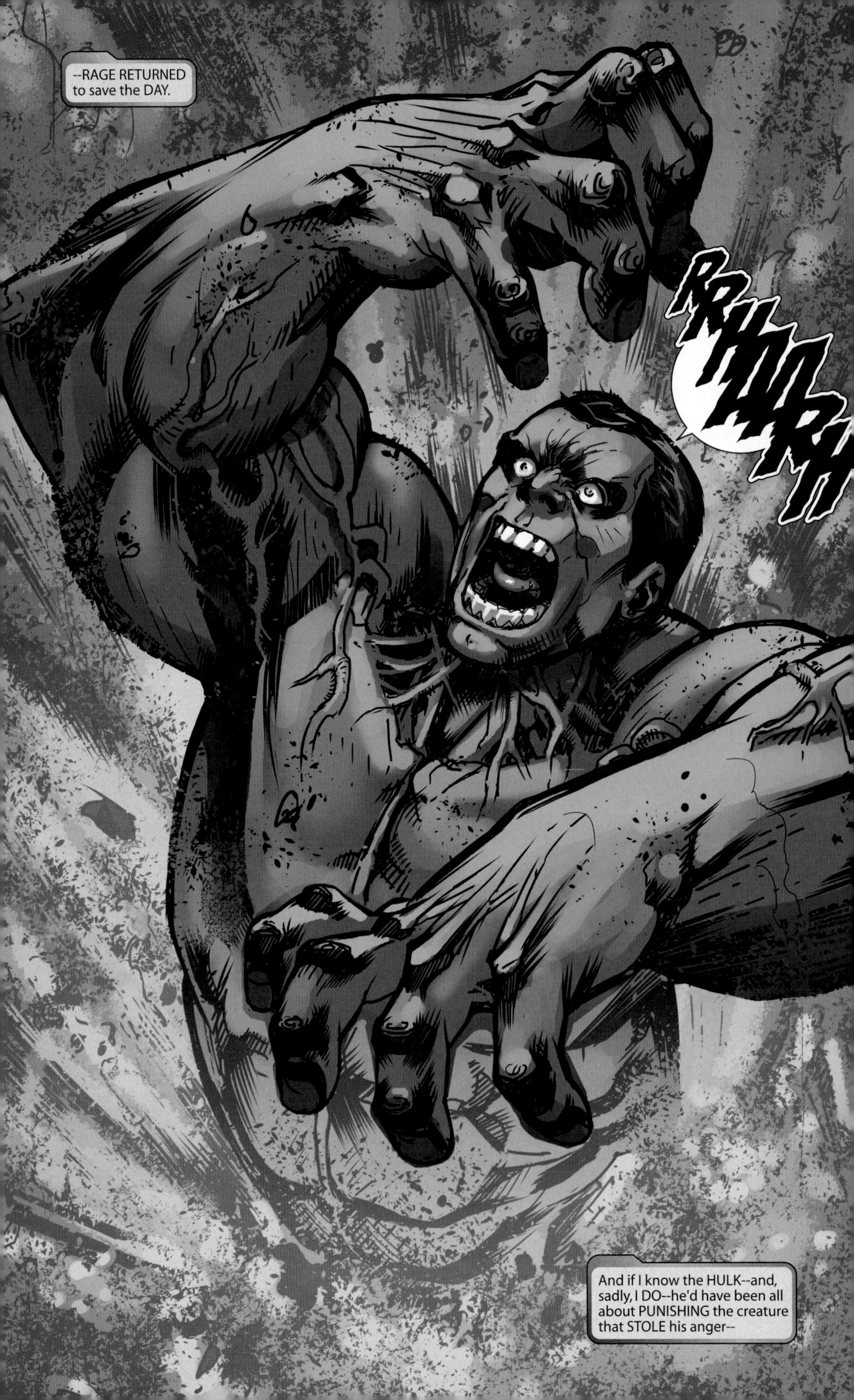
--RAGE RETURNED to save the DAY.
RRHHRRH
And if I know the HULK--and, sadly, I DO--he'd have been all about PUNISHING the creature that STOLE his anger--

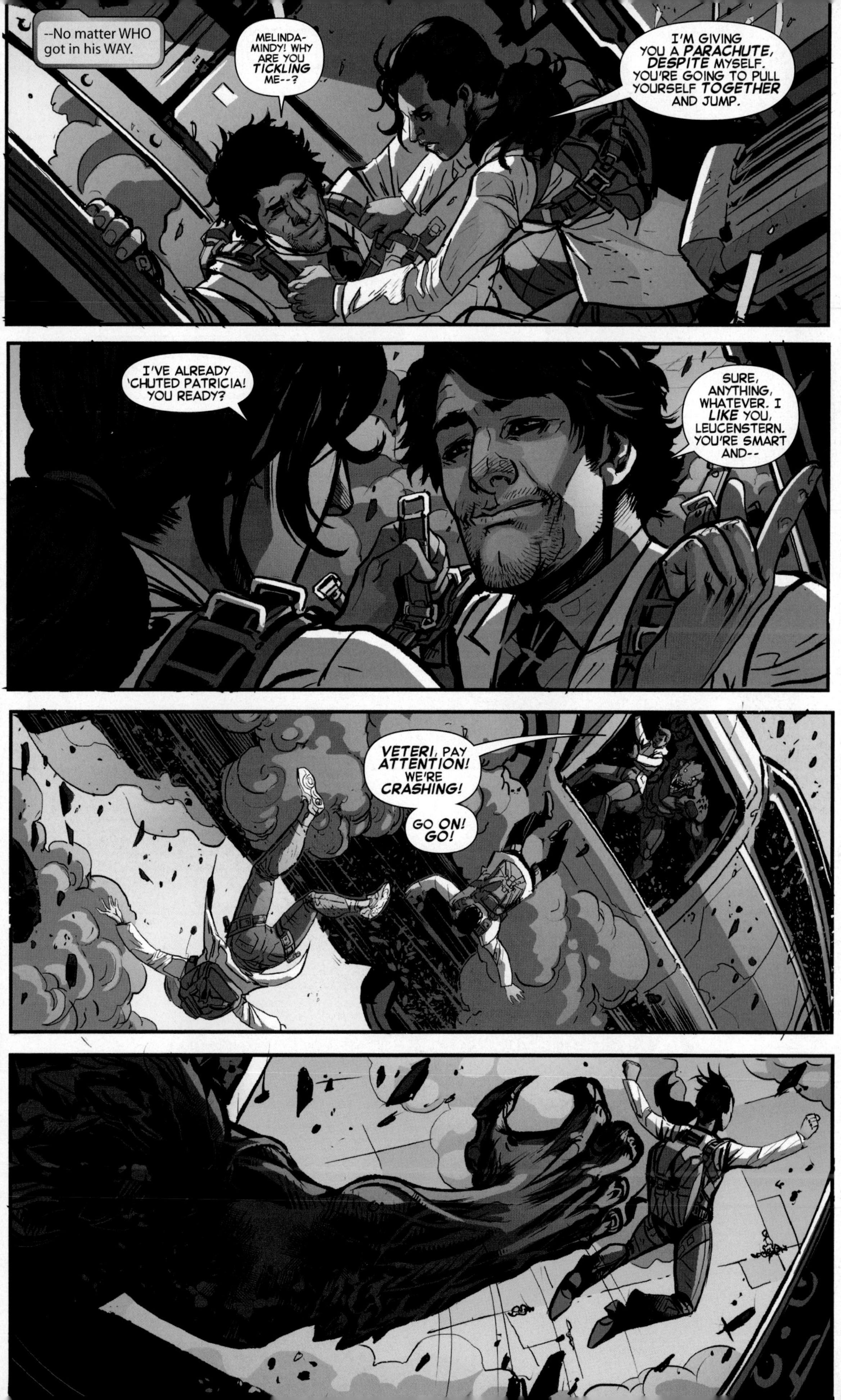
--No matter WHO got in his WAY.
MELINDA-MINDY! WHY ARE YOU TICKLING ME--?
I'M GIVING YOU A PARACHUTE, DESPITE MYSELF. YOU'RE GOING TO PULL YOURSELF TOGETHER AND JUMP.
I'VE ALREADY 'CHUTED PATRICIA! YOU READY?
SURE, ANYTHING, WHATEVER. I LIKE YOU, LEUCENSTERN. YOU'RE SMART AND--
VETERI, PAY ATTENTION! WE'RE CRASHING!
GO ON! GO!

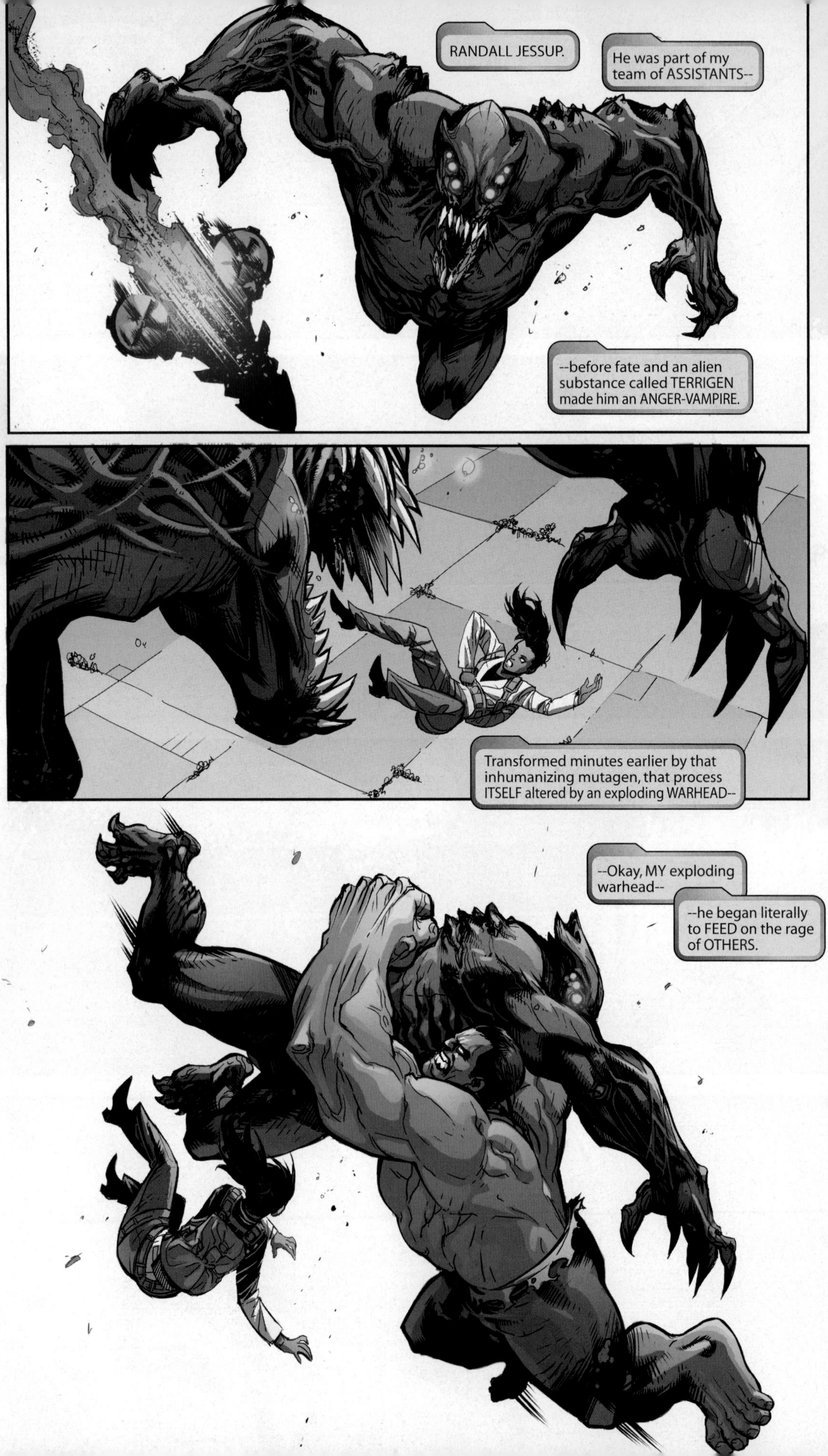
RANDALL JESSUP.
He was part of my team of ASSISTANTS--
--before fate and an alien substance called TERRIGEN made him an ANGER-VAMPIRE.
Transformed minutes earlier by that inhumanizing mutagen, that process ITSELF altered by an exploding WARHEAD--
--Okay, MY exploding warhead--
--he began literally to FEED on the rage of OTHERS.

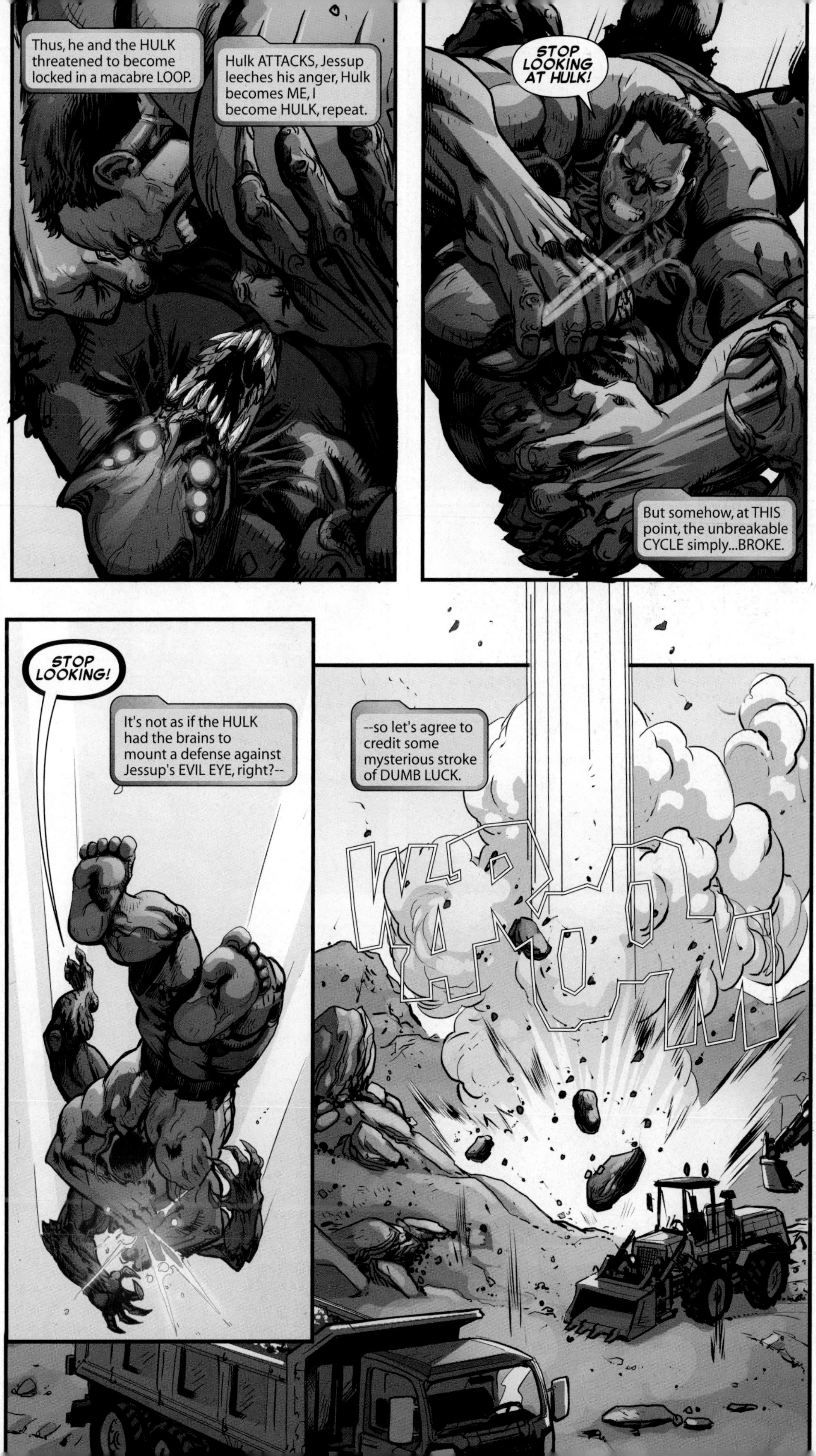
Thus, he and the HULK threatened to become locked in a macabre LOOP.
Hulk ATTACKS, Jessup leeches his anger, Hulk becomes ME, I become HULK, repeat.
STOP LOOKING AT HULK!
But somehow, at THIS point, the unbreakable CYCLE simply...BROKE.
STOP LOOKING!
It's not as if the HULK had the brains to mount a defense against Jessup's EVIL EYE, right?--
--so let's agree to credit some mysterious stroke of DUMB LUCK.

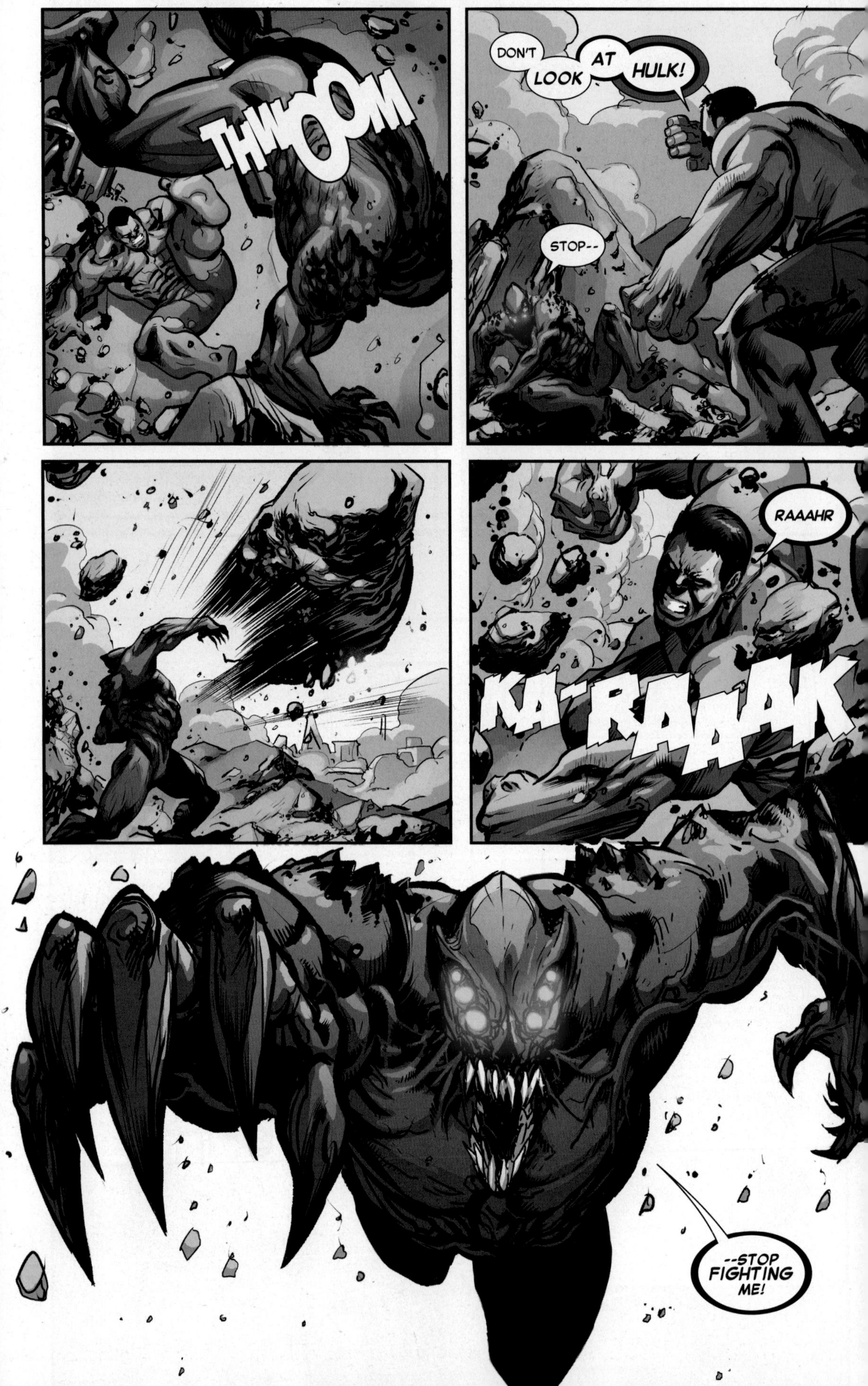
THWOOM
DON'T
LOOK
AT
HULK!
STOP--
RAAAHR
KA-RAAAAK
--STOP FIGHTING ME!

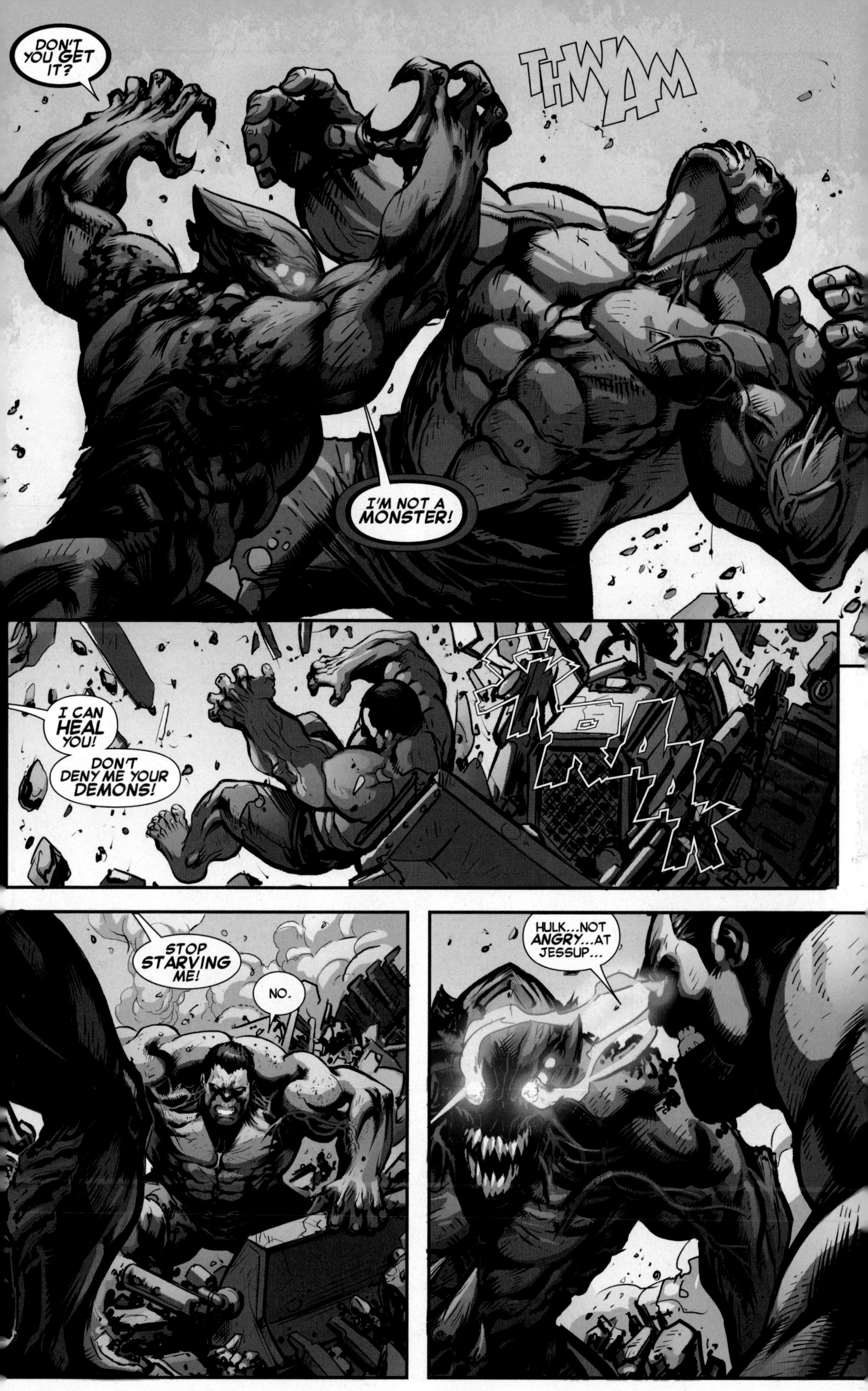
DON'T YOU GET IT?
THWAM
I'M NOT A MONSTER!
I CAN HEAL YOU!
DON'T DENY ME YOUR DEMONS!
STOP STARVING ME!
NO.
HULK...NOT ANGRY...AT JESSUP...

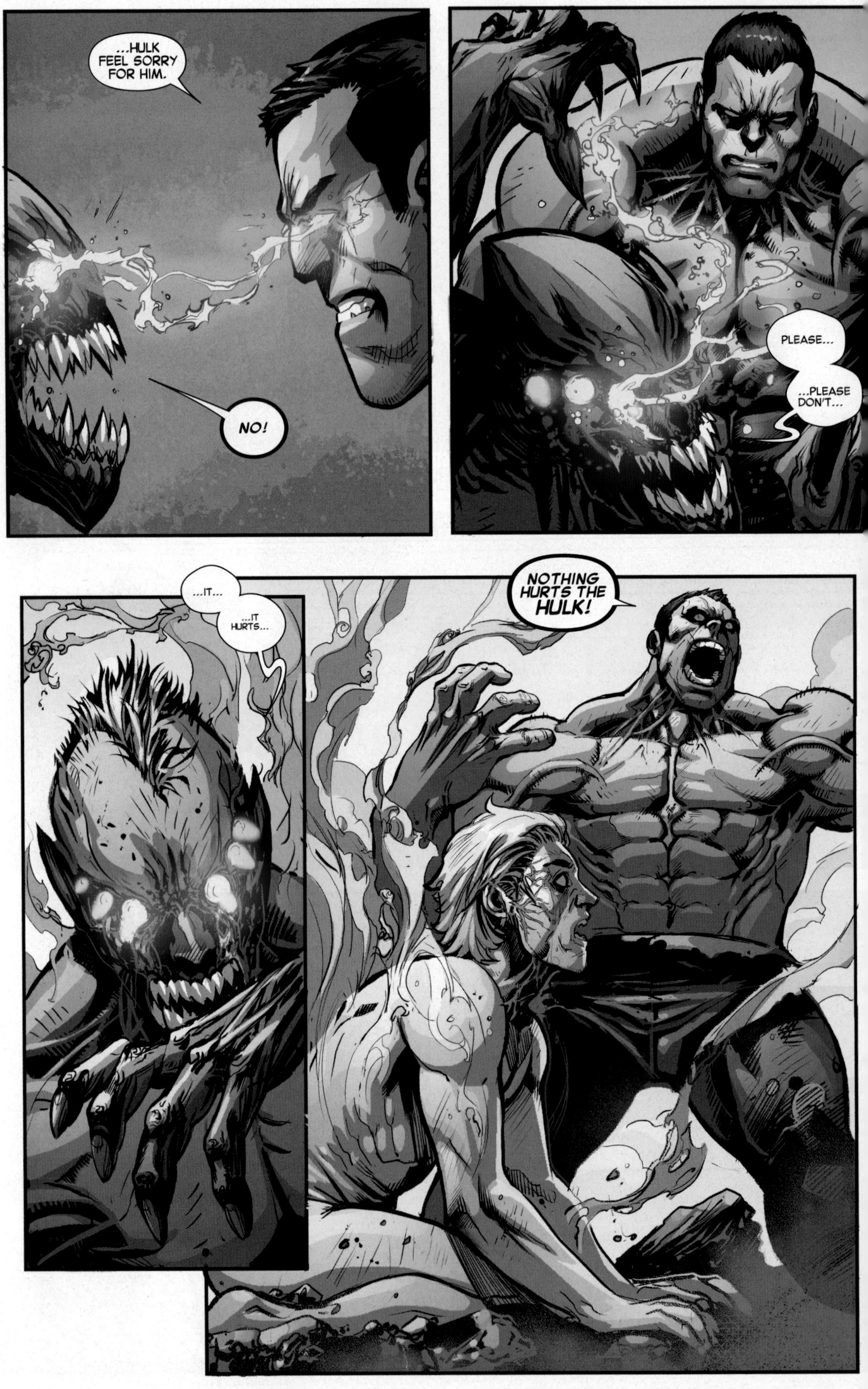
...HULK FEEL SORRY FOR HIM.
NO!
PLEASE...
...PLEASE DON'T...
...IT...
...IT HURTS...
NOTHING HURTS THE HULK!

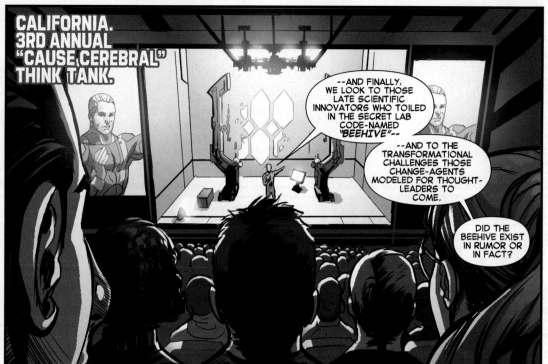

CALIFORNIA. 3RD ANNUAL "CAUSE CEREBRAL" THINK TANK.

--AND FINALLY, WE LOOK TO THOSE LATE SCIENTIFIC INNOVATORS WHO TOILED IN THE SECRET LAB CODE-NAMED *"BEEHIVE"*--

--AND TO THE TRANSFORMATIONAL CHALLENGES THOSE CHANGE-AGENTS MODELED FOR THOUGHT-LEADERS TO COME.

DID THE BEEHIVE EXIST IN RUMOR OR IN FACT?

DID AN ENCLAVE OF SCIENCE-ENTREPRENEURS SECRETLY DEVELOP A HUMAN UPGRADE?

DID THAT SENTIENT BREAKTHROUGH EMERGE FROM ITS COCOON AND DELETE ITS MAKERS IN A PASSION OF CREATIVE DESTRUCTION?

THE ANSWER IS, IT DOESN'T *MATTER.* FACTS *DIE,* BUT *IDEAS* BREATHE FOREVER...

...AND NEW *COCOONS* MATERIALIZE EVERY DAY.

BRAVO!

ENCORE!

CLAPCLAPCLAPCLAPCLAPCLAPCLAP

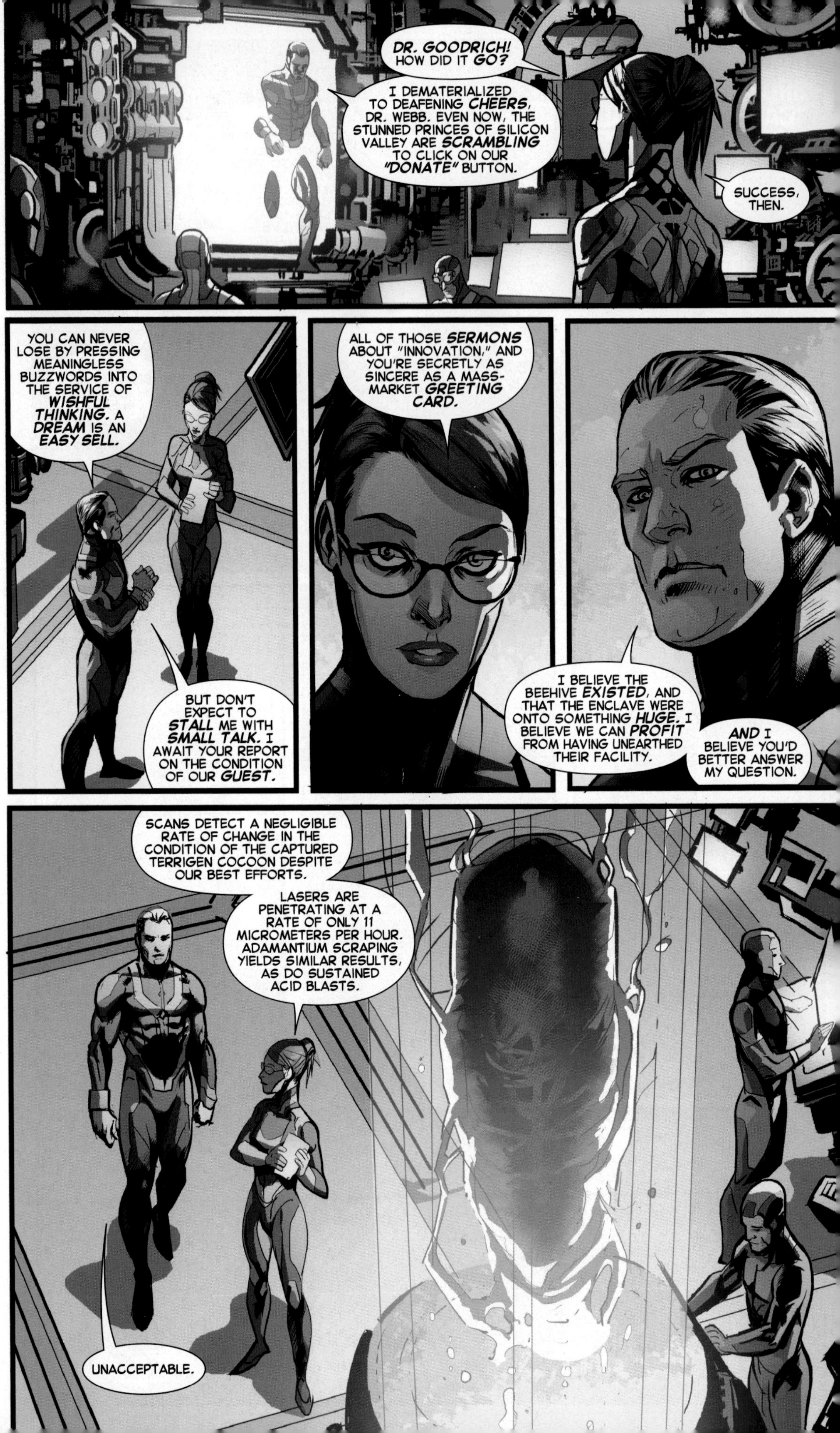
DR. GOODRICH! HOW DID IT GO?
I DEMATERIALIZED TO DEAFENING CHEERS, DR. WEBB. EVEN NOW, THE STUNNED PRINCES OF SILICON VALLEY ARE SCRAMBLING TO CLICK ON OUR "DONATE" BUTTON.
SUCCESS, THEN.
YOU CAN NEVER LOSE BY PRESSING MEANINGLESS BUZZWORDS INTO THE SERVICE OF WISHFUL THINKING. A DREAM IS AN EASY SELL.
BUT DON'T EXPECT TO STALL ME WITH SMALL TALK. I AWAIT YOUR REPORT ON THE CONDITION OF OUR GUEST.
ALL OF THOSE SERMONS ABOUT "INNOVATION," AND YOU'RE SECRETLY AS SINCERE AS A MASS-MARKET GREETING CARD.
I BELIEVE THE BEEHIVE EXISTED, AND THAT THE ENCLAVE WERE ONTO SOMETHING HUGE. I BELIEVE WE CAN PROFIT FROM HAVING UNEARTHED THEIR FACILITY.
AND I BELIEVE YOU'D BETTER ANSWER MY QUESTION.
SCANS DETECT A NEGLIGIBLE RATE OF CHANGE IN THE CONDITION OF THE CAPTURED TERRIGEN COCOON DESPITE OUR BEST EFFORTS.
LASERS ARE PENETRATING AT A RATE OF ONLY 11 MICROMETERS PER HOUR. ADAMANTIUM SCRAPING YIELDS SIMILAR RESULTS, AS DO SUSTAINED ACID BLASTS.
UNACCEPTABLE.

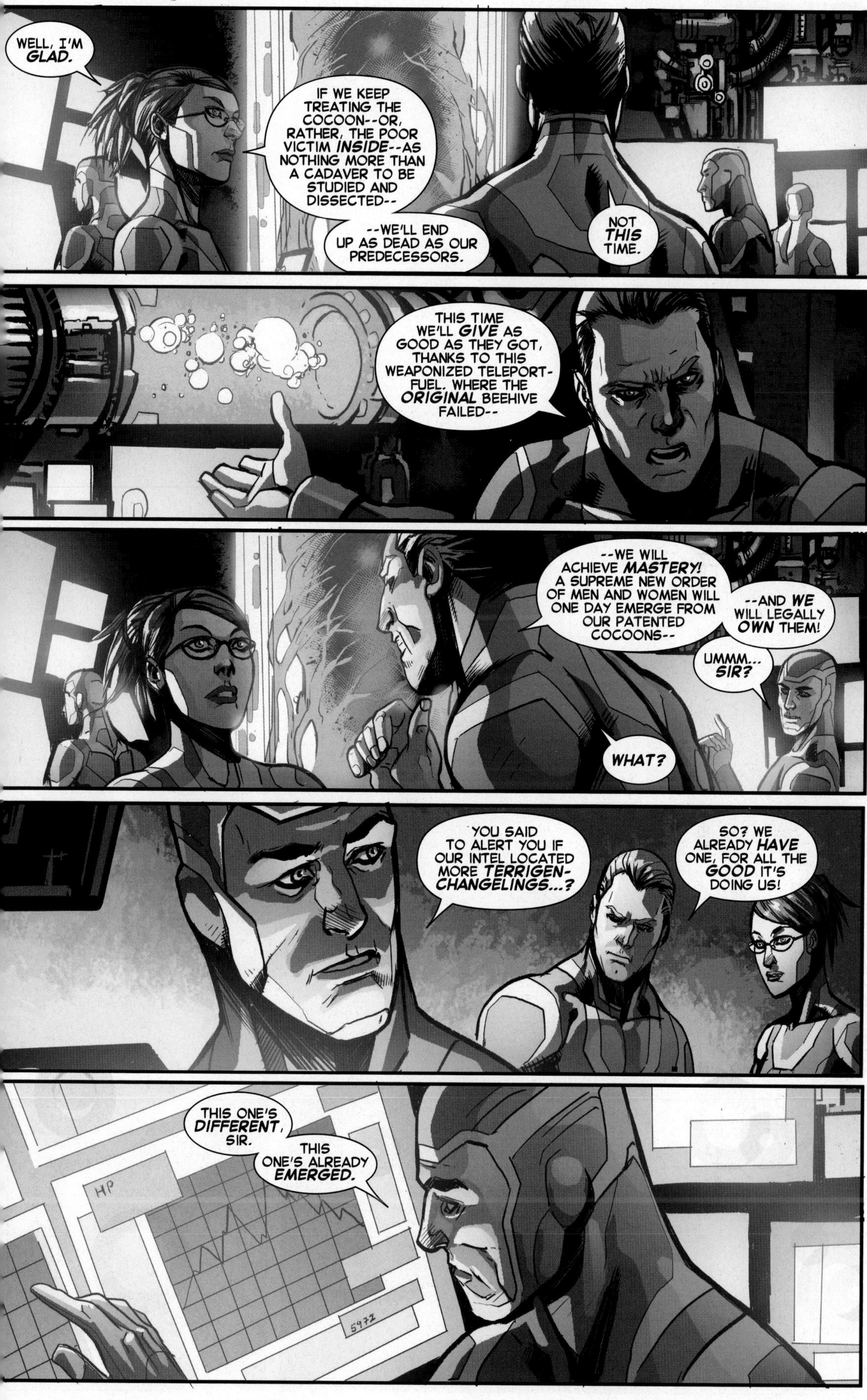
WELL, I'M GLAD.
IF WE KEEP TREATING THE COCOON--OR, RATHER, THE POOR VICTIM INSIDE--AS NOTHING MORE THAN A CADAVER TO BE STUDIED AND DISSECTED--
--WE'LL END UP AS DEAD AS OUR PREDECESSORS.
NOT THIS TIME.
THIS TIME WE'LL GIVE AS GOOD AS THEY GOT, THANKS TO THIS WEAPONIZED TELEPORT-FUEL. WHERE THE ORIGINAL BEEHIVE FAILED--
--WE WILL ACHIEVE MASTERY! A SUPREME NEW ORDER OF MEN AND WOMEN WILL ONE DAY EMERGE FROM OUR PATENTED COCOONS--
--AND WE WILL LEGALLY OWN THEM!
UMMM... SIR?
WHAT?
YOU SAID TO ALERT YOU IF OUR INTEL LOCATED MORE TERRIGEN-CHANGELINGS...?
SO? WE ALREADY HAVE ONE, FOR ALL THE GOOD IT'S DOING US!
THIS ONE'S DIFFERENT, SIR.
THIS ONE'S ALREADY EMERGED.

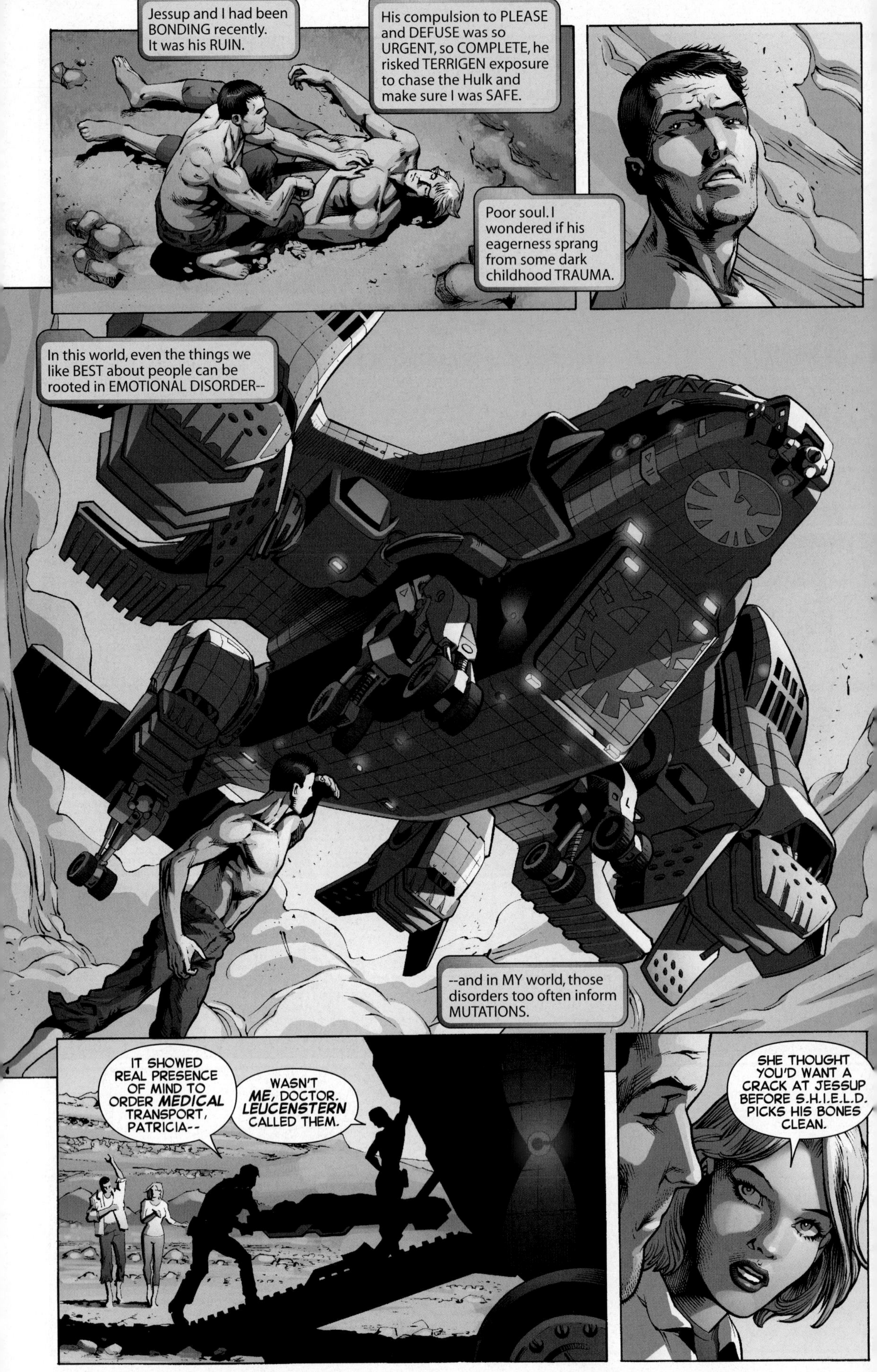

Jessup and I had been BONDING recently. It was his RUIN.
His compulsion to PLEASE and DEFUSE was so URGENT, so COMPLETE, he risked TERRIGEN exposure to chase the Hulk and make sure I was SAFE.
Poor soul. I wondered if his eagerness sprang from some dark childhood TRAUMA.
In this world, even the things we like BEST about people can be rooted in EMOTIONAL DISORDER--
--and in MY world, those disorders too often inform MUTATIONS.
IT SHOWED REAL PRESENCE OF MIND TO ORDER MEDICAL TRANSPORT, PATRICIA--
WASN'T ME, DOCTOR. LEUCENSTERN CALLED THEM.
SHE THOUGHT YOU'D WANT A CRACK AT JESSUP BEFORE S.H.I.E.L.D. PICKS HIS BONES CLEAN.

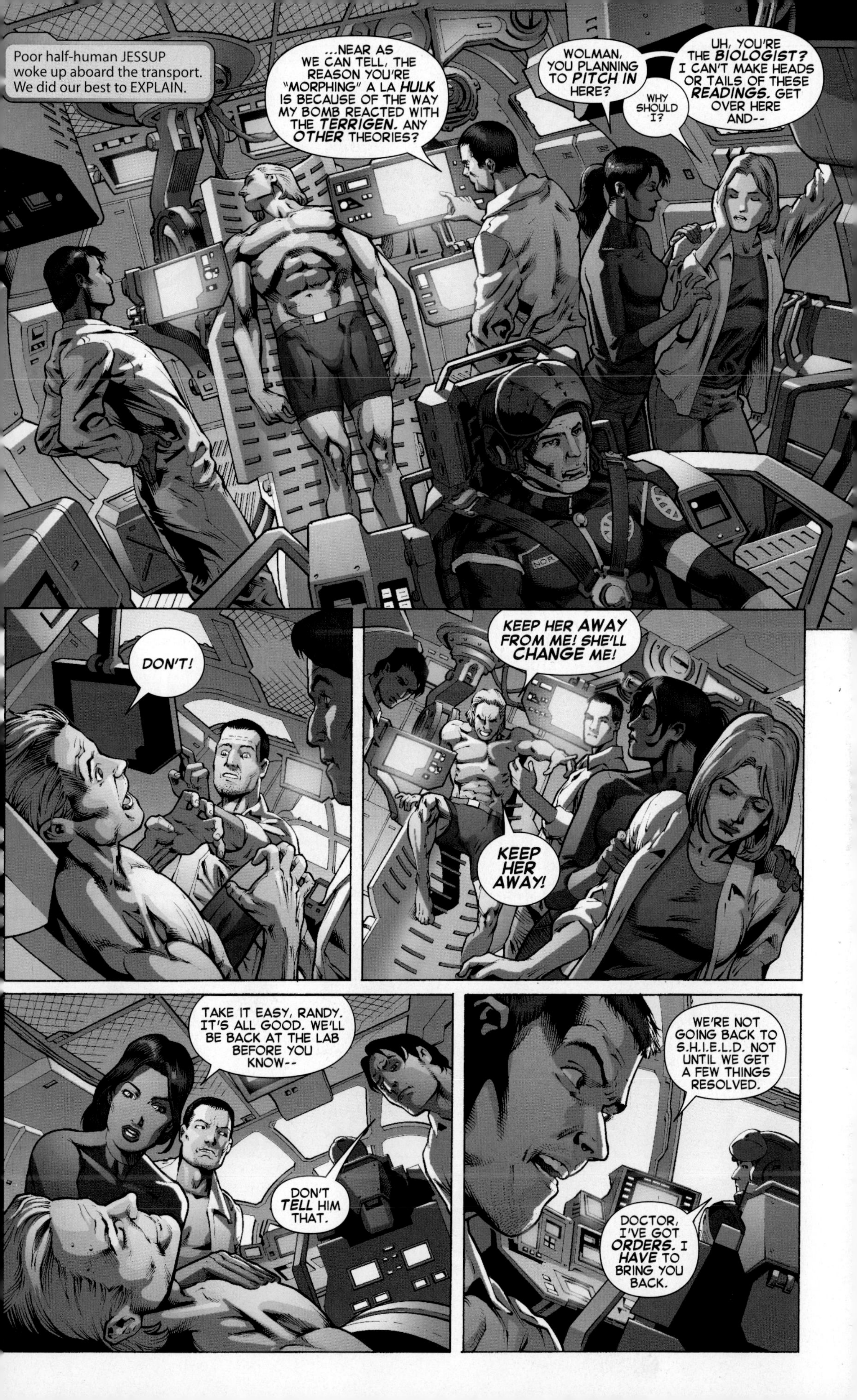
Poor half-human JESSUP woke up aboard the transport. We did our best to EXPLAIN.
...NEAR AS WE CAN TELL, THE REASON YOU'RE "MORPHING" A LA HULK IS BECAUSE OF THE WAY MY BOMB REACTED WITH THE TERRIGEN. ANY OTHER THEORIES?
WOLMAN, YOU PLANNING TO PITCH IN HERE?
WHY SHOULD I?
UH, YOU'RE THE BIOLOGIST? I CAN'T MAKE HEADS OR TAILS OF THESE READINGS. GET OVER HERE AND--
DON'T!
KEEP HER AWAY FROM ME! SHE'LL CHANGE ME!
KEEP HER AWAY!
TAKE IT EASY, RANDY. IT'S ALL GOOD. WE'LL BE BACK AT THE LAB BEFORE YOU KNOW--
DON'T TELL HIM THAT.
WE'RE NOT GOING BACK TO S.H.I.E.L.D. NOT UNTIL WE GET A FEW THINGS RESOLVED.
DOCTOR, I'VE GOT ORDERS. I HAVE TO BRING YOU BACK.

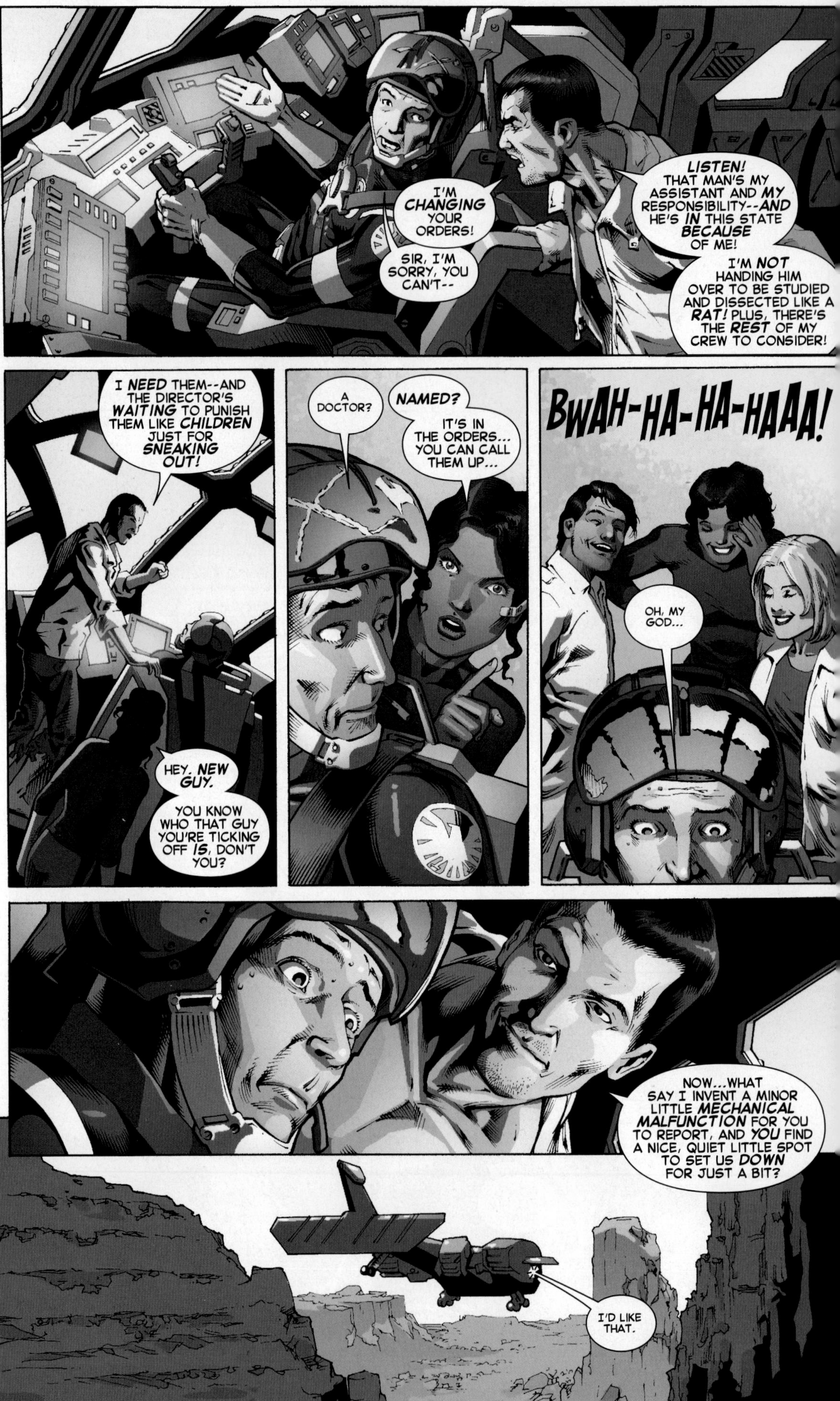
I'M CHANGING YOUR ORDERS!
SIR, I'M SORRY, YOU CAN'T--
LISTEN! THAT MAN'S MY ASSISTANT AND MY RESPONSIBILITY--AND HE'S IN THIS STATE BECAUSE OF ME!
I'M NOT HANDING HIM OVER TO BE STUDIED AND DISSECTED LIKE A RAT! PLUS, THERE'S THE REST OF MY CREW TO CONSIDER!
I NEED THEM--AND THE DIRECTOR'S WAITING TO PUNISH THEM LIKE CHILDREN JUST FOR SNEAKING OUT!
HEY. NEW GUY.
YOU KNOW WHO THAT GUY YOU'RE TICKING OFF IS, DON'T YOU?
A DOCTOR?
NAMED?
IT'S IN THE ORDERS... YOU CAN CALL THEM UP...
BWAH-HA-HA-HAAA!
OH, MY GOD...
NOW...WHAT SAY I INVENT A MINOR LITTLE MECHANICAL MALFUNCTION FOR YOU TO REPORT, AND YOU FIND A NICE, QUIET LITTLE SPOT TO SET US DOWN FOR JUST A BIT?
I'D LIKE THAT.

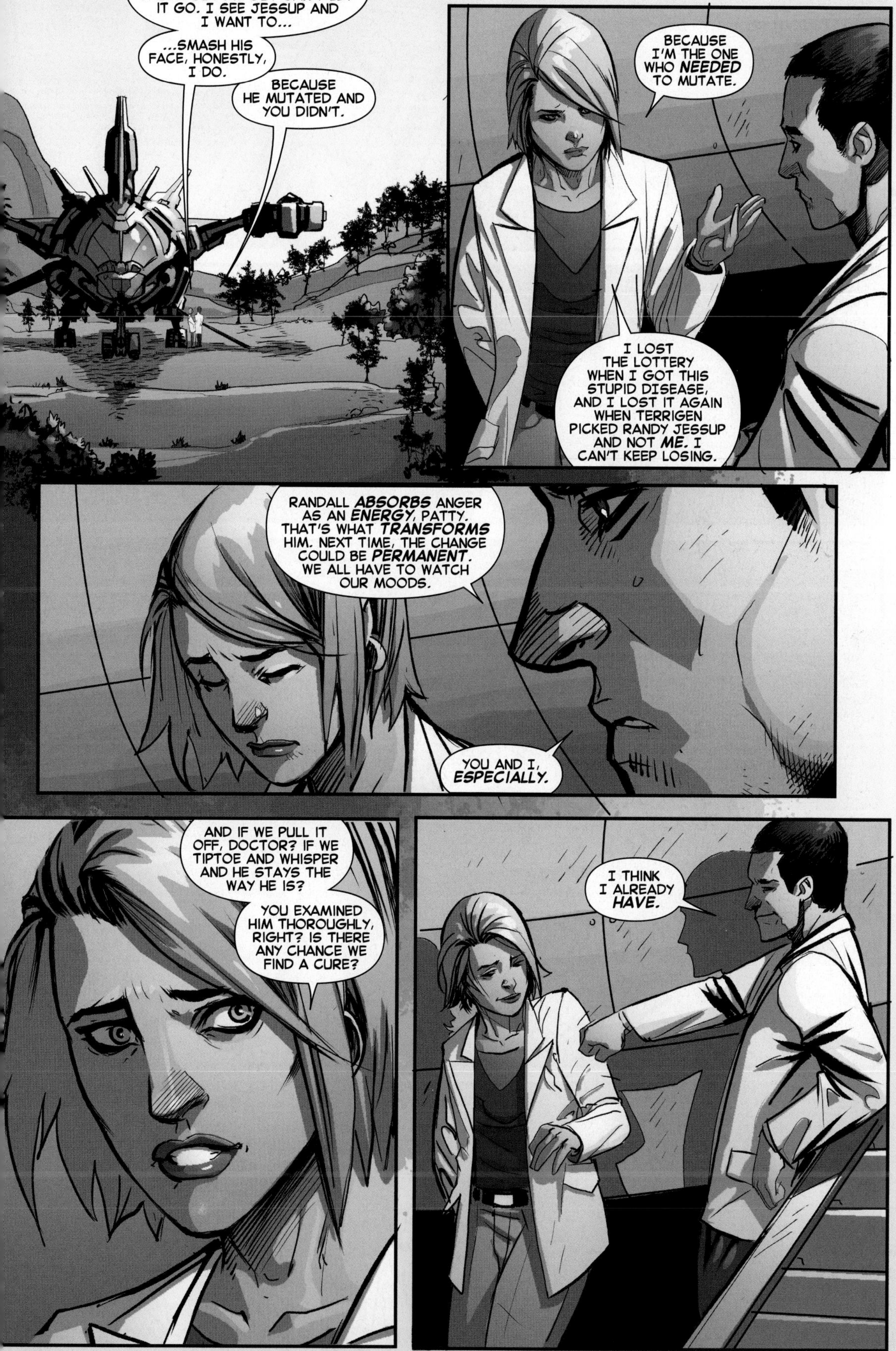
INTELLECTUALLY, I REALIZE IT'S UNFOUNDED, DR. BANNER. THAT IT'S NOT HIS FAULT. BUT MY GUT CAN'T LET IT GO. I SEE JESSUP AND I WANT TO...
...SMASH HIS FACE, HONESTLY, I DO.
BECAUSE HE MUTATED AND YOU DIDN'T.
BECAUSE I'M THE ONE WHO NEEDED TO MUTATE.
I LOST THE LOTTERY WHEN I GOT THIS STUPID DISEASE, AND I LOST IT AGAIN WHEN TERRIGEN PICKED RANDY JESSUP AND NOT ME. I CAN'T KEEP LOSING.
RANDALL ABSORBS ANGER AS AN ENERGY, PATTY. THAT'S WHAT TRANSFORMS HIM. NEXT TIME, THE CHANGE COULD BE PERMANENT. WE ALL HAVE TO WATCH OUR MOODS.
YOU AND I, ESPECIALLY.
AND IF WE PULL IT OFF, DOCTOR? IF WE TIPTOE AND WHISPER AND HE STAYS THE WAY HE IS?
YOU EXAMINED HIM THOROUGHLY, RIGHT? IS THERE ANY CHANCE WE FIND A CURE?
I THINK I ALREADY HAVE.

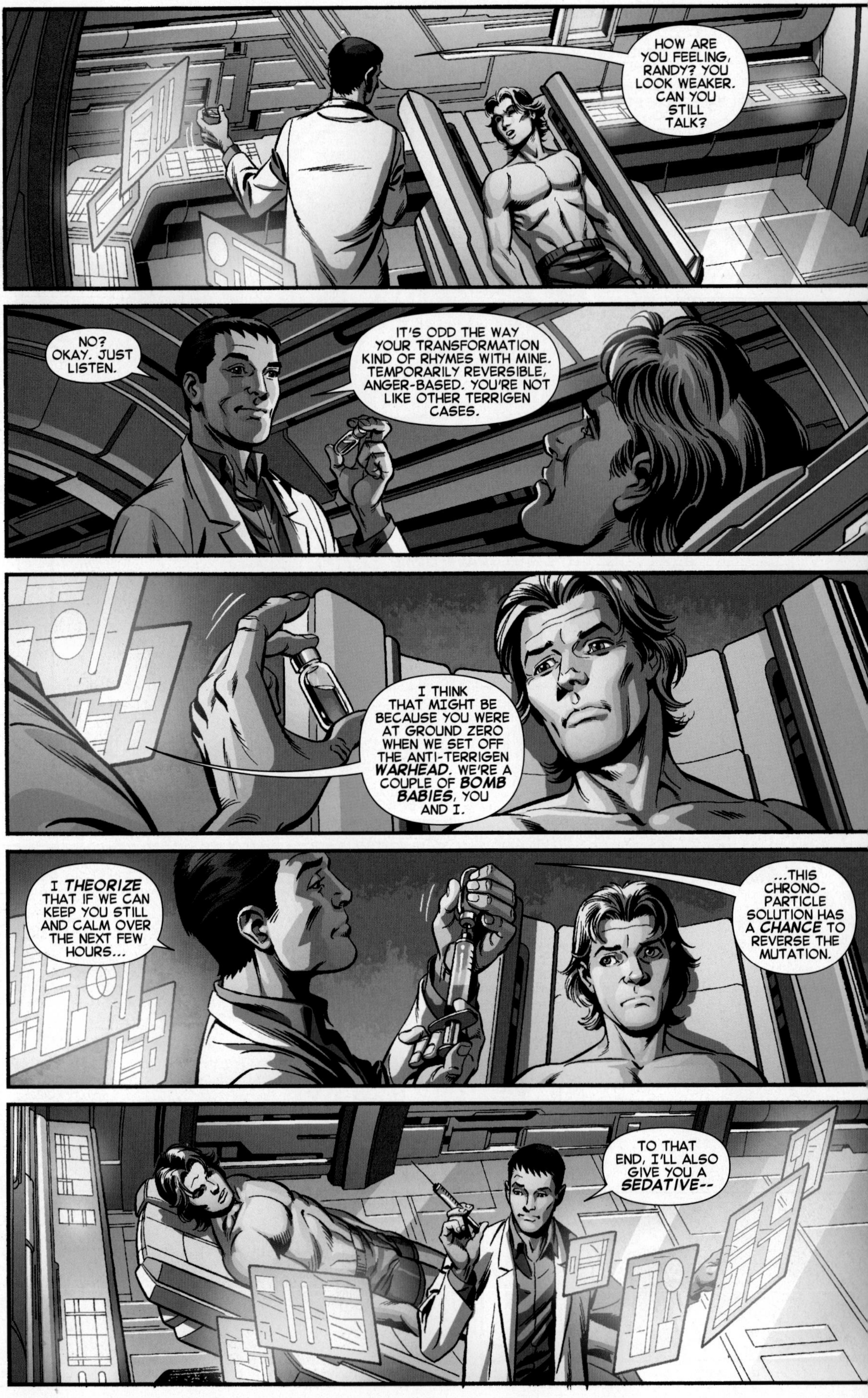
HOW ARE YOU FEELING, RANDY? YOU LOOK WEAKER. CAN YOU STILL TALK?
NO? OKAY. JUST LISTEN.
IT'S ODD THE WAY YOUR TRANSFORMATION KIND OF RHYMES WITH MINE. TEMPORARILY REVERSIBLE, ANGER-BASED. YOU'RE NOT LIKE OTHER TERRIGEN CASES.
I THINK THAT MIGHT BE BECAUSE YOU WERE AT GROUND ZERO WHEN WE SET OFF THE ANTI-TERRIGEN WARHEAD. WE'RE A COUPLE OF BOMB BABIES, YOU AND I.
I THEORIZE THAT IF WE CAN KEEP YOU STILL AND CALM OVER THE NEXT FEW HOURS...
...THIS CHRONO-PARTICLE SOLUTION HAS A CHANCE TO REVERSE THE MUTATION.
TO THAT END, I'LL ALSO GIVE YOU A SEDATIVE--

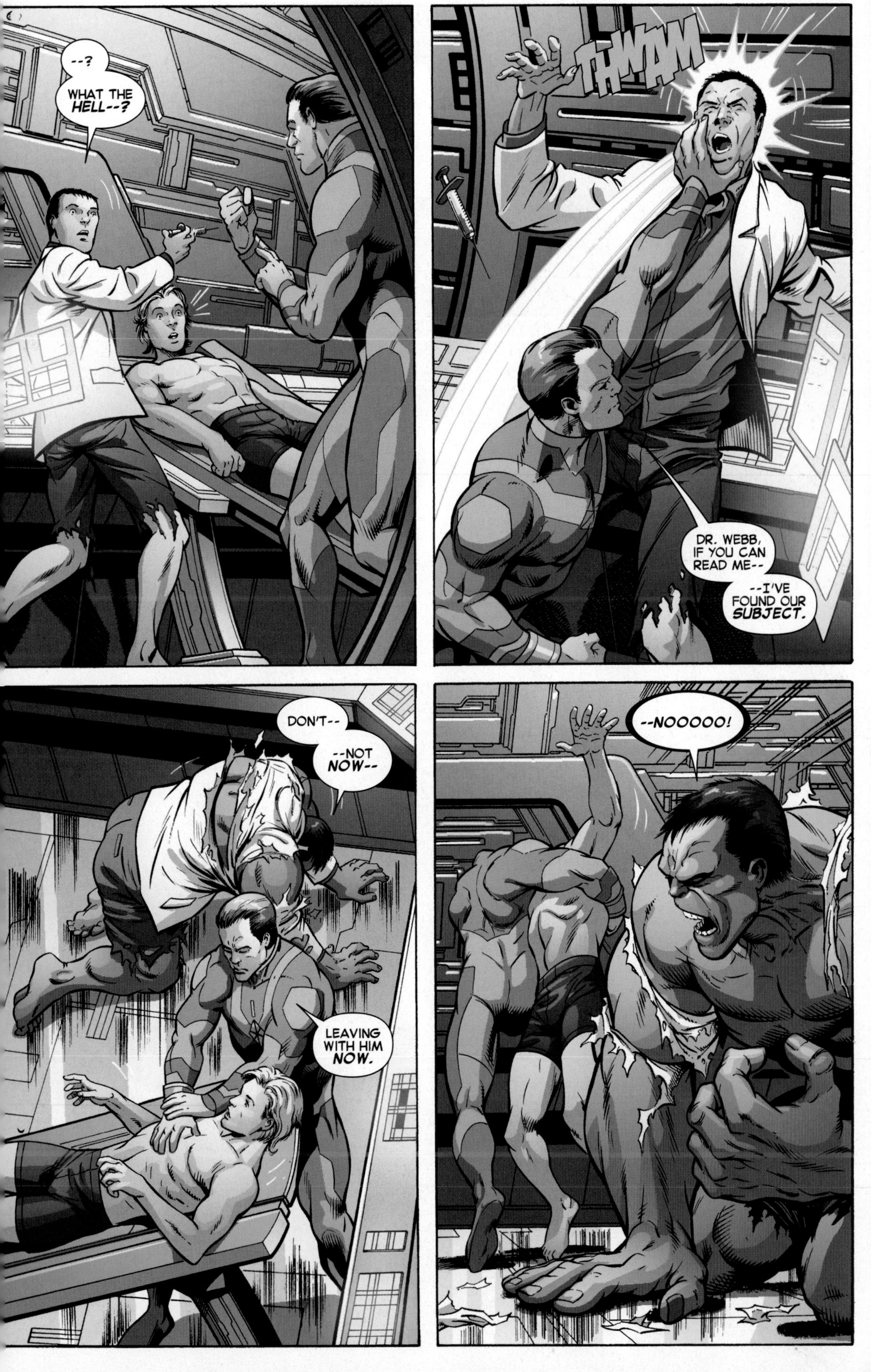
--?
WHAT THE HELL--?
THWAM
DR. WEBB, IF YOU CAN READ ME--
--I'VE FOUND OUR SUBJECT.
DON'T--
--NOT NOW--
LEAVING WITH HIM NOW.
--NOOOOO!

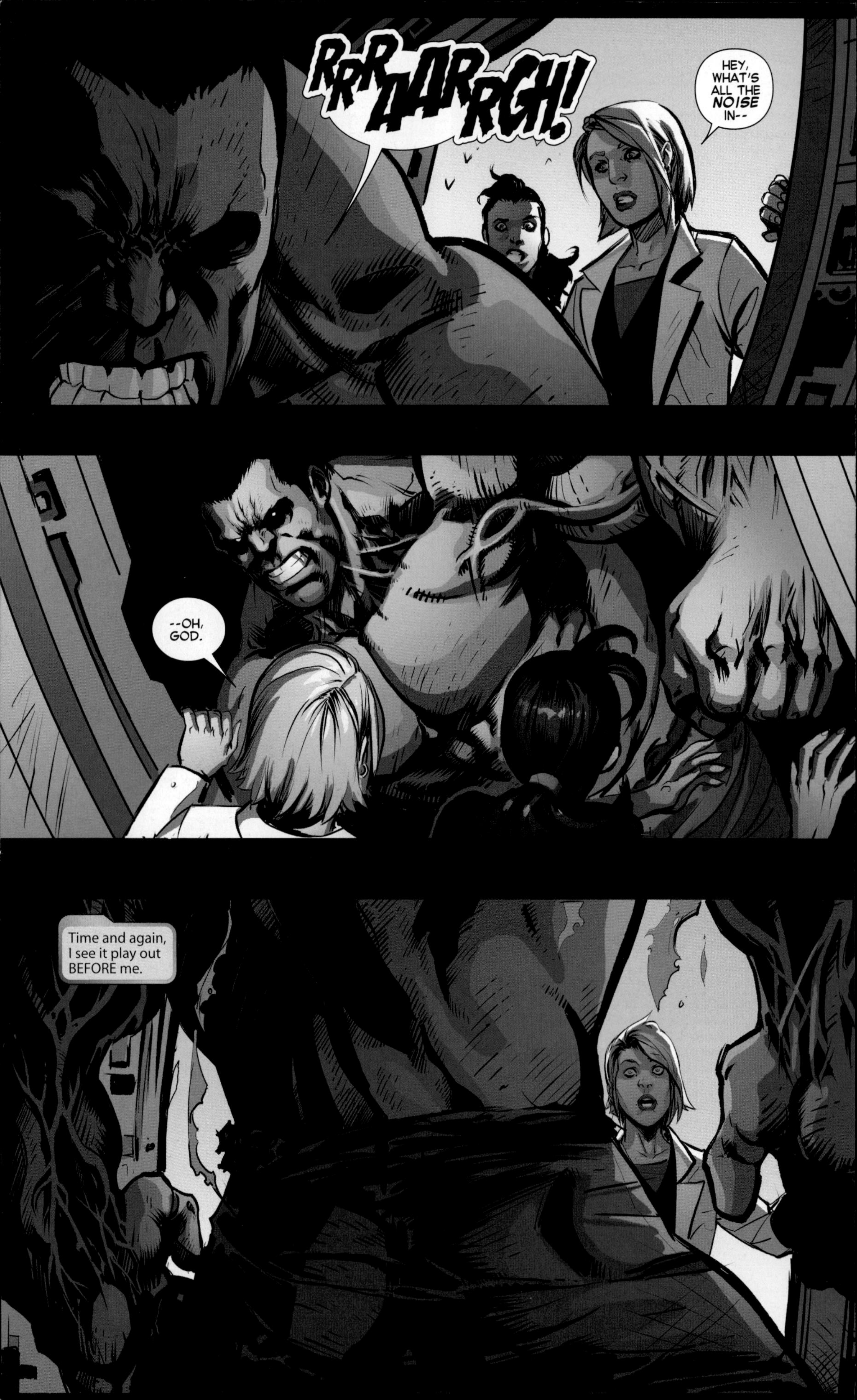
RRRAARRRGH!
HEY, WHAT'S ALL THE NOISE IN--
--OH, GOD.
Time and again, I see it play out BEFORE me.

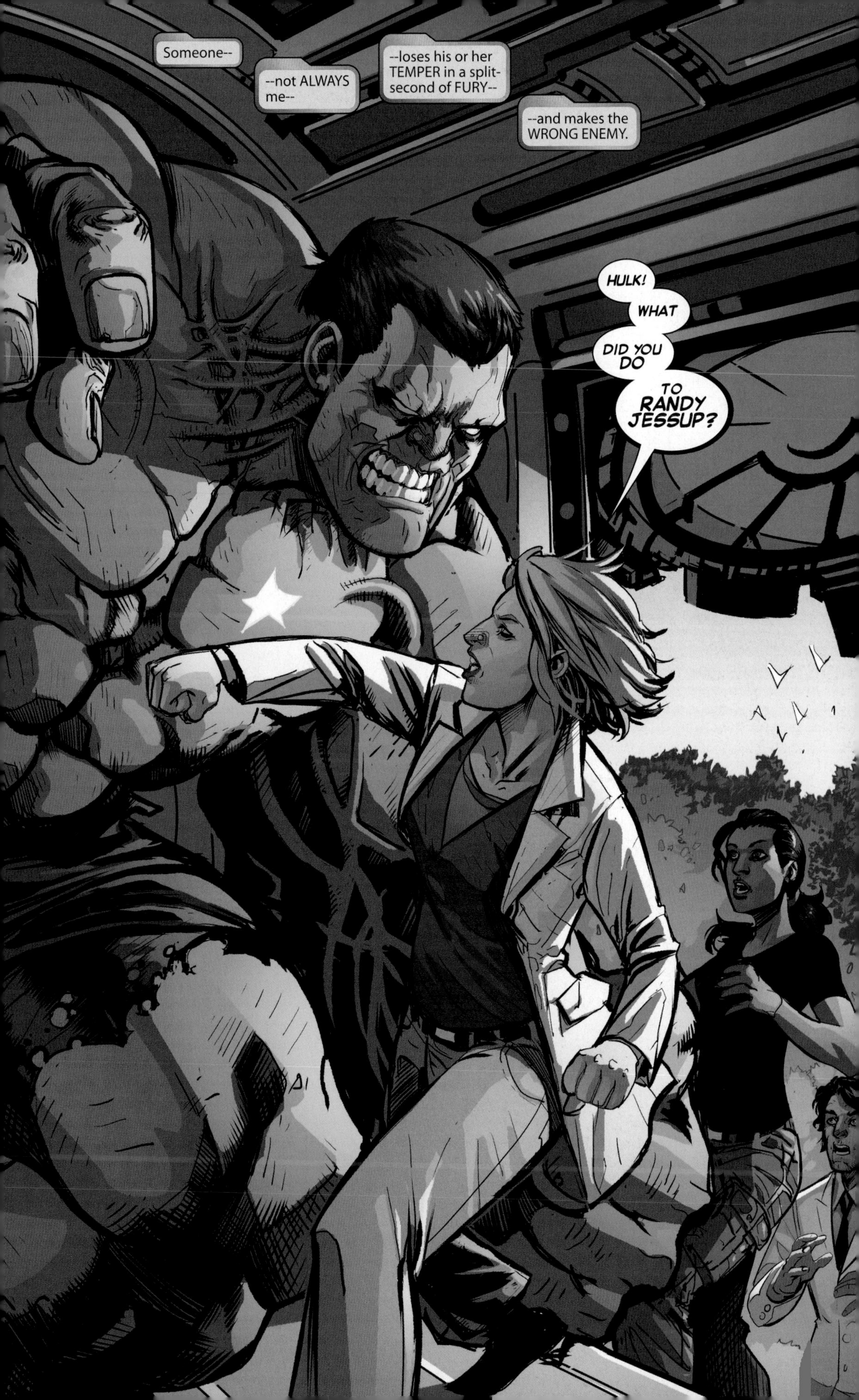
Someone--
--not ALWAYS me--
--loses his or her TEMPER in a split-second of FURY--
--and makes the WRONG ENEMY.
HULK!
WHAT
DID YOU DO
TO RANDY JESSUP?

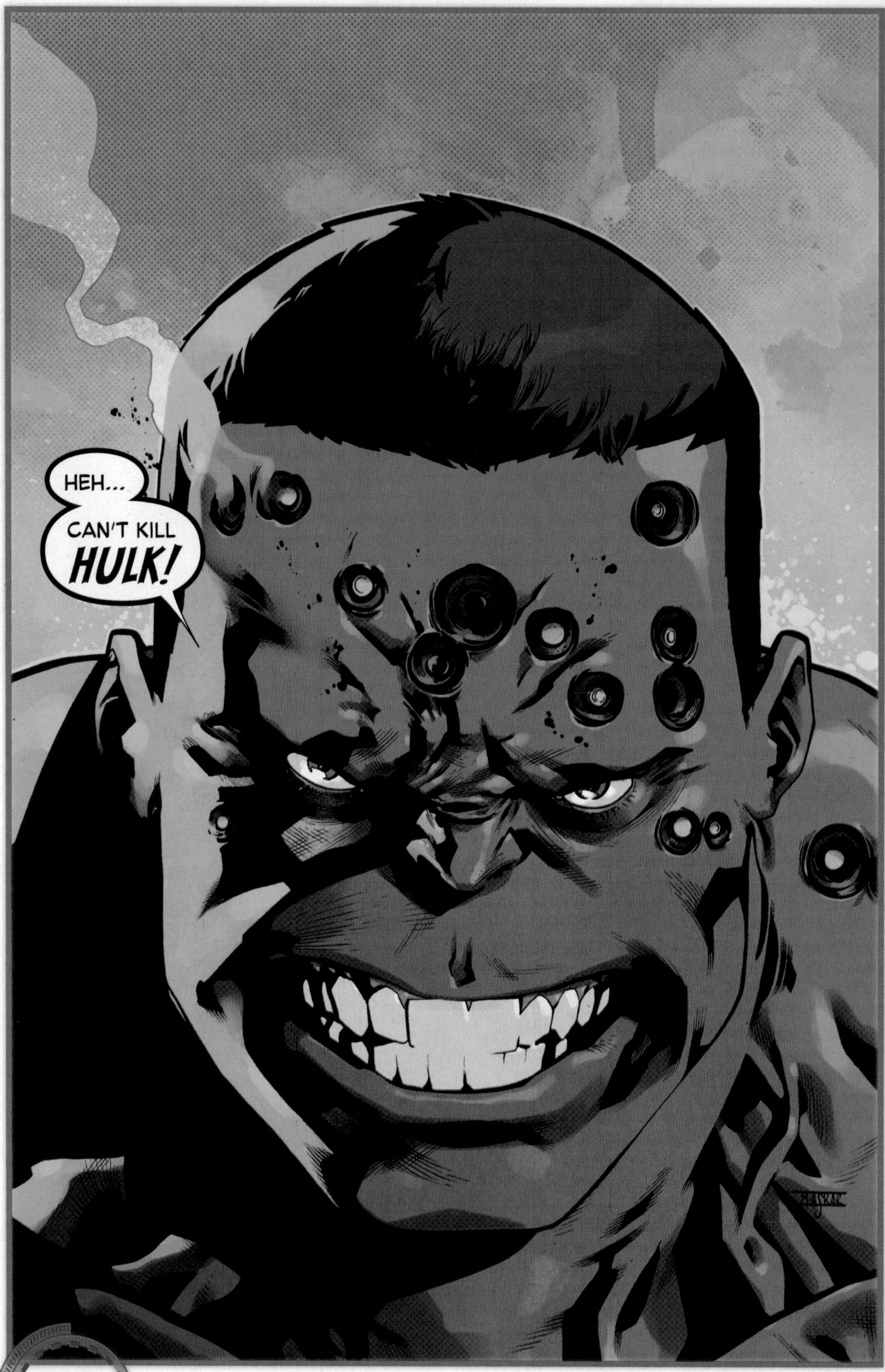
HEH...
CAN'T KILL HULK!
MAJKAK

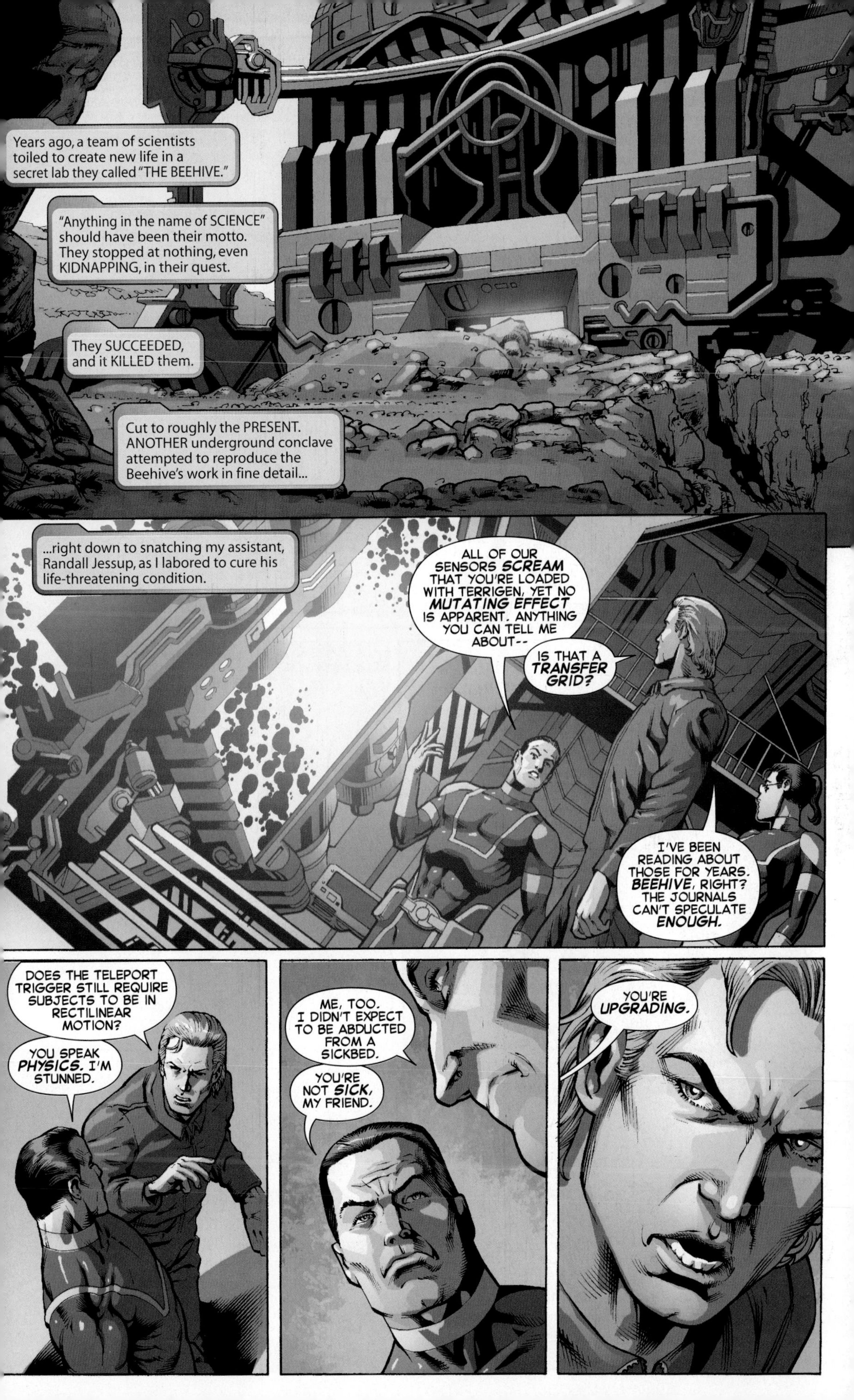

Years ago, a team of scientists toiled to create new life in a secret lab they called "THE BEEHIVE."
"Anything in the name of SCIENCE" should have been their motto. They stopped at nothing, even KIDNAPPING, in their quest.
They SUCCEEDED, and it KILLED them.
Cut to roughly the PRESENT. ANOTHER underground conclave attempted to reproduce the Beehive's work in fine detail...
...right down to snatching my assistant, Randall Jessup, as I labored to cure his life-threatening condition.
ALL OF OUR SENSORS SCREAM THAT YOU'RE LOADED WITH TERRIGEN, YET NO MUTATING EFFECT IS APPARENT. ANYTHING YOU CAN TELL ME ABOUT--
IS THAT A TRANSFER GRID?
I'VE BEEN READING ABOUT THOSE FOR YEARS. BEEHIVE, RIGHT? THE JOURNALS CAN'T SPECULATE ENOUGH.
DOES THE TELEPORT TRIGGER STILL REQUIRE SUBJECTS TO BE IN RECTILINEAR MOTION?
YOU SPEAK PHYSICS. I'M STUNNED.
ME, TOO. I DIDN'T EXPECT TO BE ABDUCTED FROM A SICKBED.
YOU'RE NOT SICK, MY FRIEND.
YOU'RE UPGRADING.

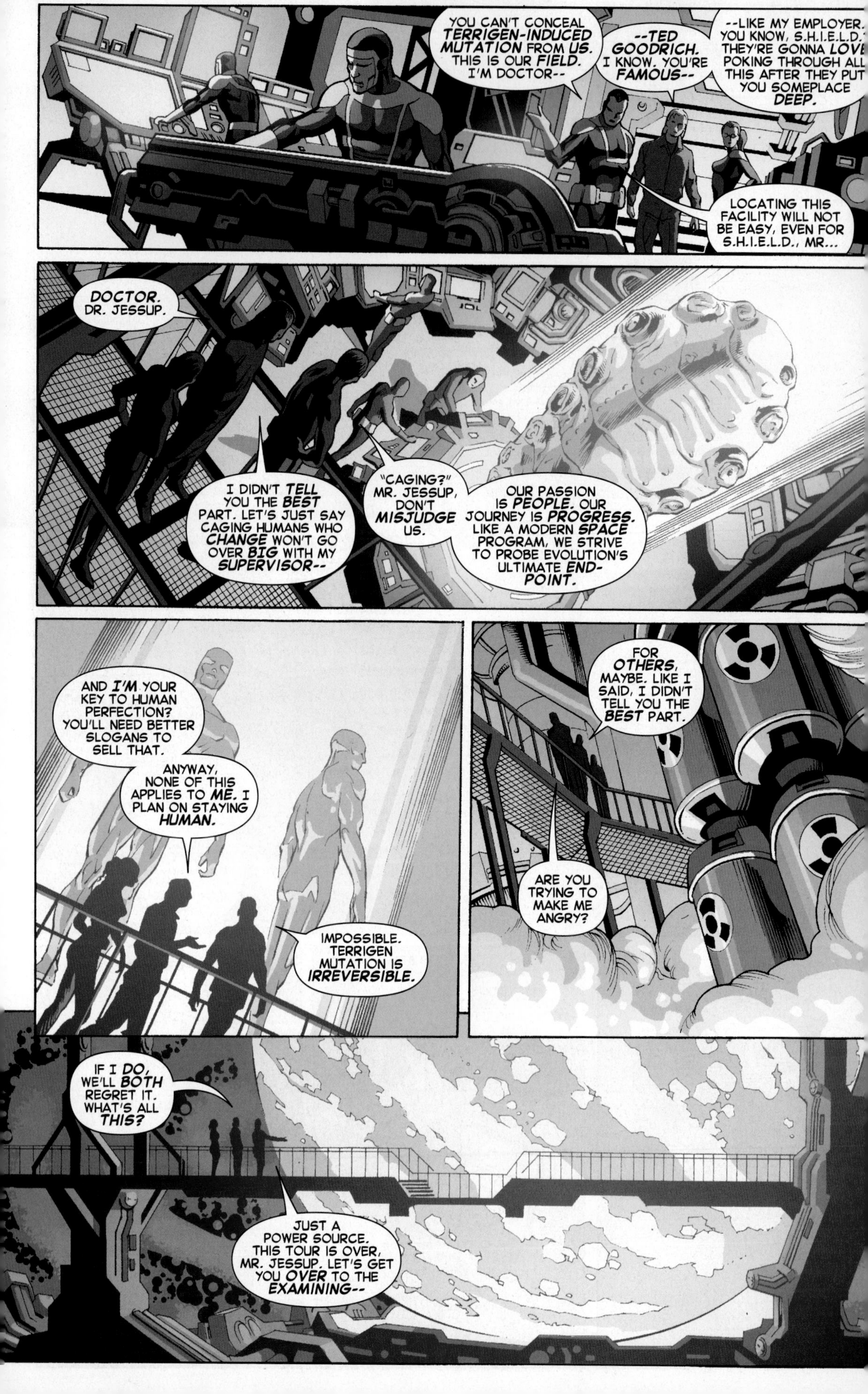
YOU CAN'T CONCEAL TERRIGEN-INDUCED MUTATION FROM US. THIS IS OUR FIELD. I'M DOCTOR--
--TED GOODRICH. I KNOW. YOU'RE FAMOUS--
--LIKE MY EMPLOYER. YOU KNOW, S.H.I.E.L.D. THEY'RE GONNA LOVE POKING THROUGH ALL THIS AFTER THEY PUT YOU SOMEPLACE DEEP.
LOCATING THIS FACILITY WILL NOT BE EASY, EVEN FOR S.H.I.E.L.D., MR...
DOCTOR. DR. JESSUP.
I DIDN'T TELL YOU THE BEST PART. LET'S JUST SAY CAGING HUMANS WHO CHANGE WON'T GO OVER BIG WITH MY SUPERVISOR--
"CAGING?" MR. JESSUP, DON'T MISJUDGE US.
OUR PASSION IS PEOPLE. OUR JOURNEY IS PROGRESS. LIKE A MODERN SPACE PROGRAM, WE STRIVE TO PROBE EVOLUTION'S ULTIMATE END-POINT.
AND I'M YOUR KEY TO HUMAN PERFECTION? YOU'LL NEED BETTER SLOGANS TO SELL THAT.
ANYWAY, NONE OF THIS APPLIES TO ME. I PLAN ON STAYING HUMAN.
IMPOSSIBLE. TERRIGEN MUTATION IS IRREVERSIBLE.
FOR OTHERS, MAYBE. LIKE I SAID, I DIDN'T TELL YOU THE BEST PART.
ARE YOU TRYING TO MAKE ME ANGRY?
IF I DO, WE'LL BOTH REGRET IT. WHAT'S ALL THIS?
JUST A POWER SOURCE. THIS TOUR IS OVER, MR. JESSUP. LET'S GET YOU OVER TO THE EXAMINING--

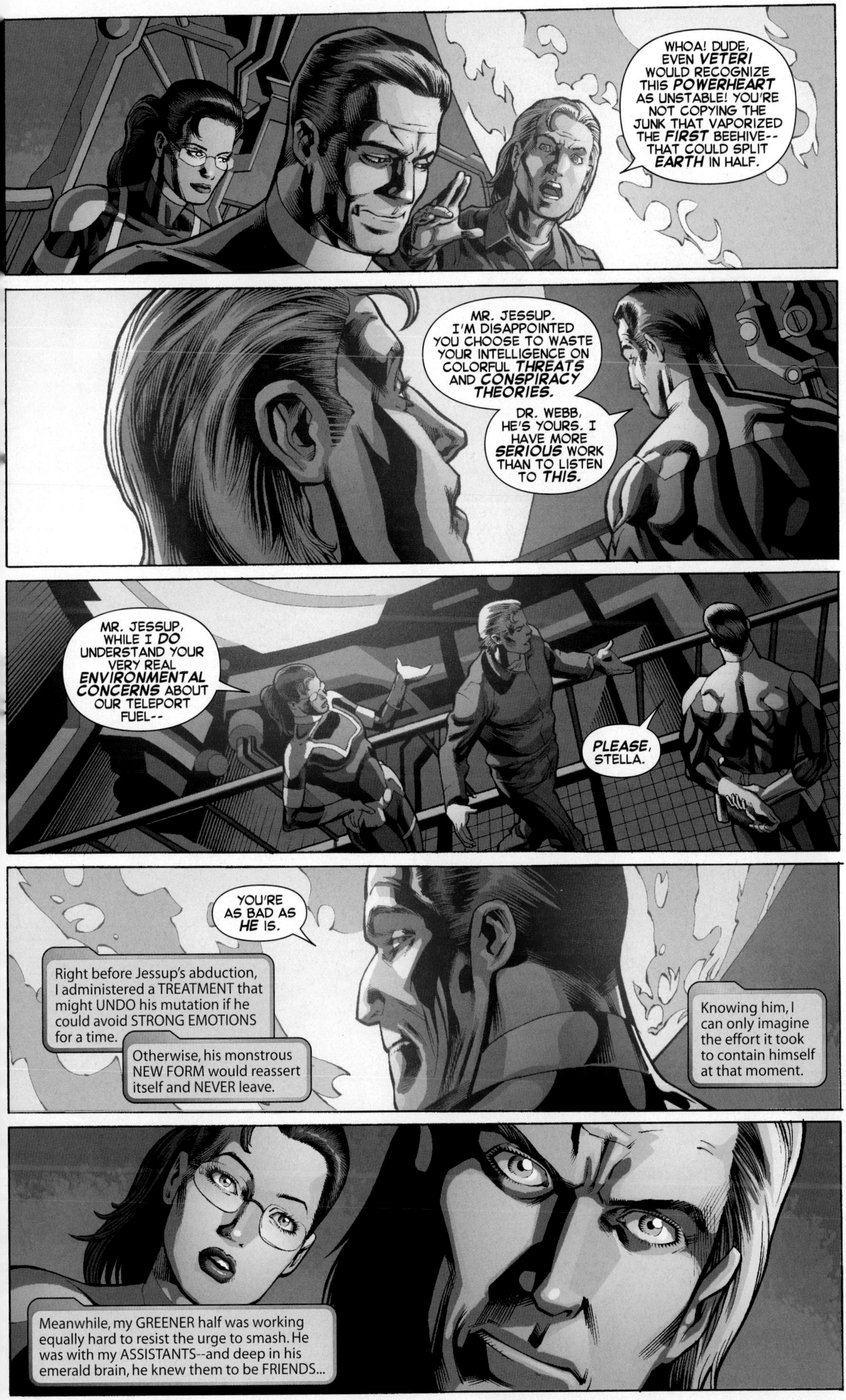

WHOA! DUDE, EVEN VETERI WOULD RECOGNIZE THIS POWERHEART AS UNSTABLE! YOU'RE NOT COPYING THE JUNK THAT VAPORIZED THE FIRST BEEHIVE-- THAT COULD SPLIT EARTH IN HALF.
MR. JESSUP. I'M DISAPPOINTED YOU CHOOSE TO WASTE YOUR INTELLIGENCE ON COLORFUL THREATS AND CONSPIRACY THEORIES.
DR. WEBB, HE'S YOURS. I HAVE MORE SERIOUS WORK THAN TO LISTEN TO THIS.
MR. JESSUP, WHILE I DO UNDERSTAND YOUR VERY REAL ENVIRONMENTAL CONCERNS ABOUT OUR TELEPORT FUEL--
PLEASE, STELLA.
YOU'RE AS BAD AS HE IS.
Right before Jessup's abduction, I administered a TREATMENT that might UNDO his mutation if he could avoid STRONG EMOTIONS for a time.
Otherwise, his monstrous NEW FORM would reassert itself and NEVER leave.
Knowing him, I can only imagine the effort it took to contain himself at that moment.
Meanwhile, my GREENER half was working equally hard to resist the urge to smash. He was with my ASSISTANTS--and deep in his emerald brain, he knew them to be FRIENDS...

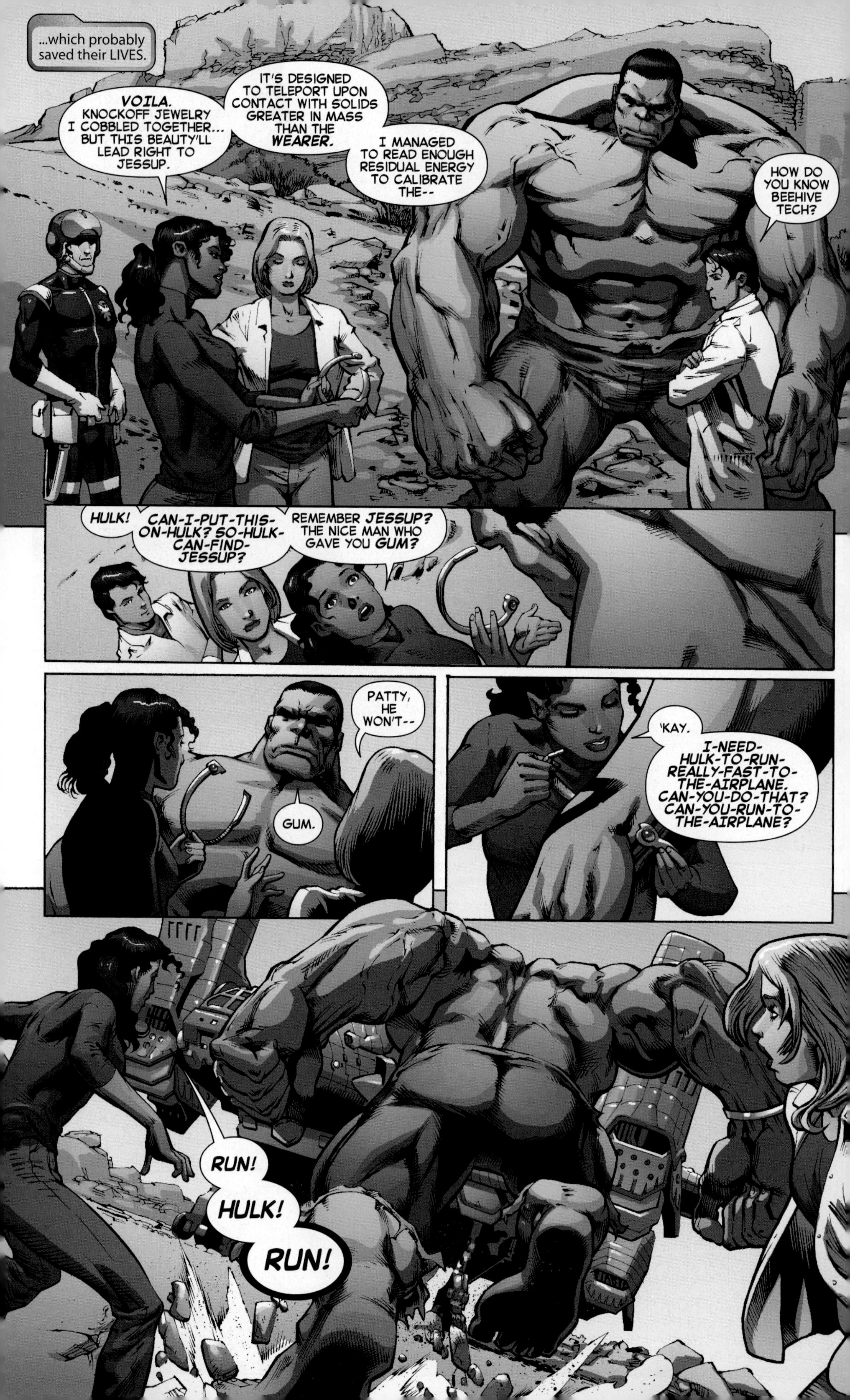
...which probably saved their LIVES.
VOILA. KNOCKOFF JEWELRY I COBBLED TOGETHER... BUT THIS BEAUTY'LL LEAD RIGHT TO JESSUP.
IT'S DESIGNED TO TELEPORT UPON CONTACT WITH SOLIDS GREATER IN MASS THAN THE WEARER.
I MANAGED TO READ ENOUGH RESIDUAL ENERGY TO CALIBRATE THE--
HOW DO YOU KNOW BEEHIVE TECH?
HULK!
CAN-I-PUT-THIS-ON-HULK? SO-HULK-CAN-FIND-JESSUP?
REMEMBER JESSUP? THE NICE MAN WHO GAVE YOU GUM?
PATTY, HE WON'T--
GUM.
'KAY.
I-NEED-HULK-TO-RUN-REALLY-FAST-TO-THE-AIRPLANE. CAN-YOU-DO-THAT? CAN-YOU-RUN-TO-THE-AIRPLANE?
RUN!
HULK!
RUN!

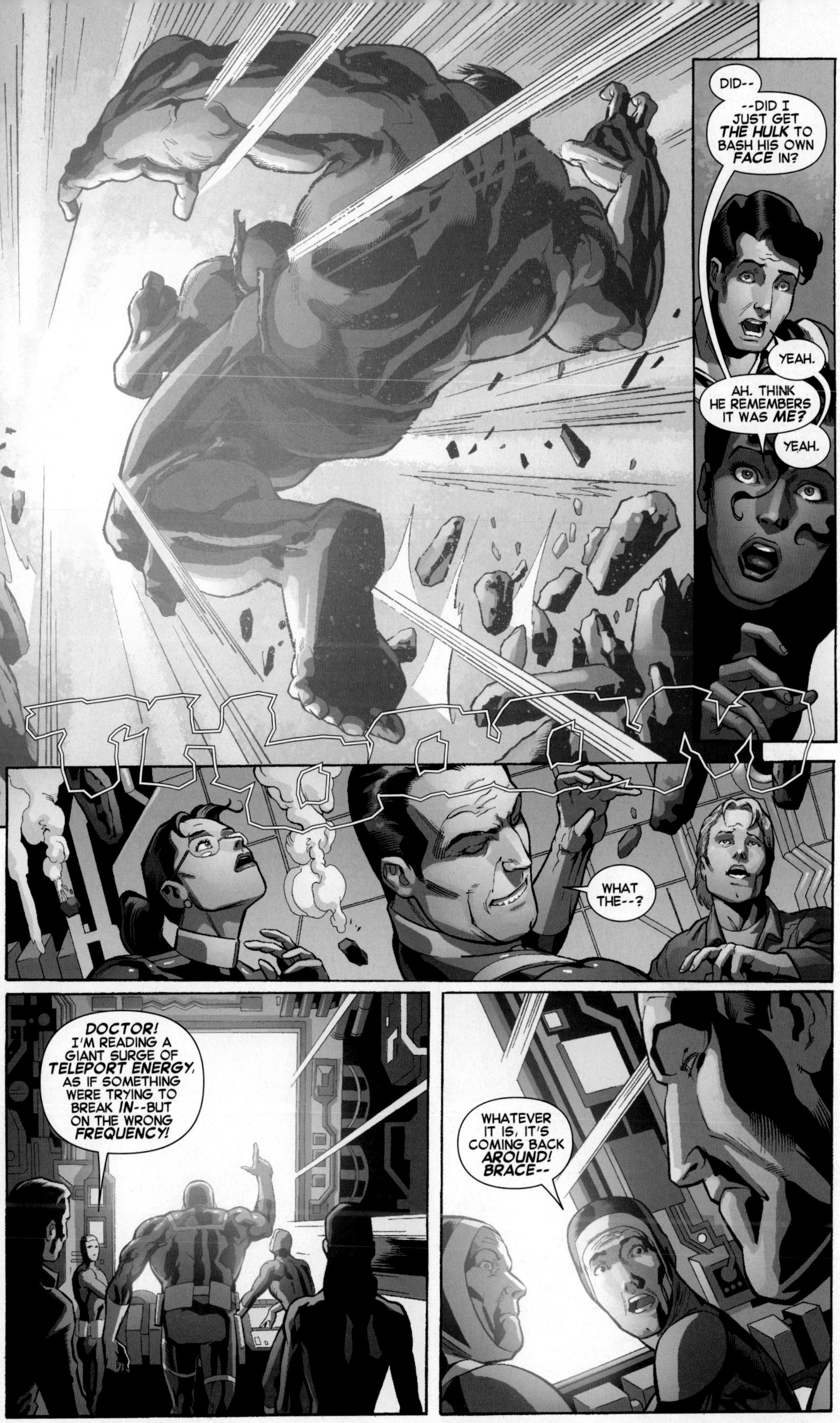
DID--
--DID I JUST GET THE HULK TO BASH HIS OWN FACE IN?
YEAH.
AH. THINK HE REMEMBERS IT WAS ME?
YEAH.
WHAT THE--?
DOCTOR! I'M READING A GIANT SURGE OF TELEPORT ENERGY, AS IF SOMETHING WERE TRYING TO BREAK IN--BUT ON THE WRONG FREQUENCY!
WHATEVER IT IS, IT'S COMING BACK AROUND! BRACE--

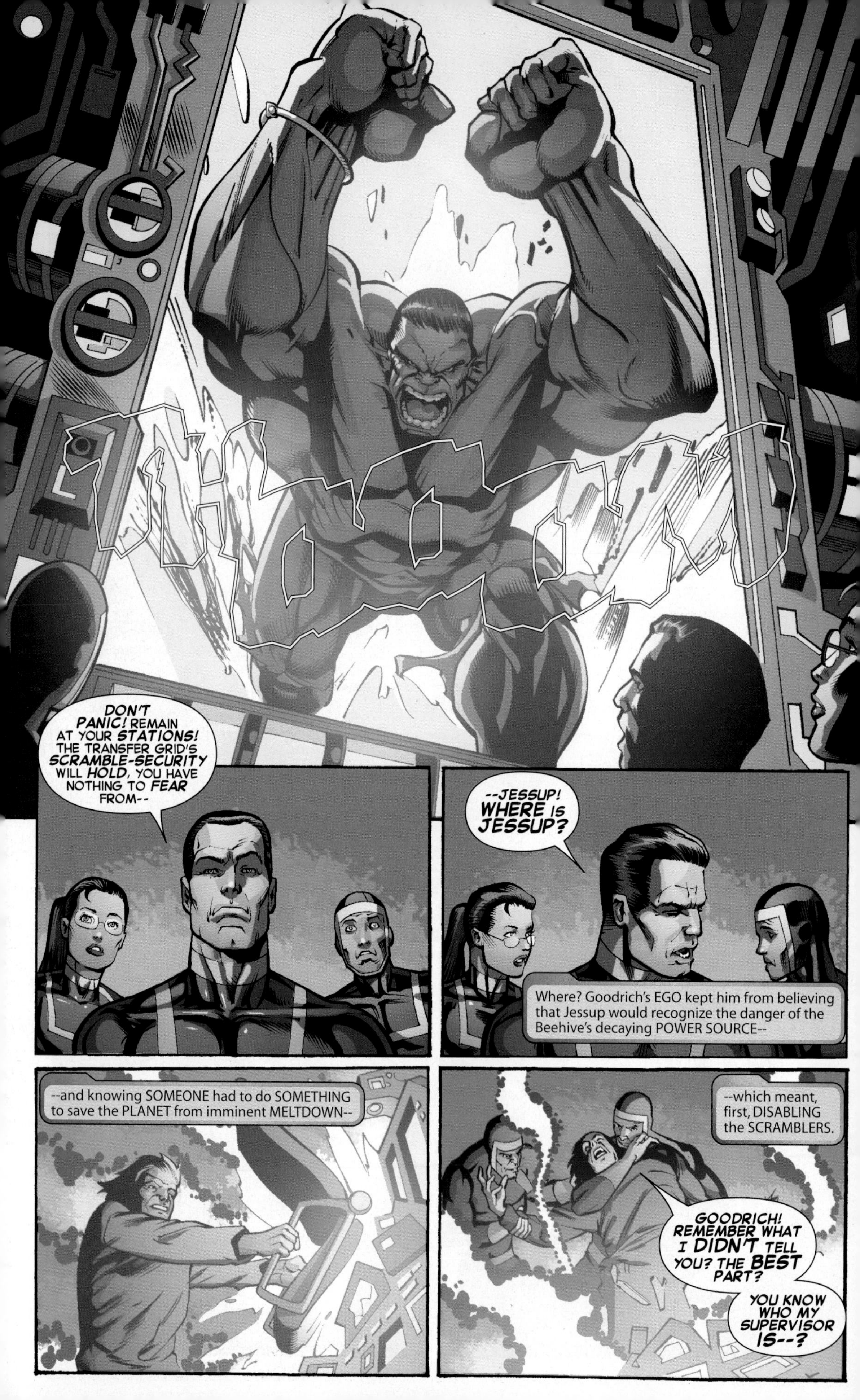
DON'T PANIC! REMAIN AT YOUR STATIONS! THE TRANSFER GRID'S SCRAMBLE-SECURITY WILL HOLD, YOU HAVE NOTHING TO FEAR FROM--
--JESSUP! WHERE IS JESSUP?
Where? Goodrich's EGO kept him from believing that Jessup would recognize the danger of the Beehive's decaying POWER SOURCE--
--and knowing SOMEONE had to do SOMETHING to save the PLANET from imminent MELTDOWN--
--which meant, first, DISABLING the SCRAMBLERS.
GOODRICH! REMEMBER WHAT I DIDN'T TELL YOU? THE BEST PART?
YOU KNOW WHO MY SUPERVISOR IS--?

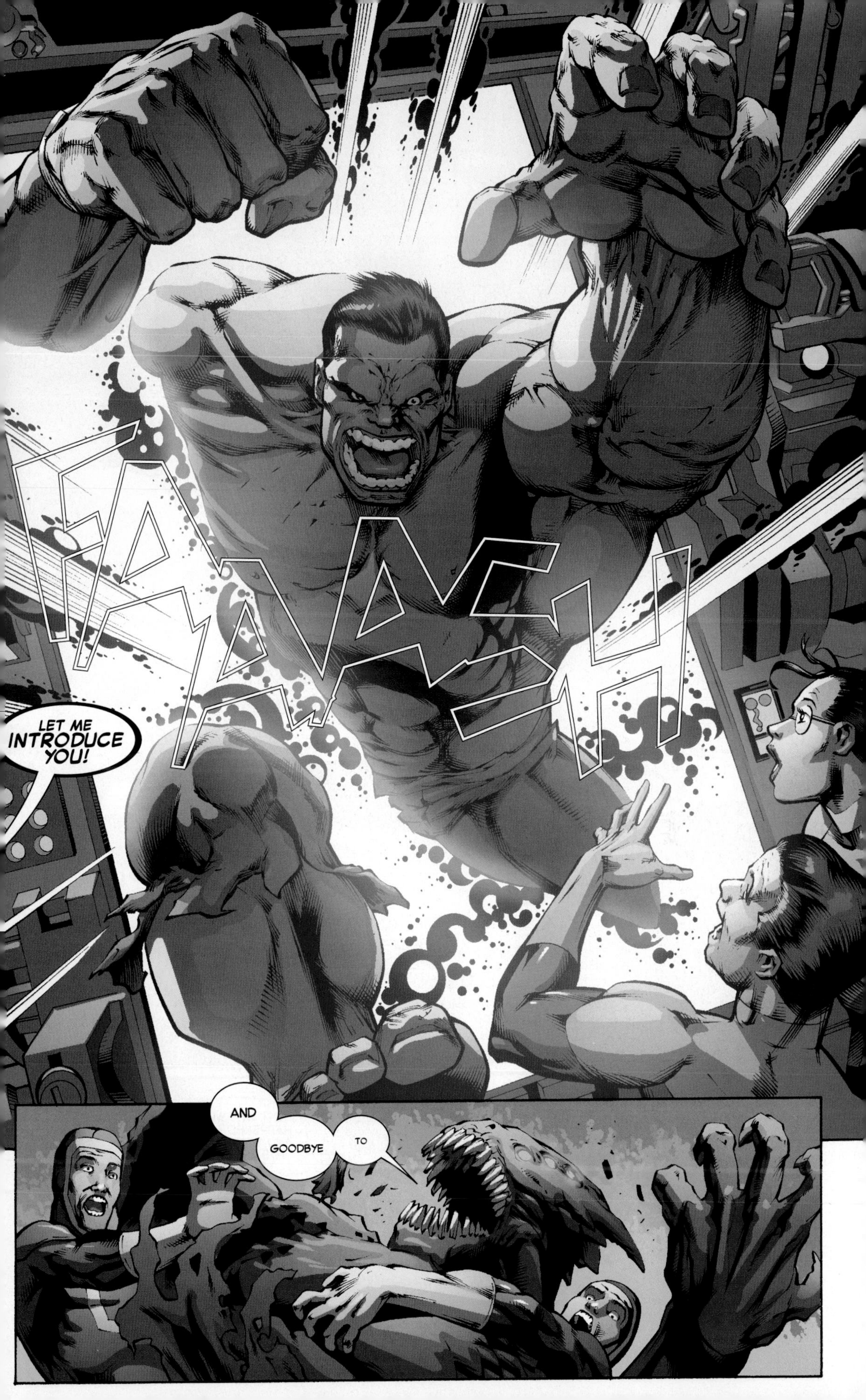
FAAASH
LET ME INTRODUCE YOU!
AND
GOODBYE
TO

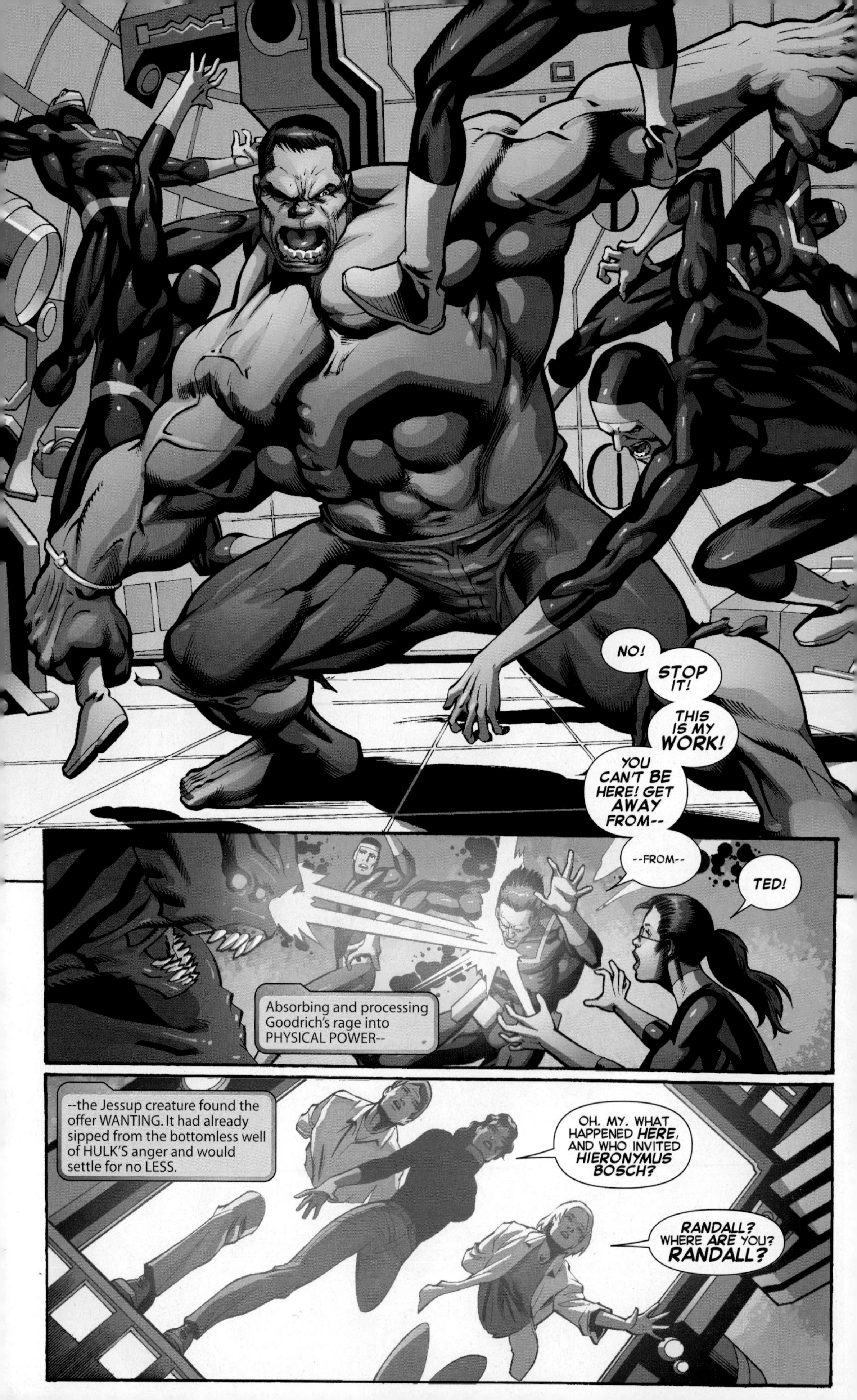
NO!
STOP IT!
THIS IS MY WORK!
YOU CAN'T BE HERE! GET AWAY FROM--
--FROM--
TED!
Absorbing and processing Goodrich's rage into PHYSICAL POWER--
--the Jessup creature found the offer WANTING. It had already sipped from the bottomless well of HULK'S anger and would settle for no LESS.
OH. MY. WHAT HAPPENED HERE, AND WHO INVITED HIERONYMUS BOSCH?
RANDALL? WHERE ARE YOU? RANDALL?

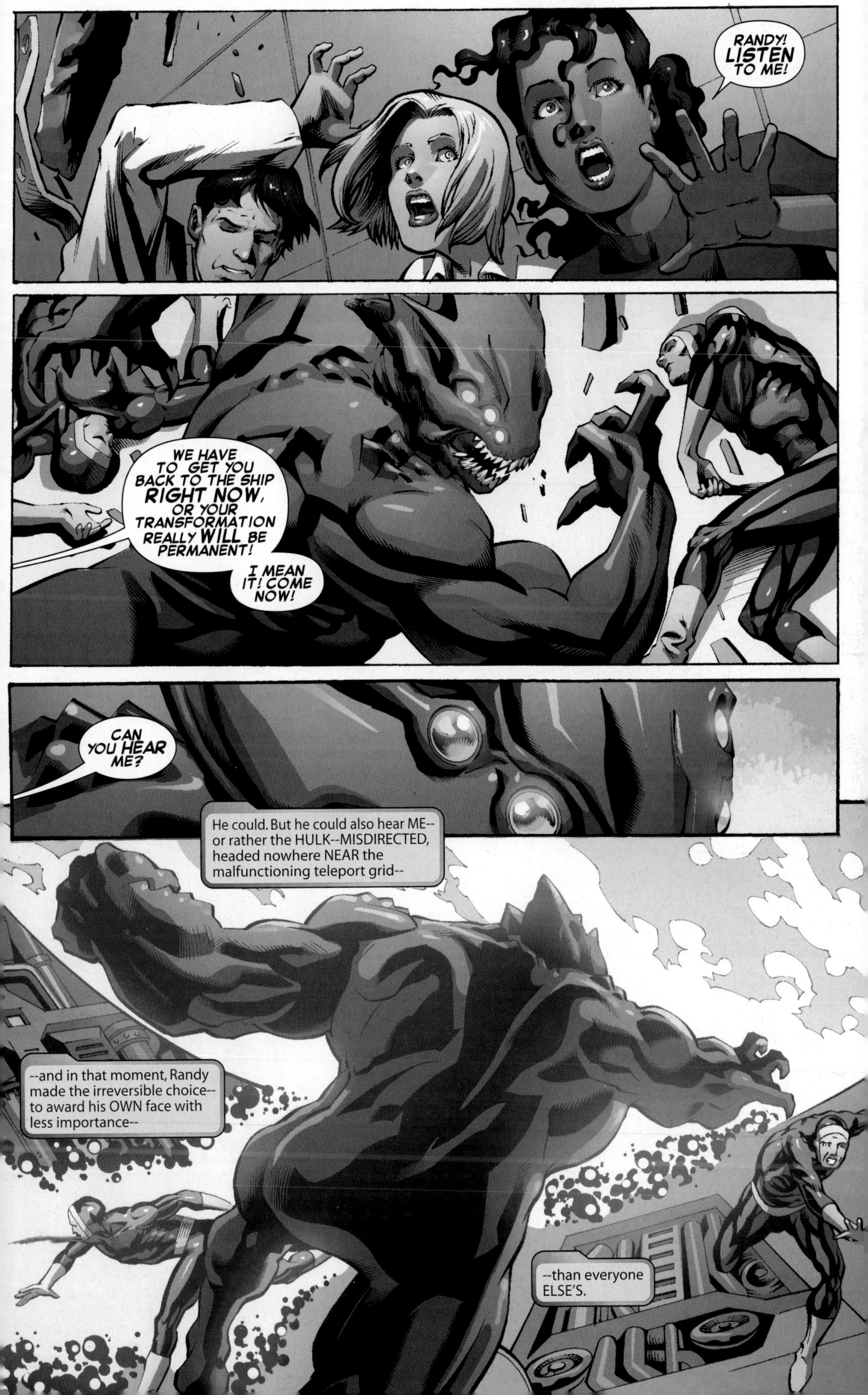
RANDY! LISTEN TO ME!
WE HAVE TO GET YOU BACK TO THE SHIP RIGHT NOW, OR YOUR TRANSFORMATION REALLY WILL BE PERMANENT!
I MEAN IT! COME NOW!
CAN YOU HEAR ME?
He could. But he could also hear ME--or rather the HULK--MISDIRECTED, headed nowhere NEAR the malfunctioning teleport grid--
--and in that moment, Randy made the irreversible choice--to award his OWN face with less importance--
--than everyone ELSE'S.

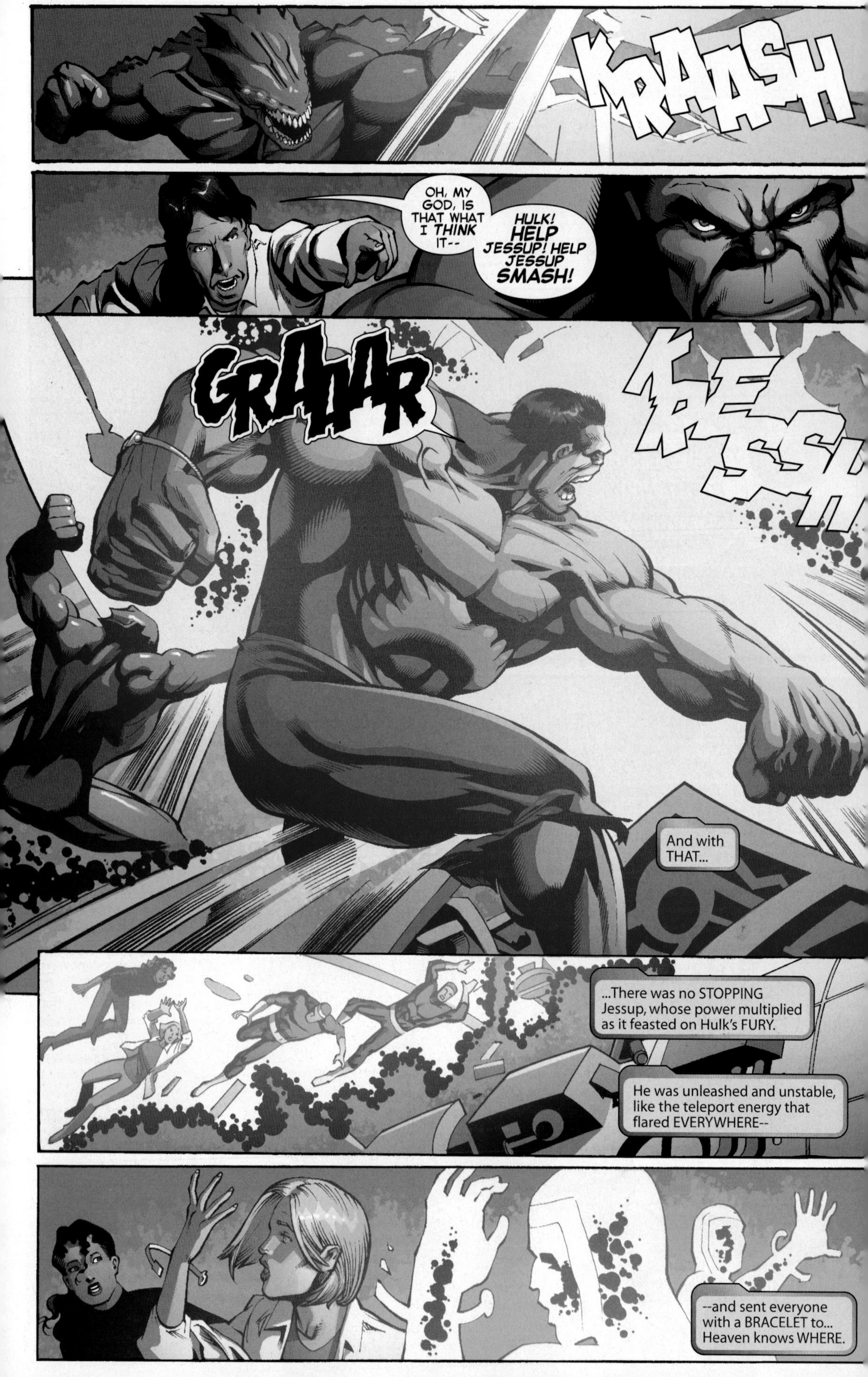
KRAASH
OH, MY GOD, IS THAT WHAT I THINK IT--
HULK! HELP JESSUP! HELP JESSUP SMASH!
GRAAAR
KRESSH
And with THAT...
...There was no STOPPING Jessup, whose power multiplied as it feasted on Hulk's FURY.
He was unleashed and unstable, like the teleport energy that flared EVERYWHERE--
--and sent everyone with a BRACELET to... Heaven knows WHERE.

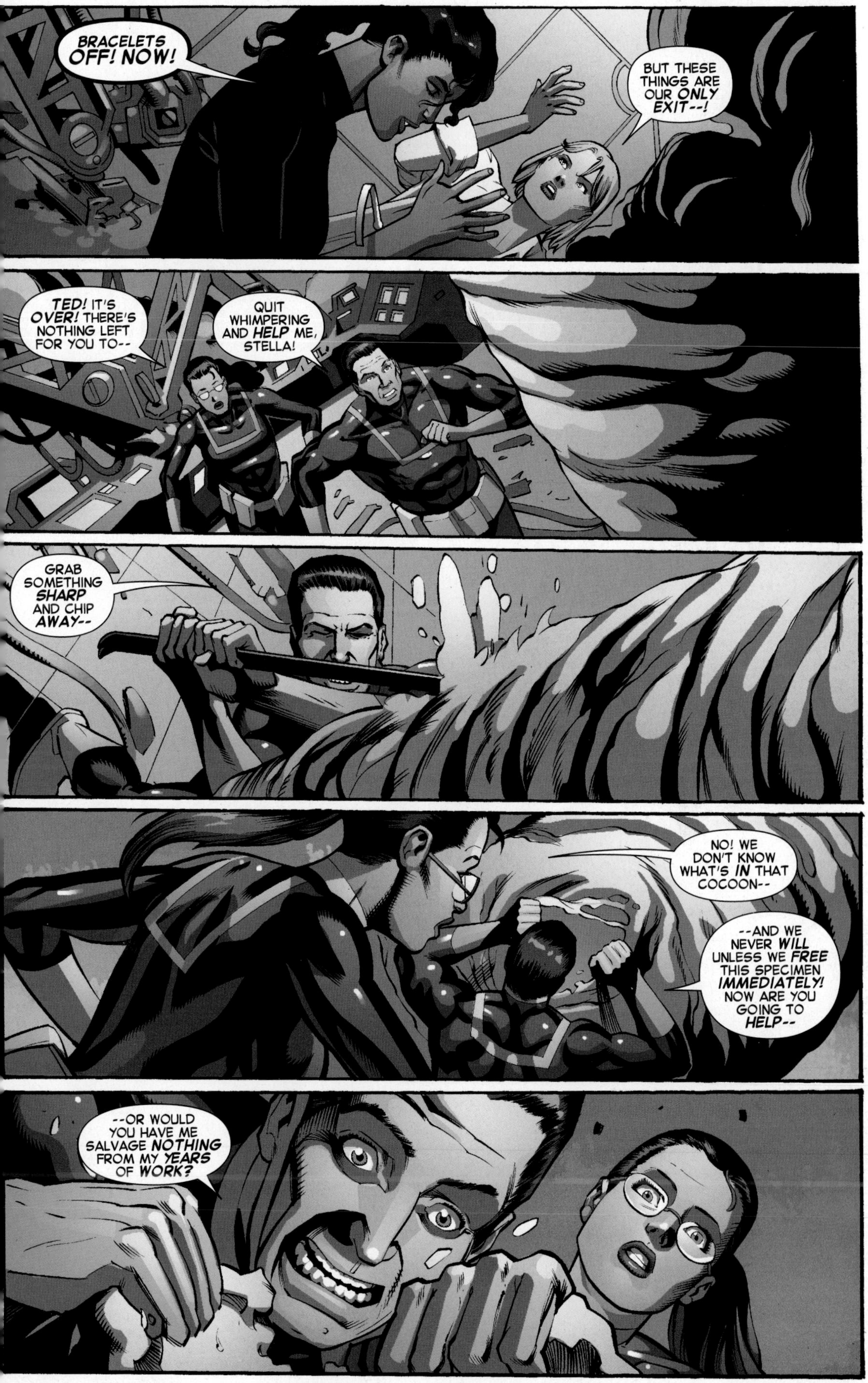
BRACELETS OFF! NOW!
BUT THESE THINGS ARE OUR ONLY EXIT--!
TED! IT'S OVER! THERE'S NOTHING LEFT FOR YOU TO--
QUIT WHIMPERING AND HELP ME, STELLA!
GRAB SOMETHING SHARP AND CHIP AWAY--
NO! WE DON'T KNOW WHAT'S IN THAT COCOON--
--AND WE NEVER WILL UNLESS WE FREE THIS SPECIMEN IMMEDIATELY! NOW ARE YOU GOING TO HELP--
--OR WOULD YOU HAVE ME SALVAGE NOTHING FROM MY YEARS OF WORK?

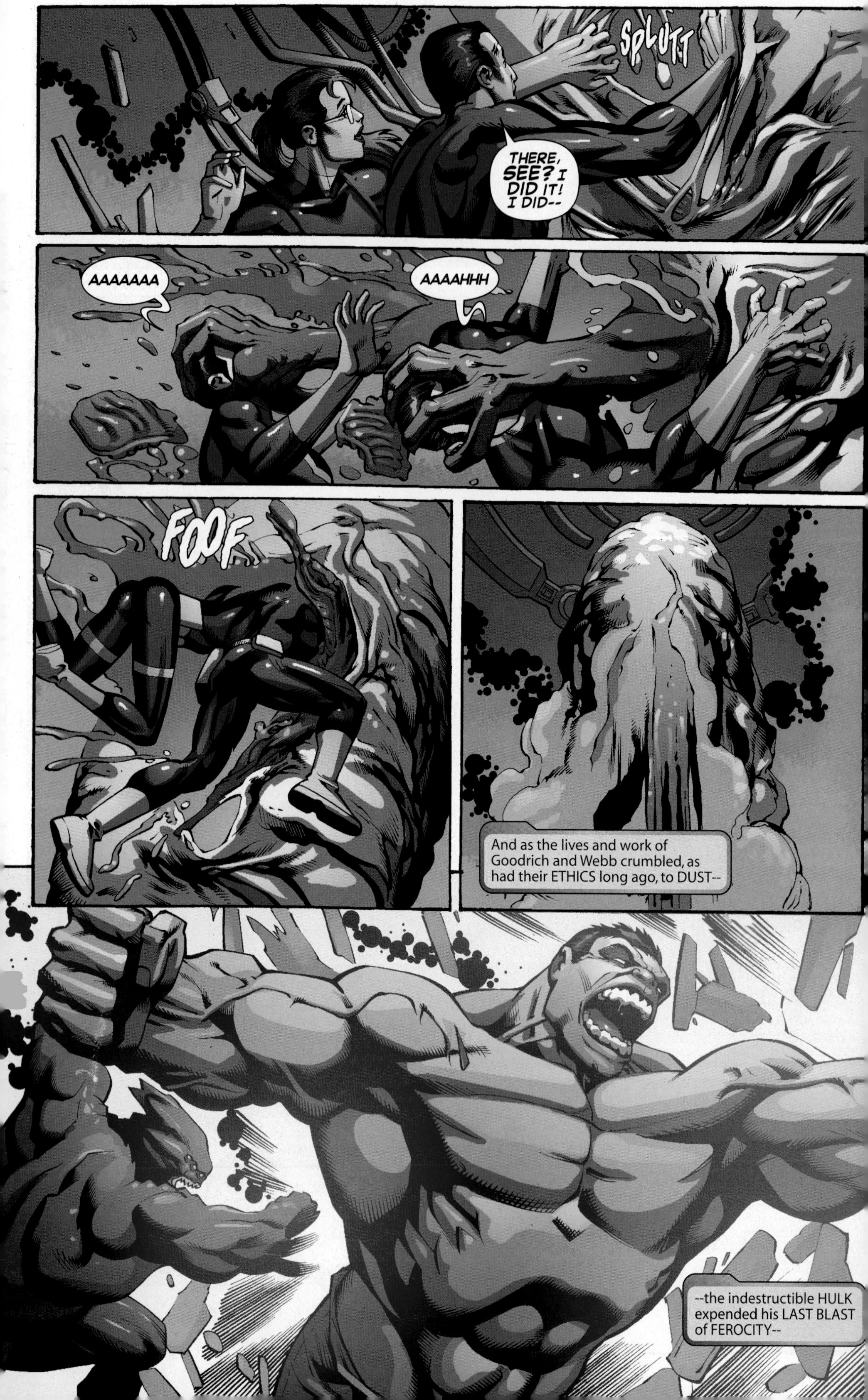
SPLUTT
THERE, SEE? I DID IT! I DID--
AAAAAAA
AAAAHHH
FOOF
And as the lives and work of Goodrich and Webb crumbled, as had their ETHICS long ago, to DUST--
--the indestructible HULK expended his LAST BLAST of FEROCITY--

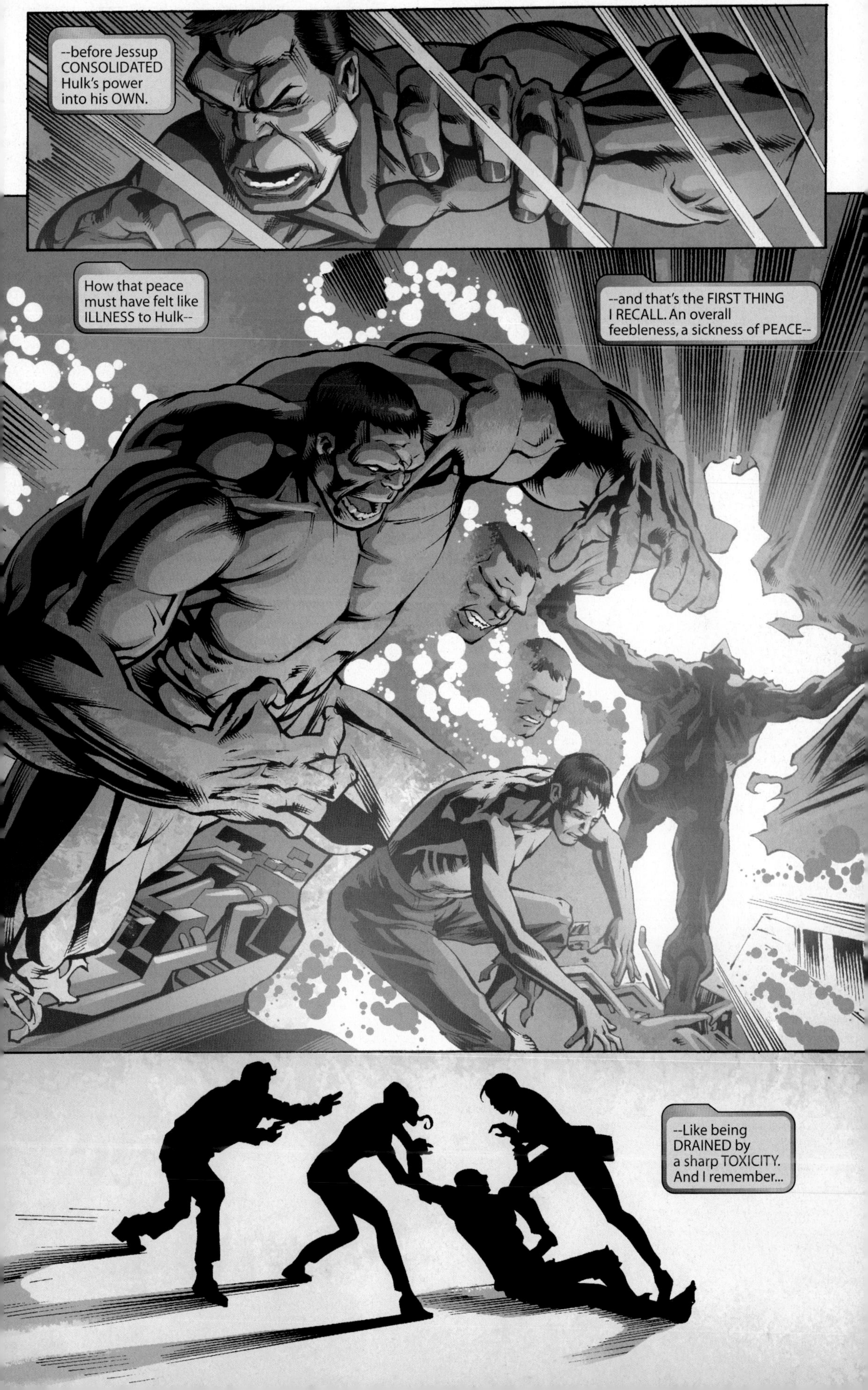
--before Jessup CONSOLIDATED Hulk's power into his OWN.
How that peace must have felt like ILLNESS to Hulk--
--and that's the FIRST THING I RECALL. An overall feebleness, a sickness of PEACE--
--Like being DRAINED by a sharp TOXICITY. And I remember...

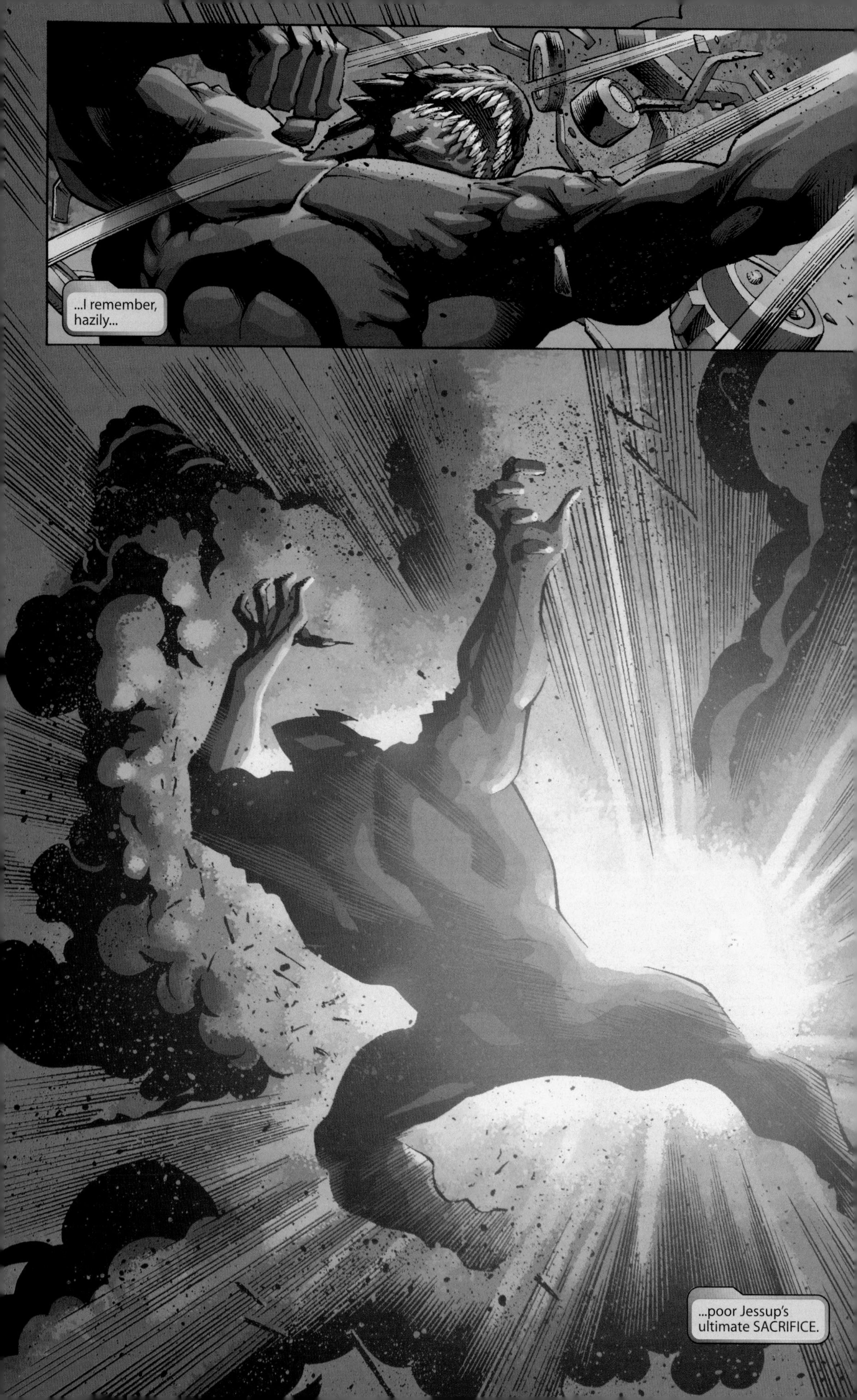
...I remember, hazily...
...poor Jessup's ultimate SACRIFICE.

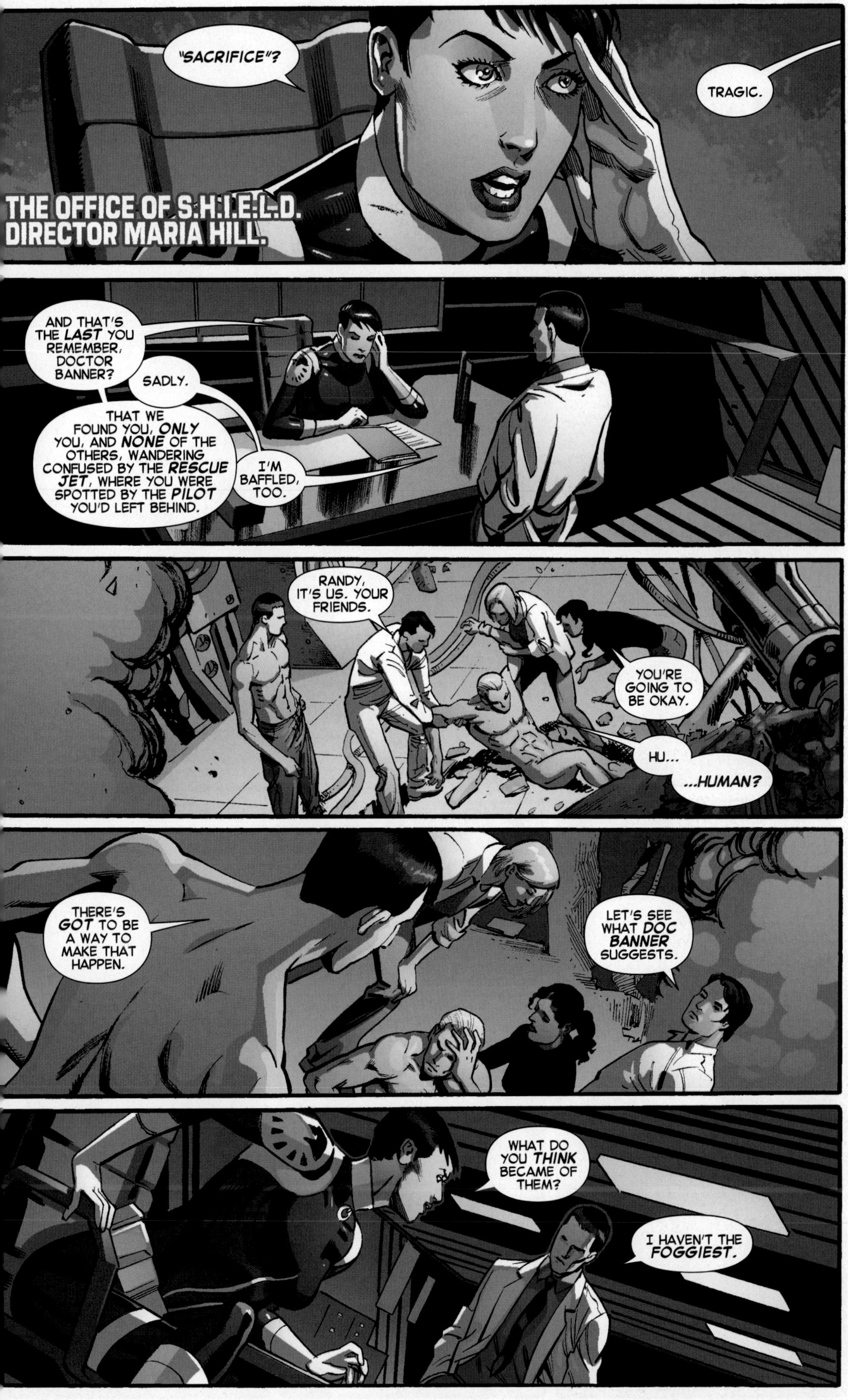
"SACRIFICE"?
TRAGIC.
THE OFFICE OF S.H.I.E.L.D. DIRECTOR MARIA HILL.
AND THAT'S THE LAST YOU REMEMBER, DOCTOR BANNER?
SADLY.
THAT WE FOUND YOU, ONLY YOU, AND NONE OF THE OTHERS, WANDERING CONFUSED BY THE RESCUE JET, WHERE YOU WERE SPOTTED BY THE PILOT YOU'D LEFT BEHIND.
I'M BAFFLED, TOO.
RANDY, IT'S US. YOUR FRIENDS.
YOU'RE GOING TO BE OKAY.
HU...
...HUMAN?
THERE'S GOT TO BE A WAY TO MAKE THAT HAPPEN.
LET'S SEE WHAT DOC BANNER SUGGESTS.
WHAT DO YOU THINK BECAME OF THEM?
I HAVEN'T THE FOGGIEST.

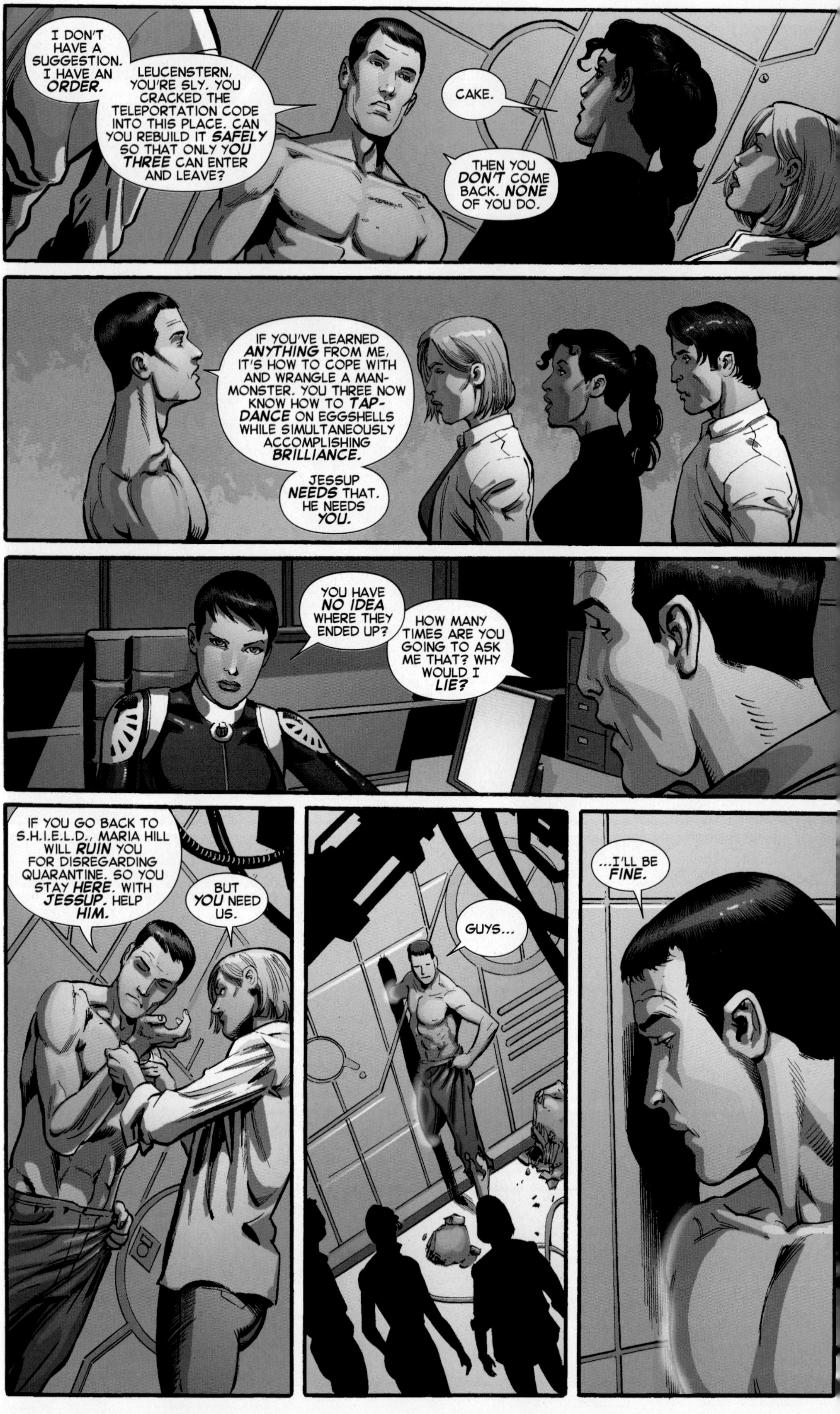
I DON'T HAVE A SUGGESTION. I HAVE AN ORDER.
LEUCENSTERN, YOU'RE SLY. YOU CRACKED THE TELEPORTATION CODE INTO THIS PLACE. CAN YOU REBUILD IT SAFELY SO THAT ONLY YOU THREE CAN ENTER AND LEAVE?
CAKE.
THEN YOU DON'T COME BACK. NONE OF YOU DO.
IF YOU'VE LEARNED ANYTHING FROM ME, IT'S HOW TO COPE WITH AND WRANGLE A MAN-MONSTER. YOU THREE NOW KNOW HOW TO TAP-DANCE ON EGGSHELLS WHILE SIMULTANEOUSLY ACCOMPLISHING BRILLIANCE.
JESSUP NEEDS THAT. HE NEEDS YOU.
YOU HAVE NO IDEA WHERE THEY ENDED UP?
HOW MANY TIMES ARE YOU GOING TO ASK ME THAT? WHY WOULD I LIE?
IF YOU GO BACK TO S.H.I.E.L.D., MARIA HILL WILL RUIN YOU FOR DISREGARDING QUARANTINE. SO YOU STAY HERE. WITH JESSUP. HELP HIM.
BUT YOU NEED US.
GUYS...
...I'LL BE FINE.

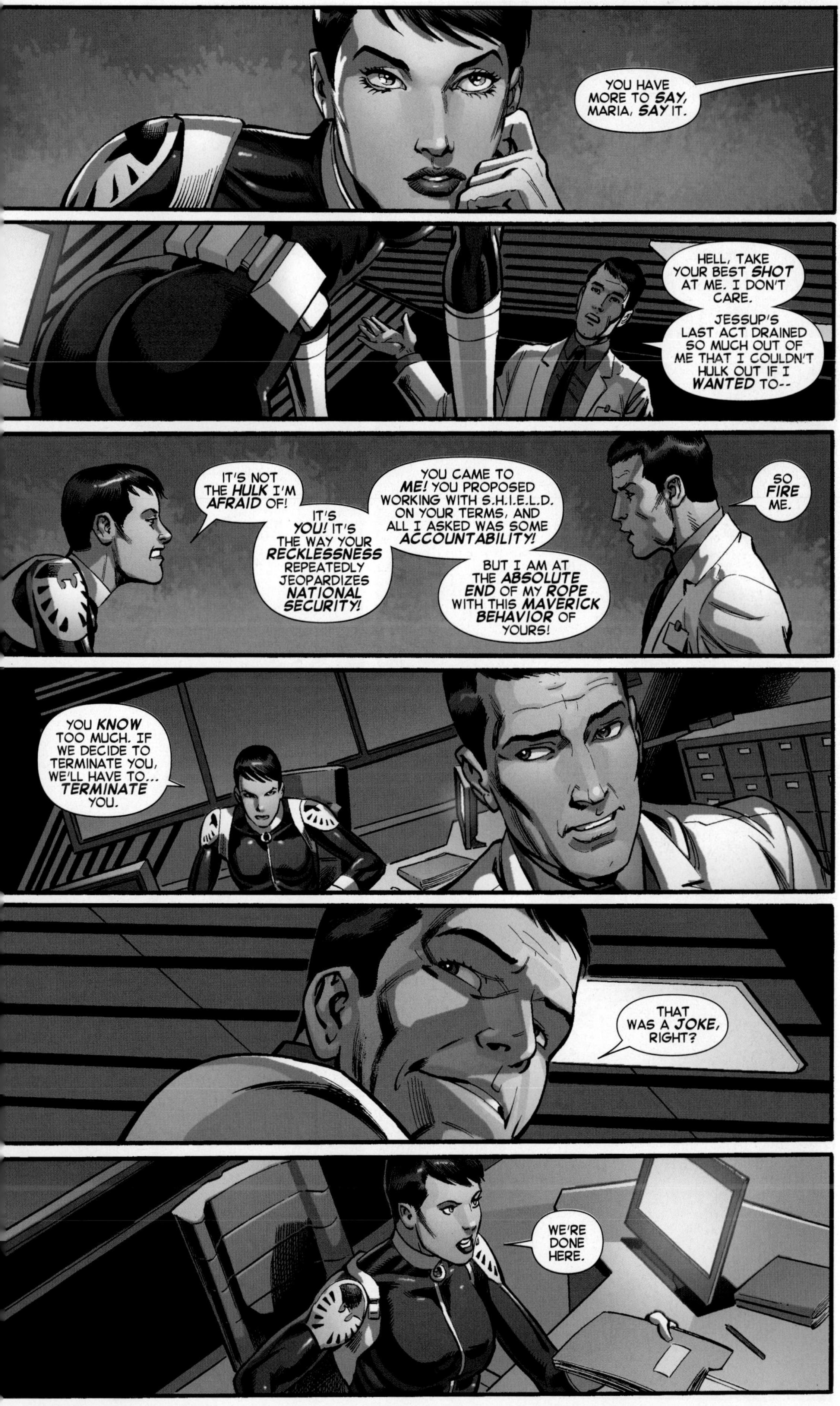
YOU HAVE MORE TO SAY, MARIA, SAY IT.
HELL, TAKE YOUR BEST SHOT AT ME. I DON'T CARE.
JESSUP'S LAST ACT DRAINED SO MUCH OUT OF ME THAT I COULDN'T HULK OUT IF I WANTED TO--
IT'S NOT THE HULK I'M AFRAID OF!
IT'S YOU! IT'S THE WAY YOUR RECKLESSNESS REPEATEDLY JEOPARDIZES NATIONAL SECURITY!
YOU CAME TO ME! YOU PROPOSED WORKING WITH S.H.I.E.L.D. ON YOUR TERMS, AND ALL I ASKED WAS SOME ACCOUNTABILITY!
BUT I AM AT THE ABSOLUTE END OF MY ROPE WITH THIS MAVERICK BEHAVIOR OF YOURS!
SO FIRE ME.
YOU KNOW TOO MUCH. IF WE DECIDE TO TERMINATE YOU, WE'LL HAVE TO... TERMINATE YOU.
THAT WAS A JOKE, RIGHT?
WE'RE DONE HERE.

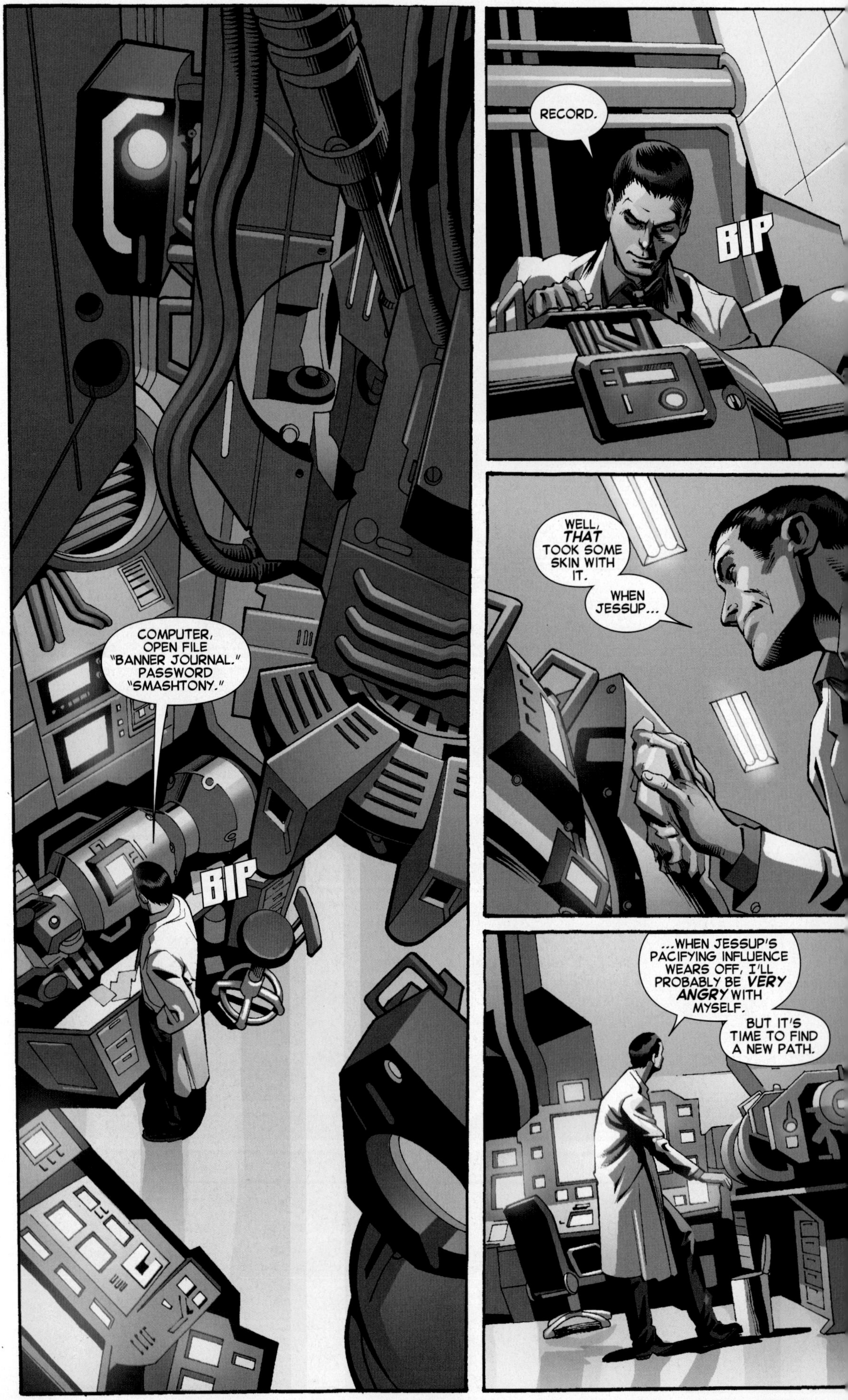

COMPUTER, OPEN FILE "BANNER JOURNAL." PASSWORD "SMASHTONY."
BIP
RECORD.
BIP
WELL, *THAT* TOOK SOME SKIN WITH IT.
WHEN JESSUP...
...WHEN JESSUP'S PACIFYING INFLUENCE WEARS OFF, I'LL PROBABLY BE *VERY ANGRY* WITH MYSELF.
BUT IT'S TIME TO FIND A NEW PATH.

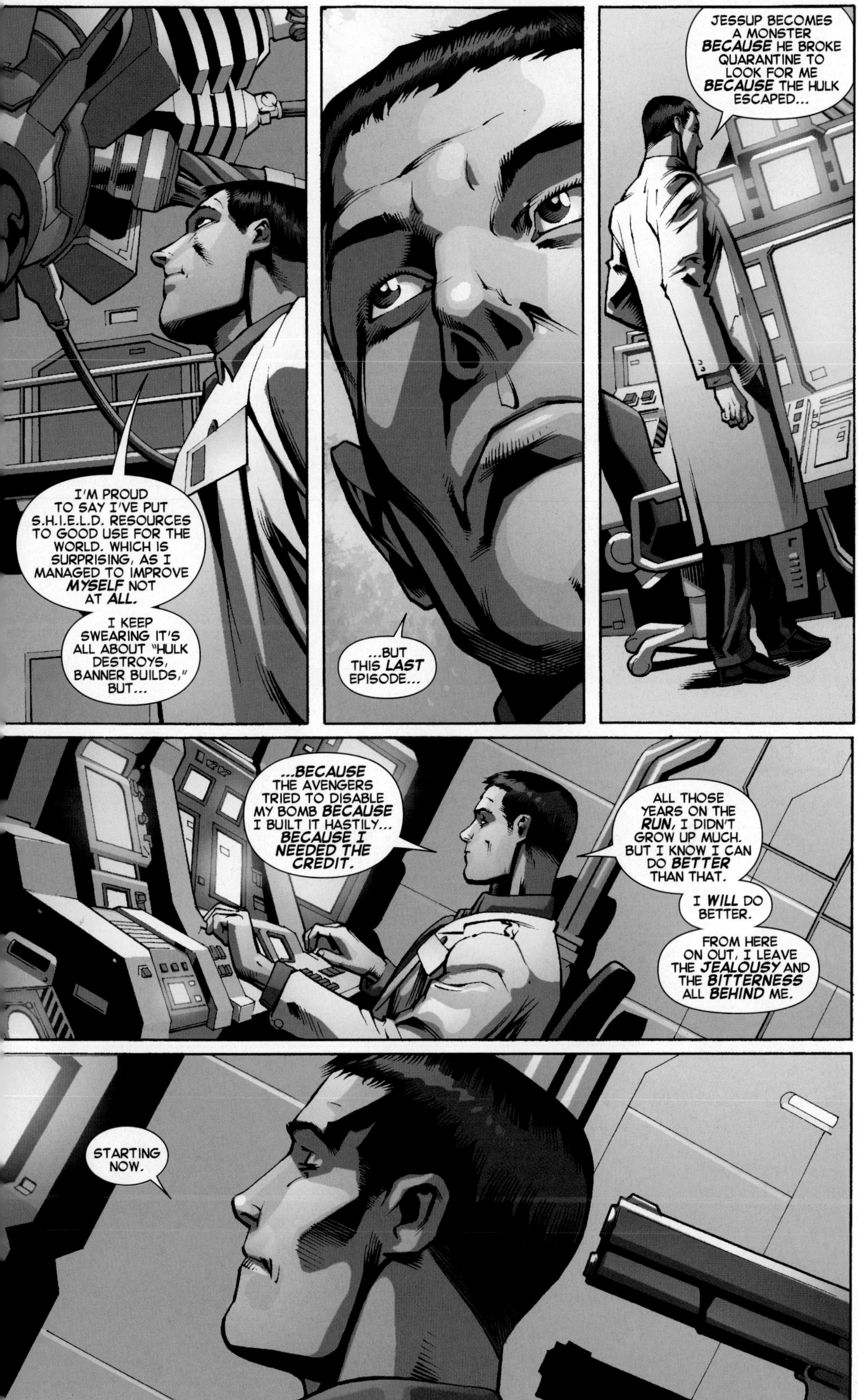
I'M PROUD TO SAY I'VE PUT S.H.I.E.L.D. RESOURCES TO GOOD USE FOR THE WORLD. WHICH IS SURPRISING, AS I MANAGED TO IMPROVE ***MYSELF*** NOT AT ***ALL.***
I KEEP SWEARING IT'S ALL ABOUT "HULK DESTROYS, BANNER BUILDS," BUT...
...BUT THIS ***LAST*** EPISODE...
JESSUP BECOMES A MONSTER ***BECAUSE*** HE BROKE QUARANTINE TO LOOK FOR ME ***BECAUSE*** THE HULK ESCAPED...
...BECAUSE THE AVENGERS TRIED TO DISABLE MY BOMB ***BECAUSE*** I BUILT IT HASTILY... ***BECAUSE I NEEDED THE CREDIT.***
ALL THOSE YEARS ON THE ***RUN,*** I DIDN'T GROW UP MUCH. BUT I KNOW I CAN DO ***BETTER*** THAN THAT.
I ***WILL*** DO BETTER.
FROM HERE ON OUT, I LEAVE THE ***JEALOUSY*** AND THE ***BITTERNESS*** ALL ***BEHIND*** ME.
STARTING NOW.

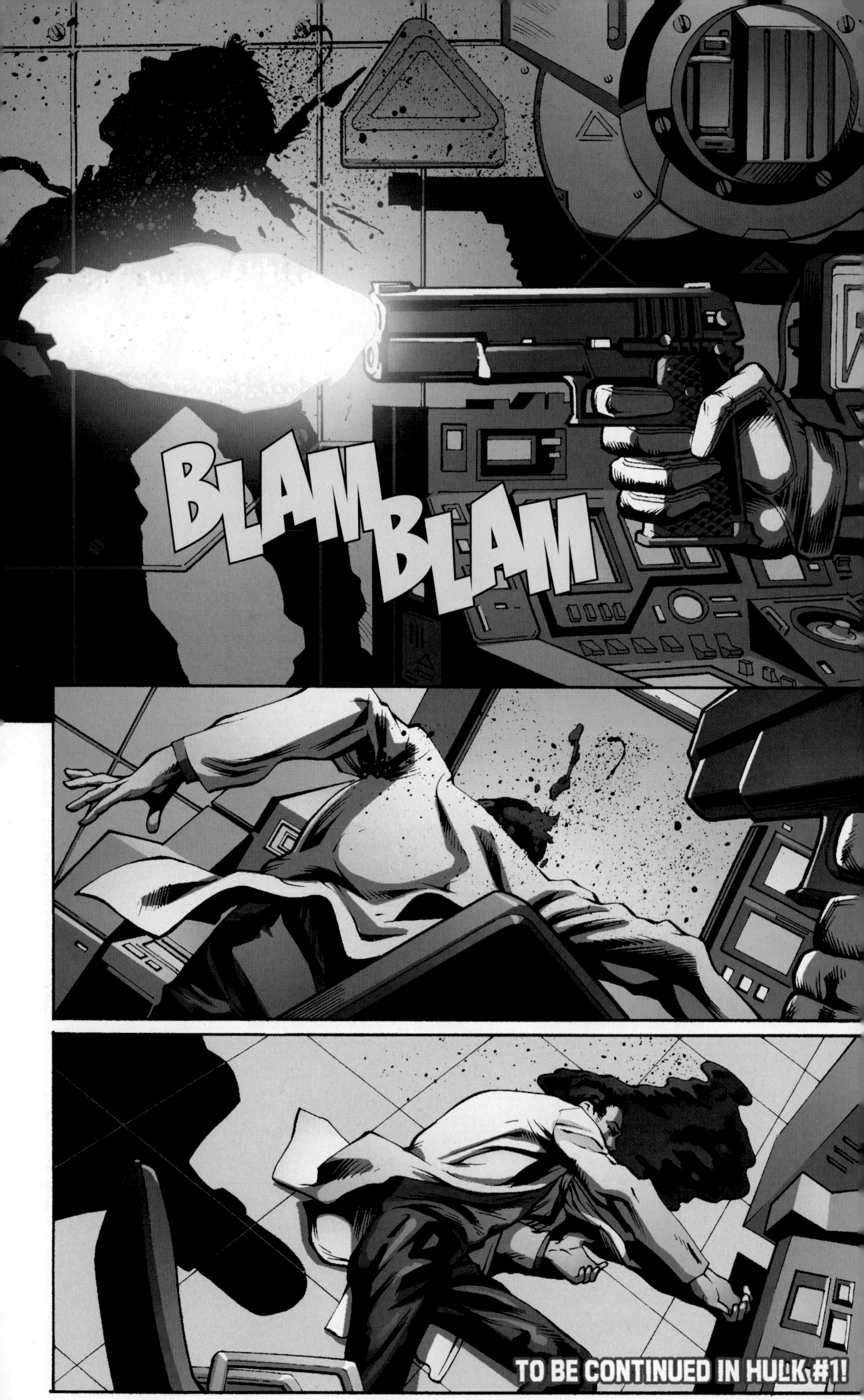
BLAM
BLAM
TO BE CONTINUED IN HULK #1!

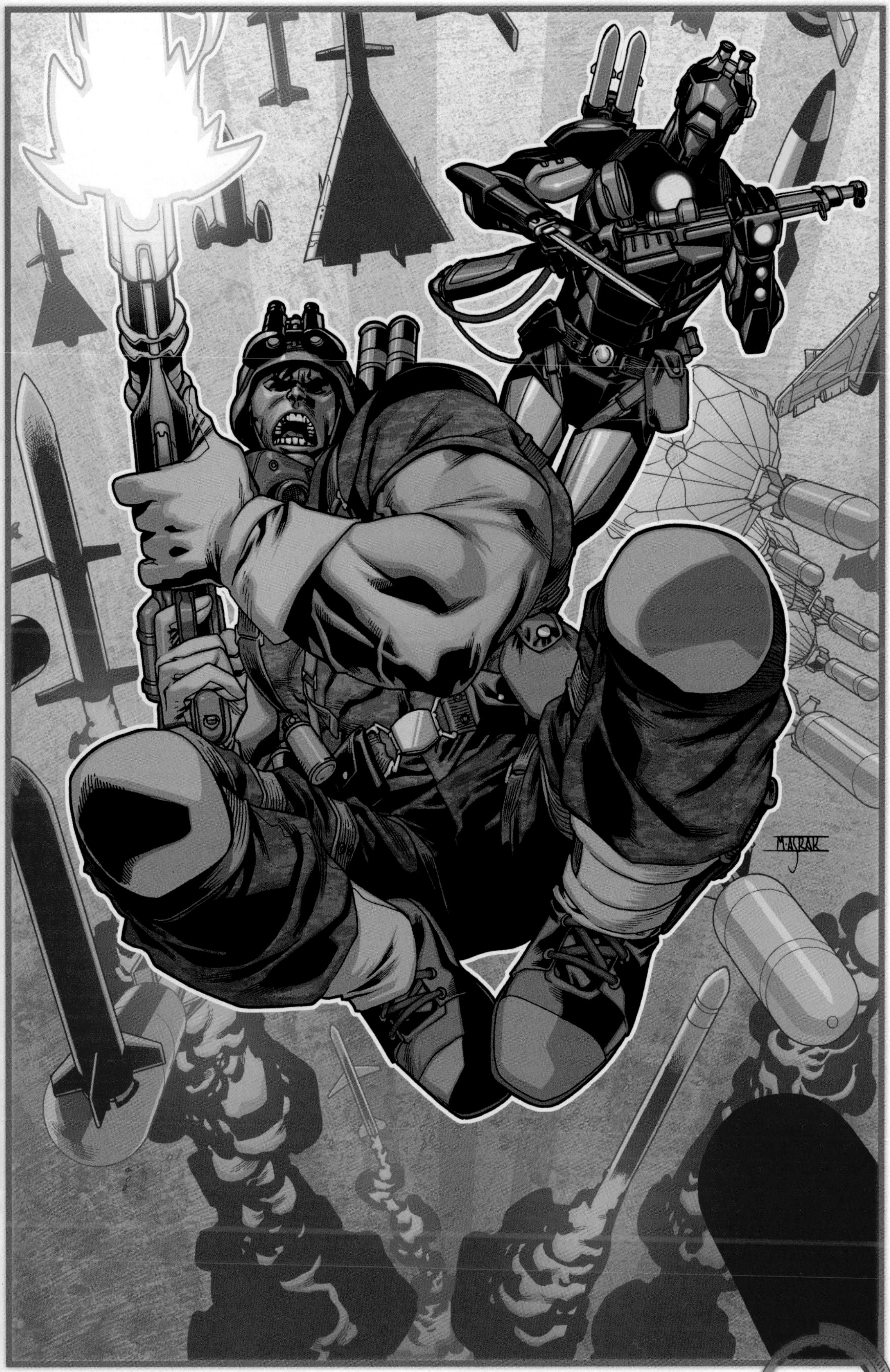

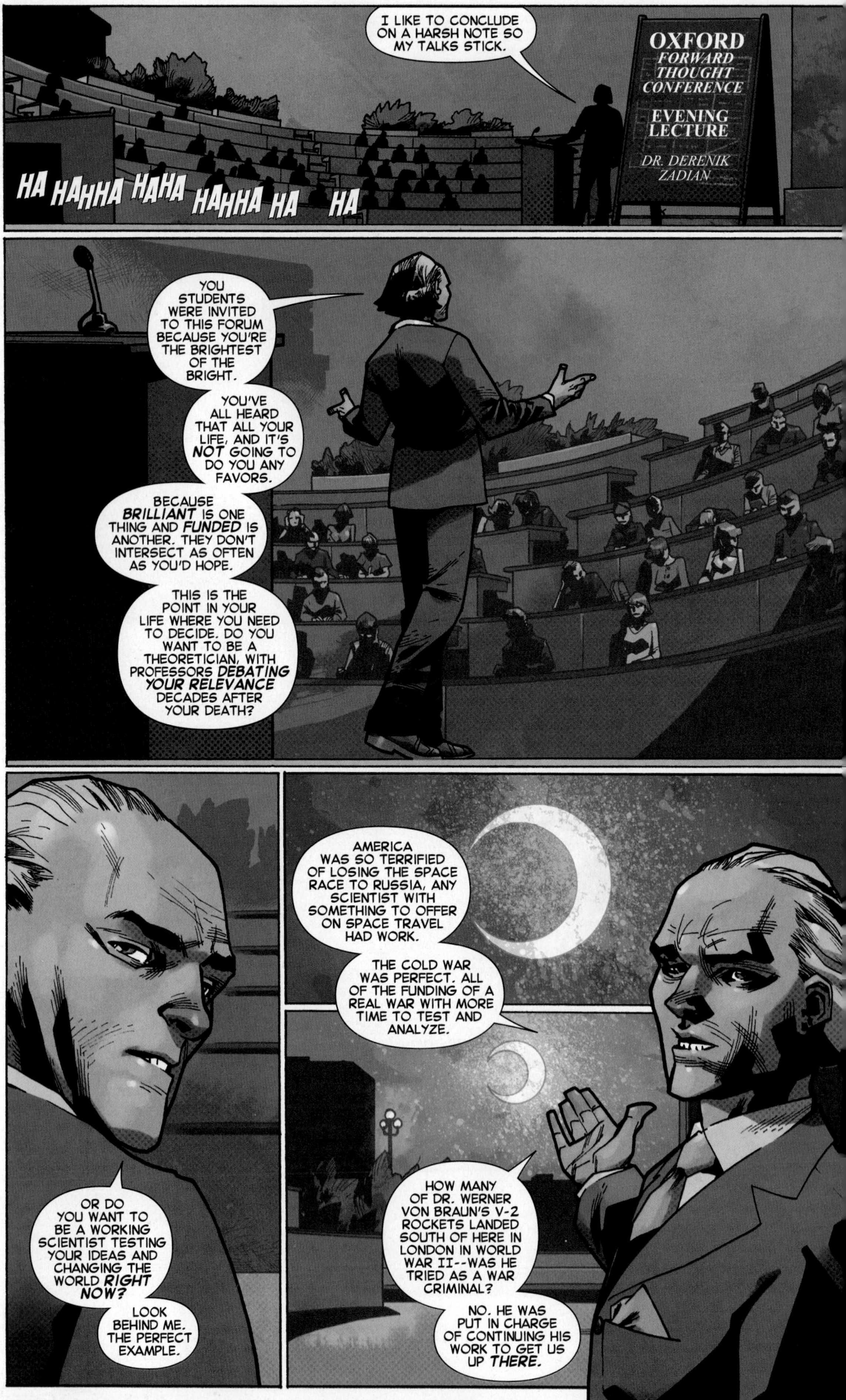
I LIKE TO CONCLUDE ON A HARSH NOTE SO MY TALKS STICK.
OXFORD
FORWARD THOUGHT CONFERENCE
EVENING LECTURE
DR. DERENIK ZADIAN
HA HAHHA HAHA HAHHA HA HA
YOU STUDENTS WERE INVITED TO THIS FORUM BECAUSE YOU'RE THE BRIGHTEST OF THE BRIGHT.
YOU'VE ALL HEARD THAT ALL YOUR LIFE, AND IT'S NOT GOING TO DO YOU ANY FAVORS.
BECAUSE BRILLIANT IS ONE THING AND FUNDED IS ANOTHER. THEY DON'T INTERSECT AS OFTEN AS YOU'D HOPE.
THIS IS THE POINT IN YOUR LIFE WHERE YOU NEED TO DECIDE. DO YOU WANT TO BE A THEORETICIAN, WITH PROFESSORS DEBATING YOUR RELEVANCE DECADES AFTER YOUR DEATH?
OR DO YOU WANT TO BE A WORKING SCIENTIST TESTING YOUR IDEAS AND CHANGING THE WORLD RIGHT NOW?
LOOK BEHIND ME. THE PERFECT EXAMPLE.
AMERICA WAS SO TERRIFIED OF LOSING THE SPACE RACE TO RUSSIA, ANY SCIENTIST WITH SOMETHING TO OFFER ON SPACE TRAVEL HAD WORK.
THE COLD WAR WAS PERFECT. ALL OF THE FUNDING OF A REAL WAR WITH MORE TIME TO TEST AND ANALYZE.
HOW MANY OF DR. WERNER VON BRAUN'S V-2 ROCKETS LANDED SOUTH OF HERE IN LONDON IN WORLD WAR II--WAS HE TRIED AS A WAR CRIMINAL?
NO. HE WAS PUT IN CHARGE OF CONTINUING HIS WORK TO GET US UP THERE.

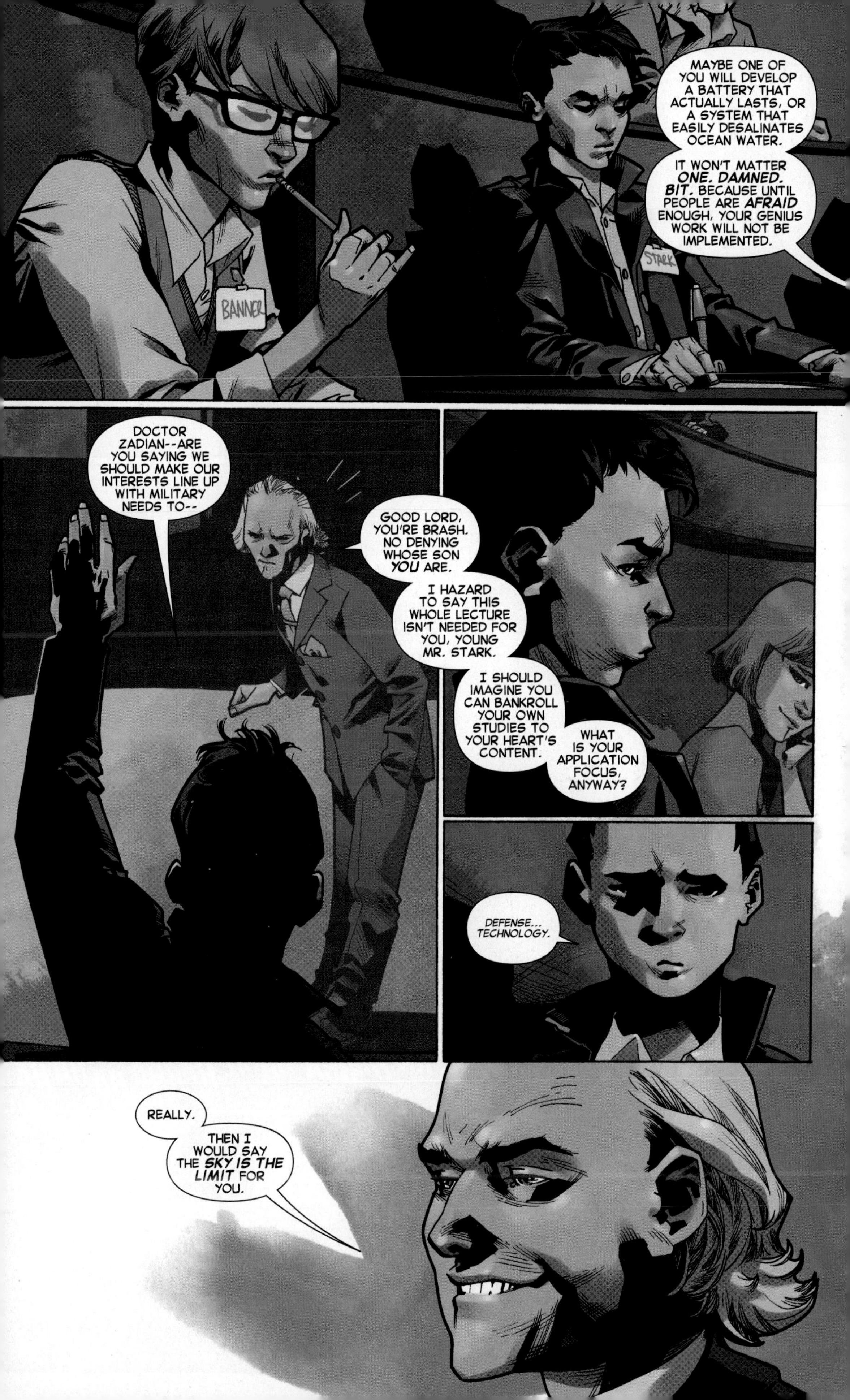
BANNER
STARK
MAYBE ONE OF YOU WILL DEVELOP A BATTERY THAT ACTUALLY LASTS, OR A SYSTEM THAT EASILY DESALINATES OCEAN WATER.
IT WON'T MATTER *ONE. DAMNED. BIT.* BECAUSE UNTIL PEOPLE ARE *AFRAID* ENOUGH, YOUR GENIUS WORK WILL NOT BE IMPLEMENTED.
DOCTOR ZADIAN--ARE YOU SAYING WE SHOULD MAKE OUR INTERESTS LINE UP WITH MILITARY NEEDS TO--
GOOD LORD, YOU'RE BRASH. NO DENYING WHOSE SON *YOU* ARE.
I HAZARD TO SAY THIS WHOLE LECTURE ISN'T NEEDED FOR YOU, YOUNG MR. STARK.
I SHOULD IMAGINE YOU CAN BANKROLL YOUR OWN STUDIES TO YOUR HEART'S CONTENT.
WHAT IS YOUR APPLICATION FOCUS, ANYWAY?
DEFENSE... TECHNOLOGY.
REALLY.
THEN I WOULD SAY THE *SKY IS THE LIMIT* FOR YOU.

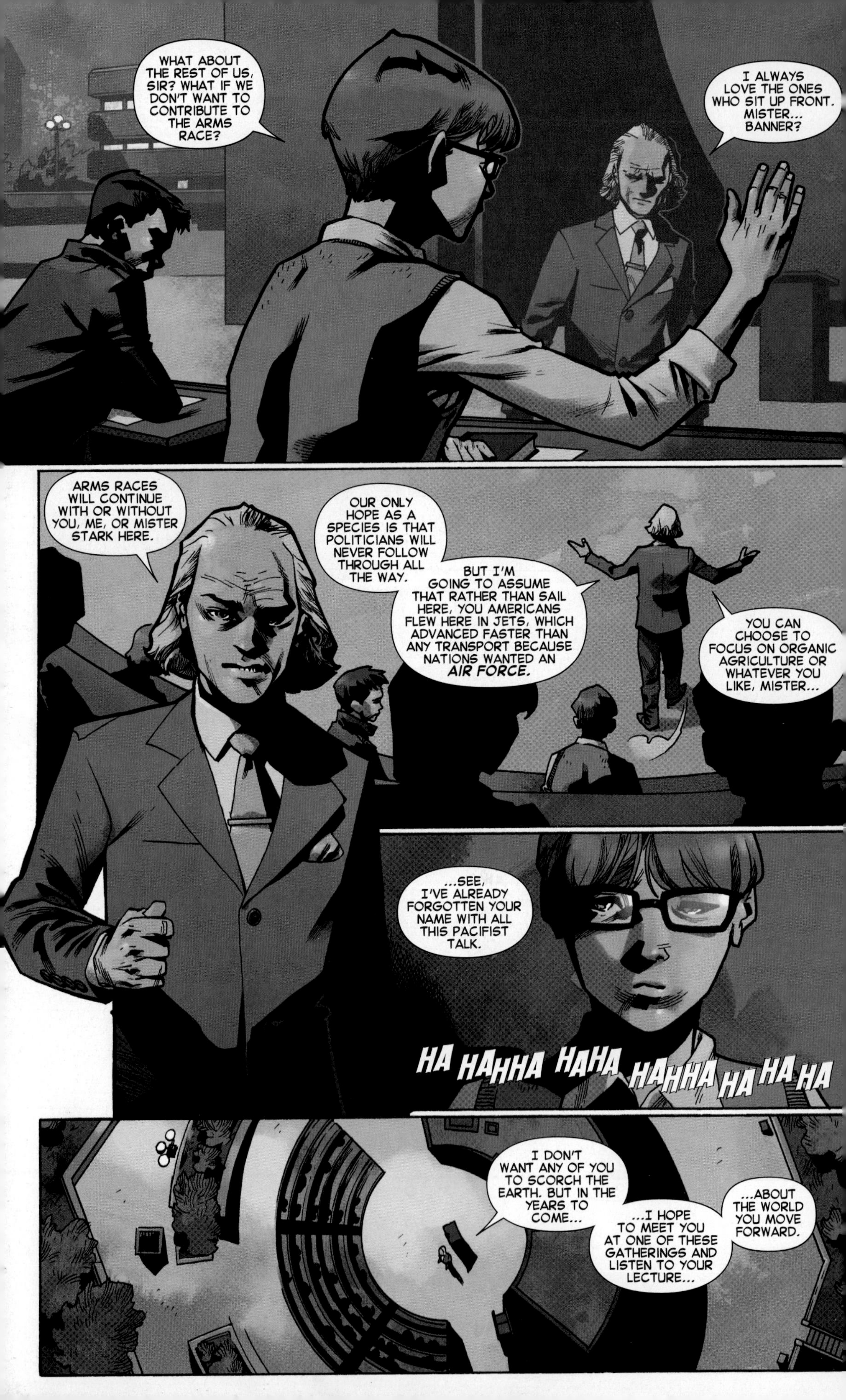
WHAT ABOUT THE REST OF US, SIR? WHAT IF WE DON'T WANT TO CONTRIBUTE TO THE ARMS RACE?
I ALWAYS LOVE THE ONES WHO SIT UP FRONT. MISTER... BANNER?
ARMS RACES WILL CONTINUE WITH OR WITHOUT YOU, ME, OR MISTER STARK HERE.
OUR ONLY HOPE AS A SPECIES IS THAT POLITICIANS WILL NEVER FOLLOW THROUGH ALL THE WAY.
BUT I'M GOING TO ASSUME THAT RATHER THAN SAIL HERE, YOU AMERICANS FLEW HERE IN JETS, WHICH ADVANCED FASTER THAN ANY TRANSPORT BECAUSE NATIONS WANTED AN *AIR FORCE.*
YOU CAN CHOOSE TO FOCUS ON ORGANIC AGRICULTURE OR WHATEVER YOU LIKE, MISTER...
...SEE, I'VE ALREADY FORGOTTEN YOUR NAME WITH ALL THIS PACIFIST TALK.
HA HAHHA HAHA HAHHA HA HA HA
I DON'T WANT ANY OF YOU TO SCORCH THE EARTH. BUT IN THE YEARS TO COME...
...I HOPE TO MEET YOU AT ONE OF THESE GATHERINGS AND LISTEN TO YOUR LECTURE...
...ABOUT THE WORLD YOU MOVE FORWARD.

JOURNEY INTO SCIENCE

WITH...

HULK

THE HULK will always be a part of Dr. Bruce Banner, but Banner wants to be remembered for his contributions to science and not for turning into a big, green force of rage and destruction. To achieve that goal, Banner has struck a mutually beneficial deal with Maria Hill, the director of S.H.I.E.L.D. She provides Banner with a lab, staff, equipment and all of the resources he needs to better mankind, and Banner provides S.H.I.E.L.D. with the Hulk for any missions that might need extra muscle.

Recently Bruce discovered his assistant Patricia Wolman suffers from a degenerative disease. She placed herself in his lab - in proximity to **THE HULK** - knowing the possibility of a fatal work result that could payout life insurance for her father.

IRON MAN

TONY STARK is a technological visionary...a famous, wealthy and unparalleled inventor, with the world's most advanced and powerful suit of armor, Stark valiantly protects the innocent as an invincible bright knight known as...IRON MAN"

Tony Stark has become aware of a plan devised by an Artifical Intelligence to put him on the path of arming the human race against eventual extraterrestrial threat. It seems he was destined to prepare for war...

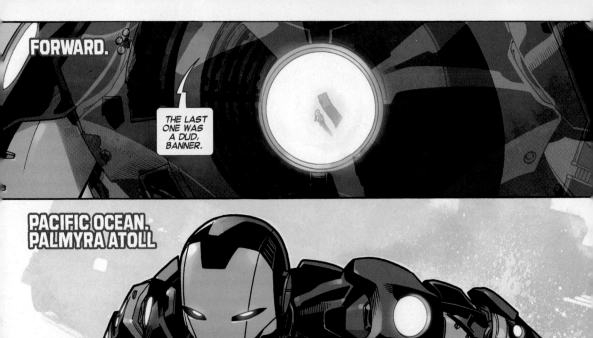

FORWARD.

THE LAST ONE WAS A DUD, BANNER.

PACIFIC OCEAN. PALMYRA ATOLL

THAT'S 33 ISLANDS WE CAN CROSS OFF.

IT LOOKS LIKE A GREAT PLACE FOR A VACATION HOME. IS IT FOR SALE?

REALLY? MY TEAM IS CERTAIN THIS IS THE PLACE.

YOU REGISTER NO SONAR, NO DEFENSES?

NO, MY ARMOR WOULD HAVE PI--

--CCCKKEEEDDDD AAAHHHHAHHHHDDDDDD--

STARK. STARK?

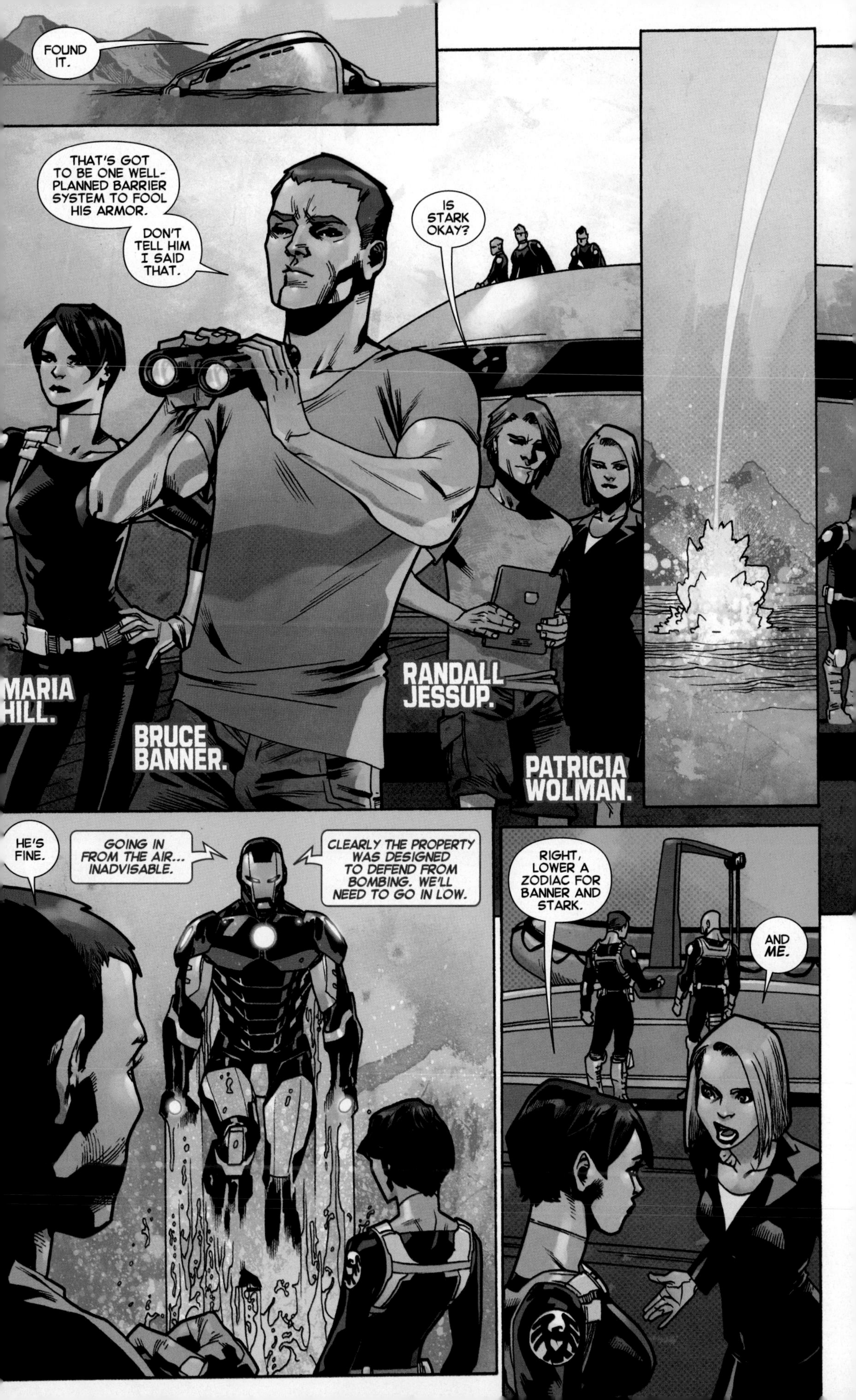
FOUND IT.
THAT'S GOT TO BE ONE WELL-PLANNED BARRIER SYSTEM TO FOOL HIS ARMOR.
DON'T TELL HIM I SAID THAT.
IS STARK OKAY?
MARIA HILL.
BRUCE BANNER.
RANDALL JESSUP.
PATRICIA WOLMAN.
HE'S FINE.
GOING IN FROM THE AIR... INADVISABLE.
CLEARLY THE PROPERTY WAS DESIGNED TO DEFEND FROM BOMBING. WE'LL NEED TO GO IN LOW.
RIGHT, LOWER A ZODIAC FOR BANNER AND STARK.
AND ME.

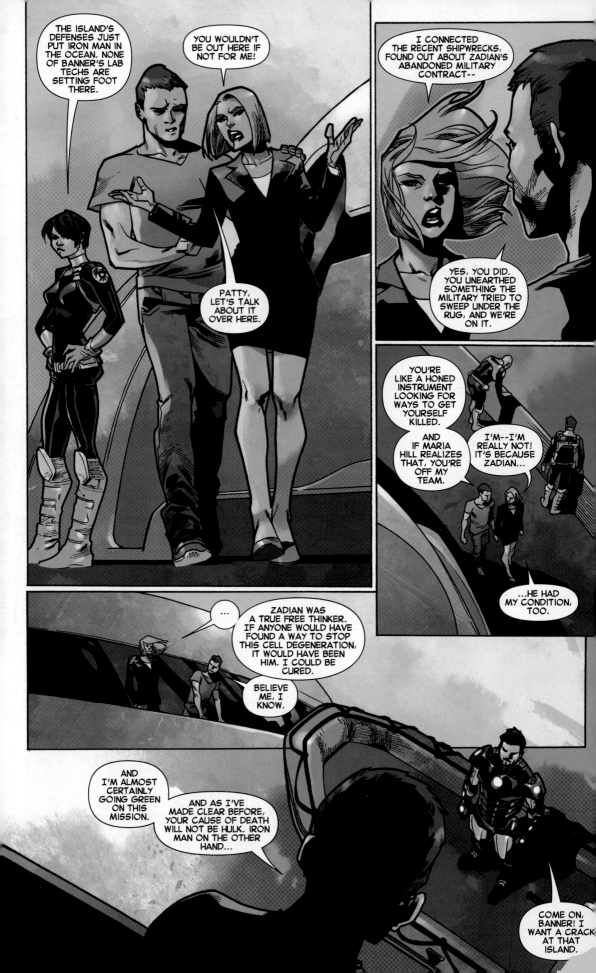

THE ISLAND'S DEFENSES JUST PUT IRON MAN IN THE OCEAN. NONE OF BANNER'S LAB TECHS ARE SETTING FOOT THERE.

YOU WOULDN'T BE OUT HERE IF NOT FOR ME!

PATTY, LET'S TALK ABOUT IT OVER HERE.

I CONNECTED THE RECENT SHIPWRECKS, FOUND OUT ABOUT ZADIAN'S ABANDONED MILITARY CONTRACT--

YES, YOU DID. YOU UNEARTHED SOMETHING THE MILITARY TRIED TO SWEEP UNDER THE RUG, AND WE'RE ON IT.

YOU'RE LIKE A HONED INSTRUMENT LOOKING FOR WAYS TO GET YOURSELF KILLED.

AND IF MARIA HILL REALIZES THAT, YOU'RE OFF MY TEAM.

I'M--I'M REALLY NOT! IT'S BECAUSE ZADIAN...

...HE HAD MY CONDITION, TOO.

...

ZADIAN WAS A TRUE FREE THINKER. IF ANYONE WOULD HAVE FOUND A WAY TO STOP THIS CELL DEGENERATION, IT WOULD HAVE BEEN HIM. I COULD BE CURED.

BELIEVE ME, I KNOW.

AND I'M ALMOST CERTAINLY GOING GREEN ON THIS MISSION.

AND AS I'VE MADE CLEAR BEFORE, YOUR CAUSE OF DEATH WILL NOT BE HULK. IRON MAN ON THE OTHER HAND...

COME ON, BANNER! I WANT A CRACK AT THAT ISLAND.

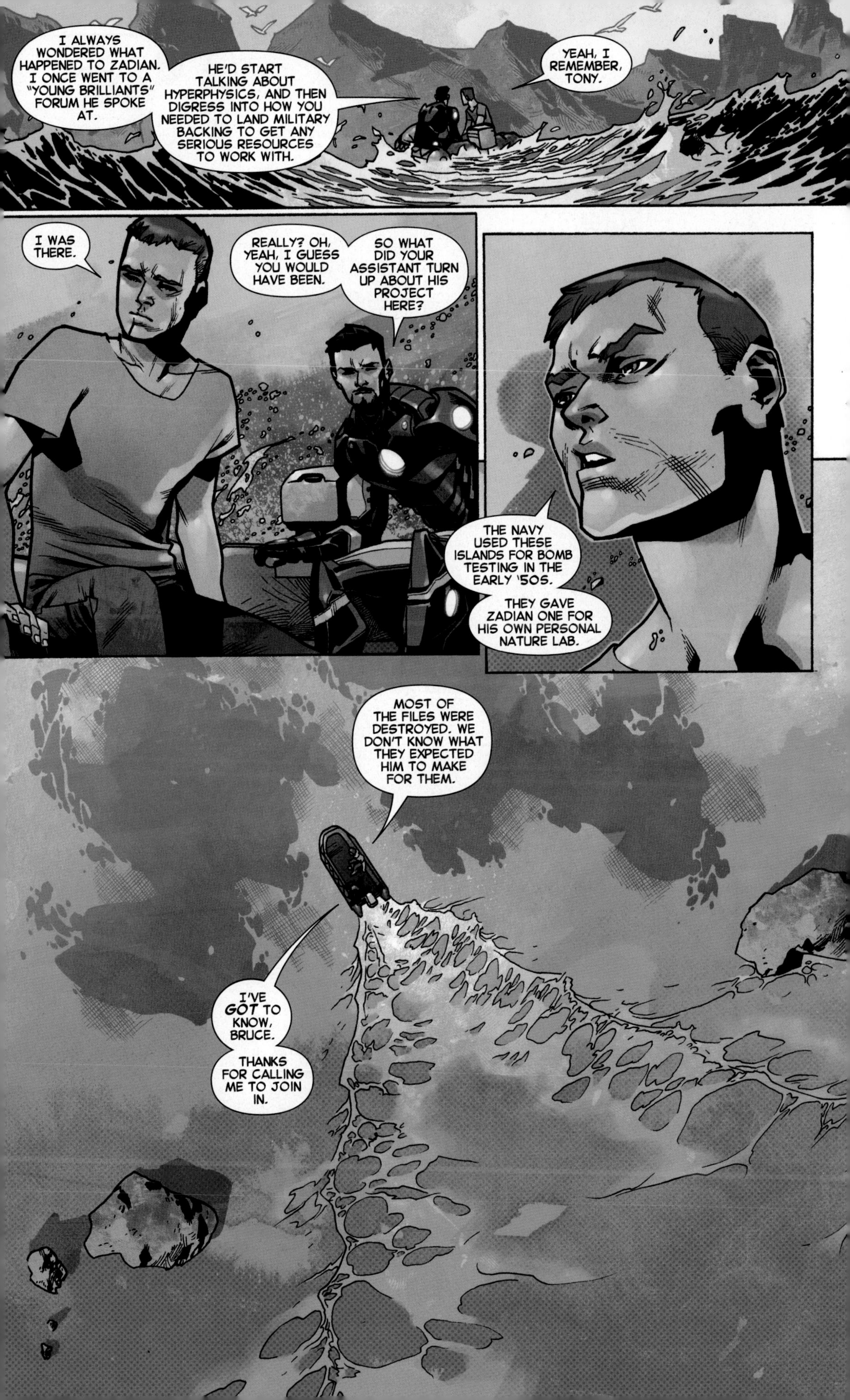
I ALWAYS WONDERED WHAT HAPPENED TO ZADIAN. I ONCE WENT TO A "YOUNG BRILLIANTS" FORUM HE SPOKE AT.
HE'D START TALKING ABOUT HYPERPHYSICS, AND THEN DIGRESS INTO HOW YOU NEEDED TO LAND MILITARY BACKING TO GET ANY SERIOUS RESOURCES TO WORK WITH.
YEAH, I REMEMBER, TONY.
I WAS THERE.
REALLY? OH, YEAH, I GUESS YOU WOULD HAVE BEEN.
SO WHAT DID YOUR ASSISTANT TURN UP ABOUT HIS PROJECT HERE?
THE NAVY USED THESE ISLANDS FOR BOMB TESTING IN THE EARLY '50S.
THEY GAVE ZADIAN ONE FOR HIS OWN PERSONAL NATURE LAB.
MOST OF THE FILES WERE DESTROYED. WE DON'T KNOW WHAT THEY EXPECTED HIM TO MAKE FOR THEM.
I'VE GOT TO KNOW, BRUCE.
THANKS FOR CALLING ME TO JOIN IN.

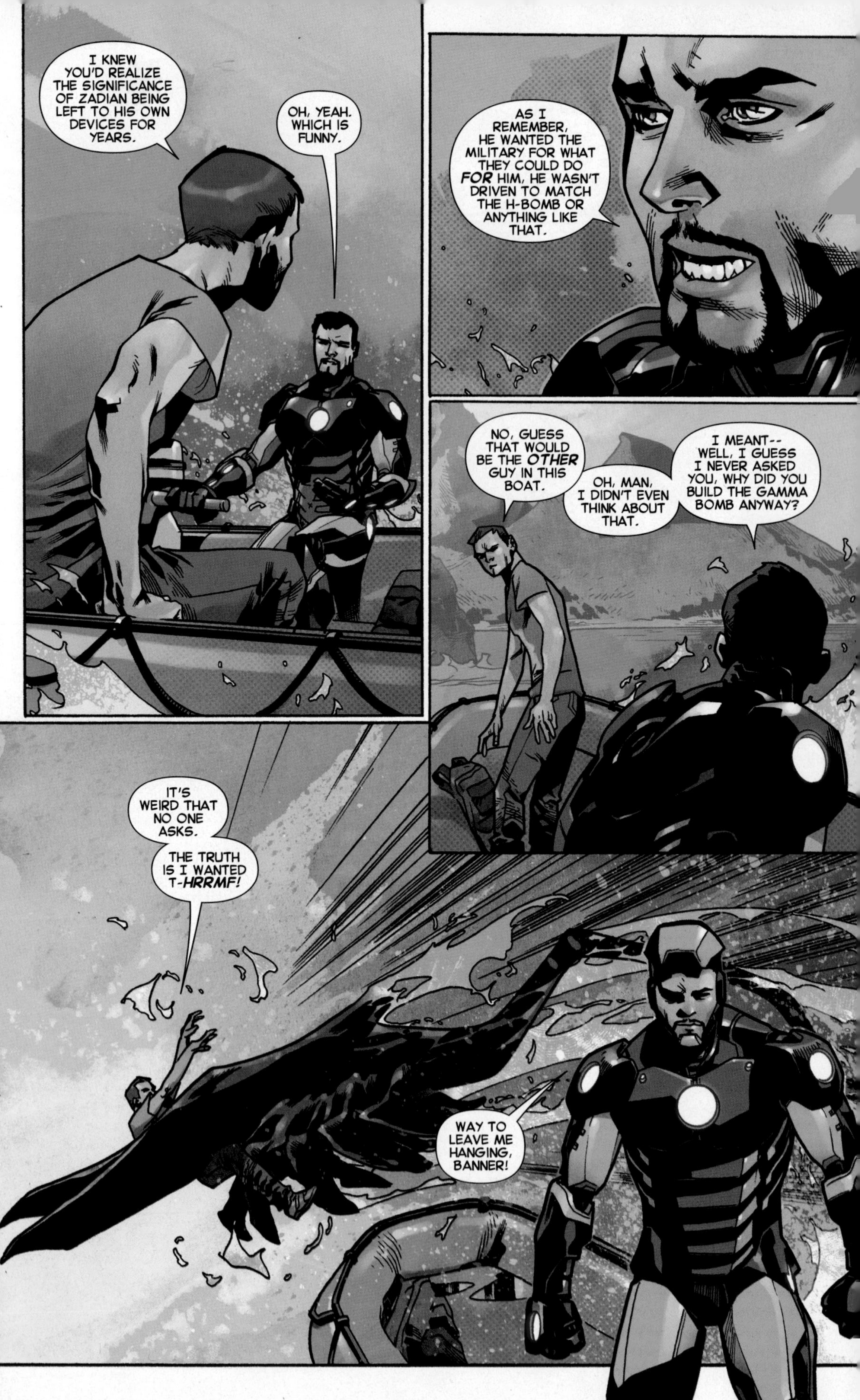

I KNEW YOU'D REALIZE THE SIGNIFICANCE OF ZADIAN BEING LEFT TO HIS OWN DEVICES FOR YEARS.
OH, YEAH. WHICH IS FUNNY.
AS I REMEMBER, HE WANTED THE MILITARY FOR WHAT THEY COULD DO *FOR* HIM, HE WASN'T DRIVEN TO MATCH THE H-BOMB OR ANYTHING LIKE THAT.
NO, GUESS THAT WOULD BE THE *OTHER* GUY IN THIS BOAT.
OH, MAN, I DIDN'T EVEN THINK ABOUT THAT.
I MEANT-- WELL, I GUESS I NEVER ASKED YOU, WHY DID YOU BUILD THE GAMMA BOMB ANYWAY?
IT'S WEIRD THAT NO ONE ASKS.
THE TRUTH IS I WANTED T-*HRRMF!*
WAY TO LEAVE ME HANGING, BANNER!

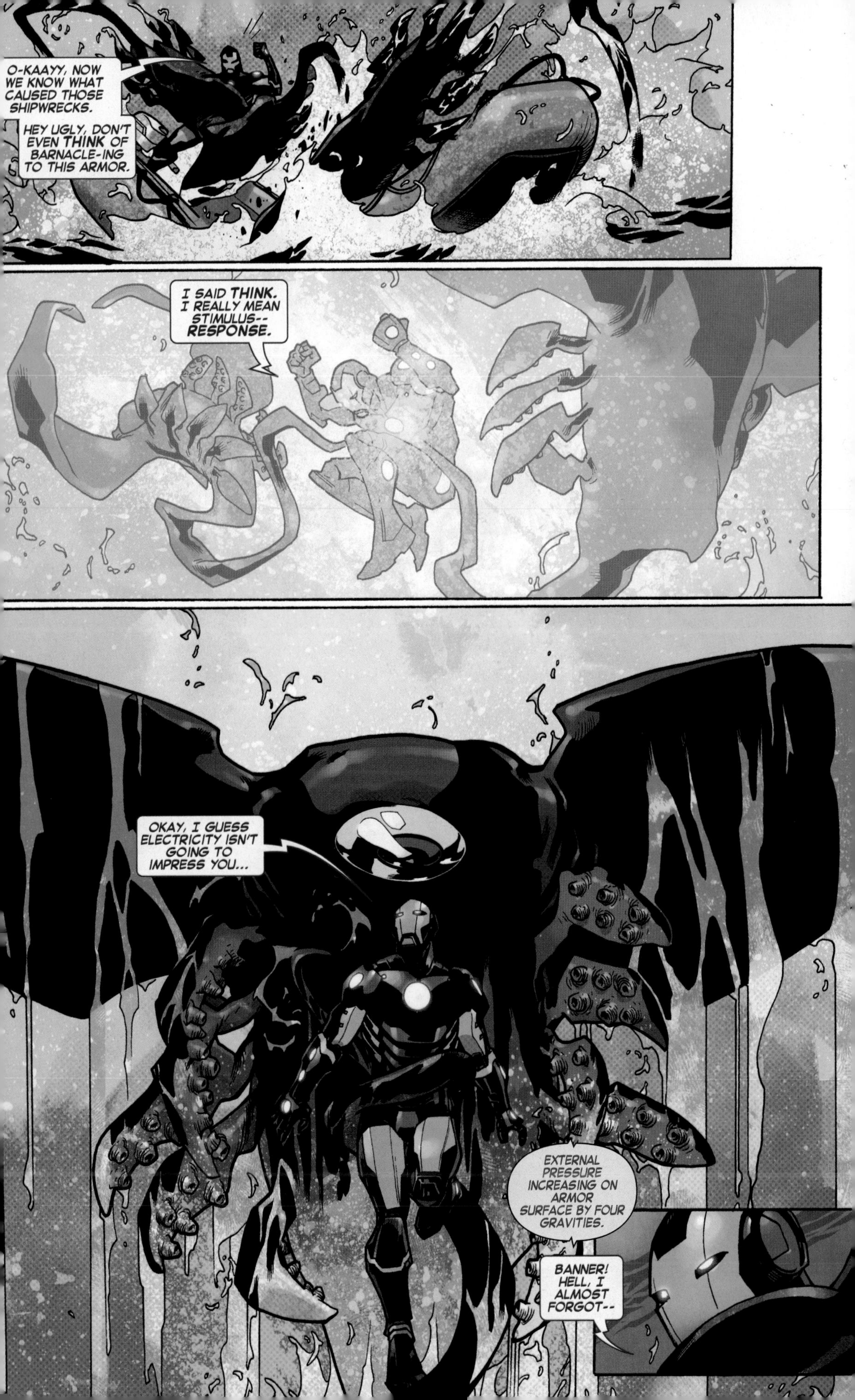
O-KAAYY, NOW WE KNOW WHAT CAUSED THOSE SHIPWRECKS.
HEY UGLY, DON'T EVEN THINK OF BARNACLE-ING TO THIS ARMOR.
I SAID THINK. I REALLY MEAN STIMULUS--RESPONSE.
OKAY, I GUESS ELECTRICITY ISN'T GOING TO IMPRESS YOU...
EXTERNAL PRESSURE INCREASING ON ARMOR SURFACE BY FOUR GRAVITIES.
BANNER! HELL, I ALMOST FORGOT--

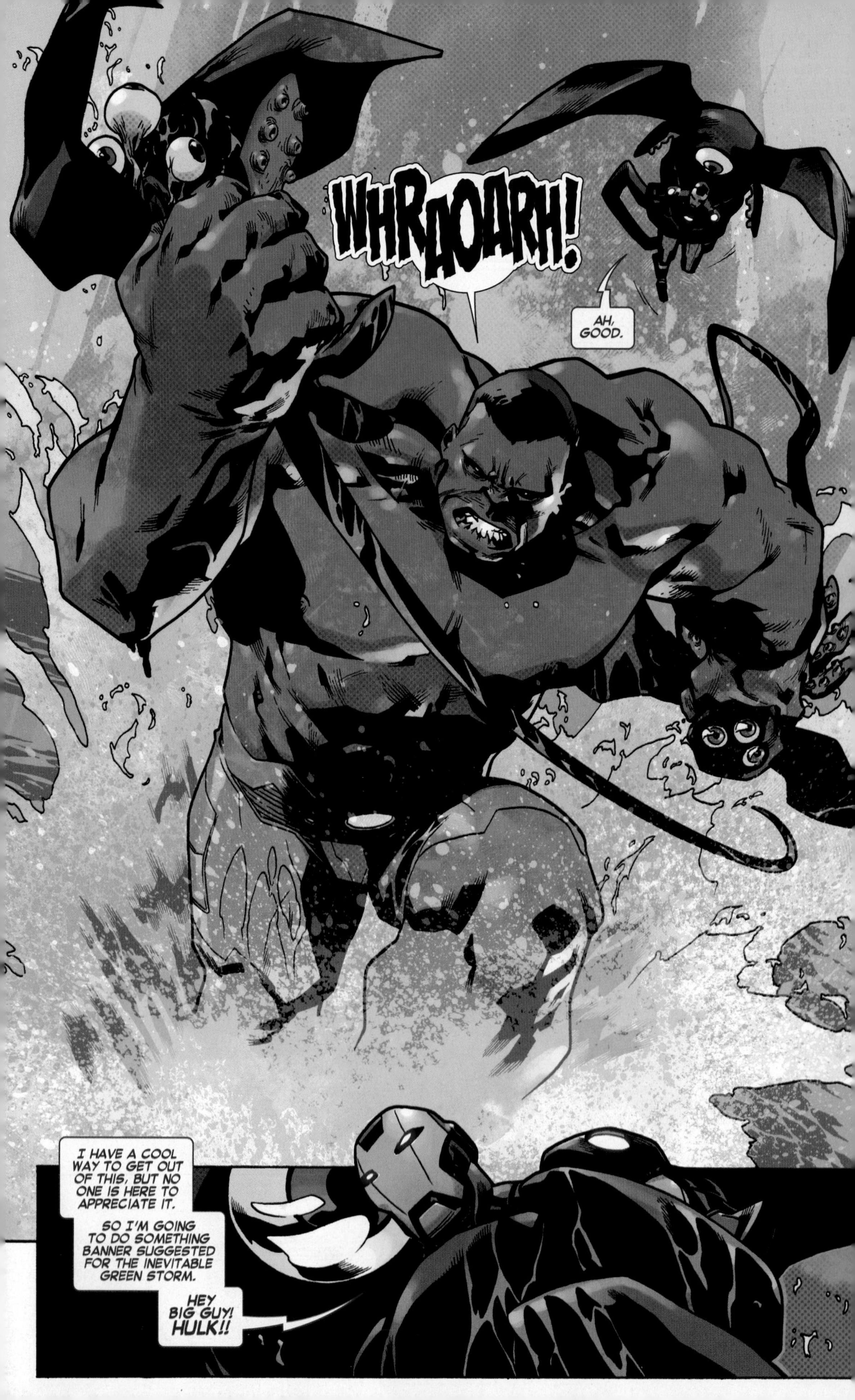
WHRAOARH!
AH, GOOD.
I HAVE A COOL WAY TO GET OUT OF THIS, BUT NO ONE IS HERE TO APPRECIATE IT.
SO I'M GOING TO DO SOMETHING BANNER SUGGESTED FOR THE INEVITABLE GREEN STORM.
HEY BIG GUY! HULK!!

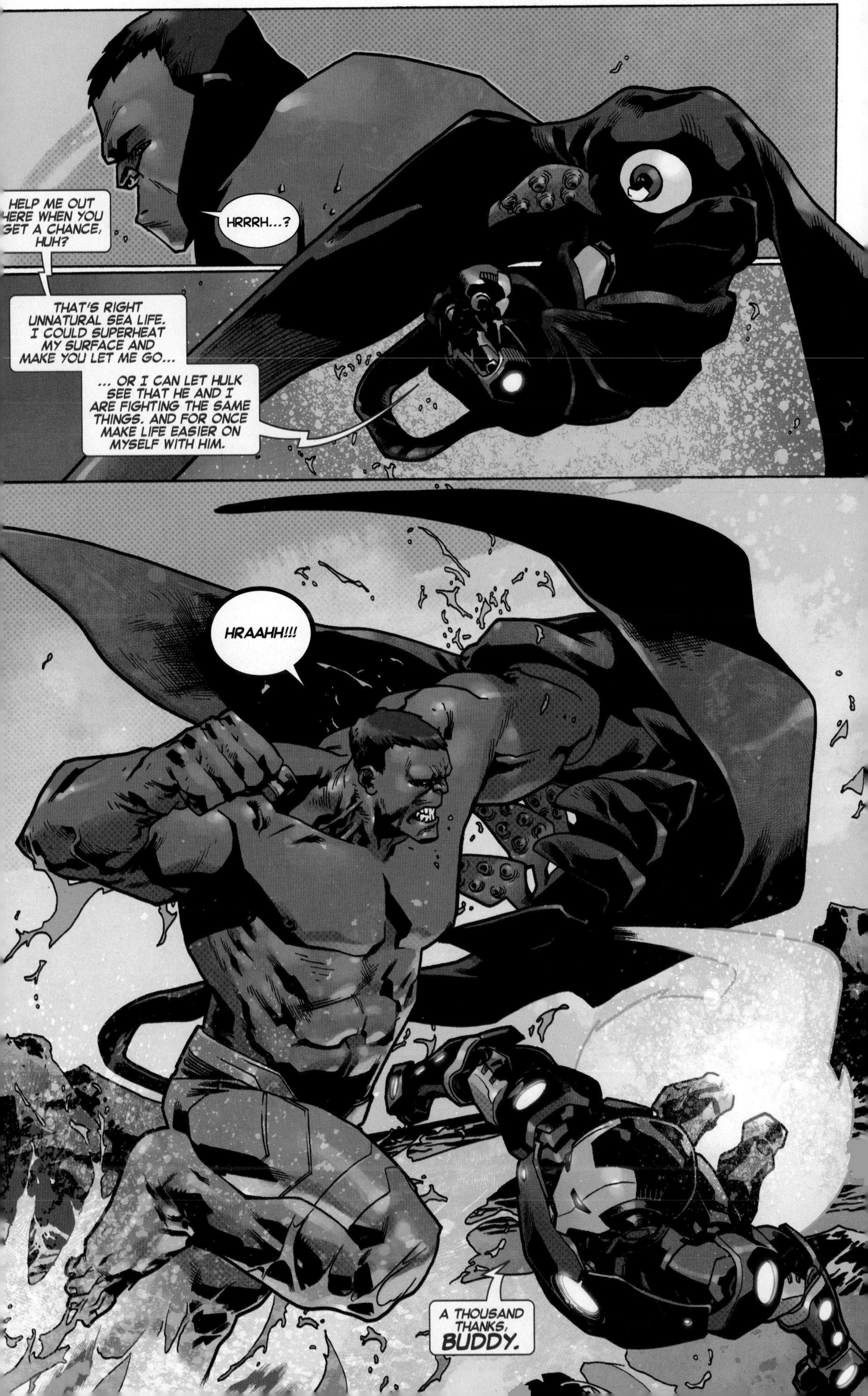
HELP ME OUT HERE WHEN YOU GET A CHANCE, HUH?
HRRRH...?
THAT'S RIGHT UNNATURAL SEA LIFE. I COULD SUPERHEAT MY SURFACE AND MAKE YOU LET ME GO...
... OR I CAN LET HULK SEE THAT HE AND I ARE FIGHTING THE SAME THINGS. AND FOR ONCE MAKE LIFE EASIER ON MYSELF WITH HIM.
HRAAHH!!!
A THOUSAND THANKS, BUDDY.

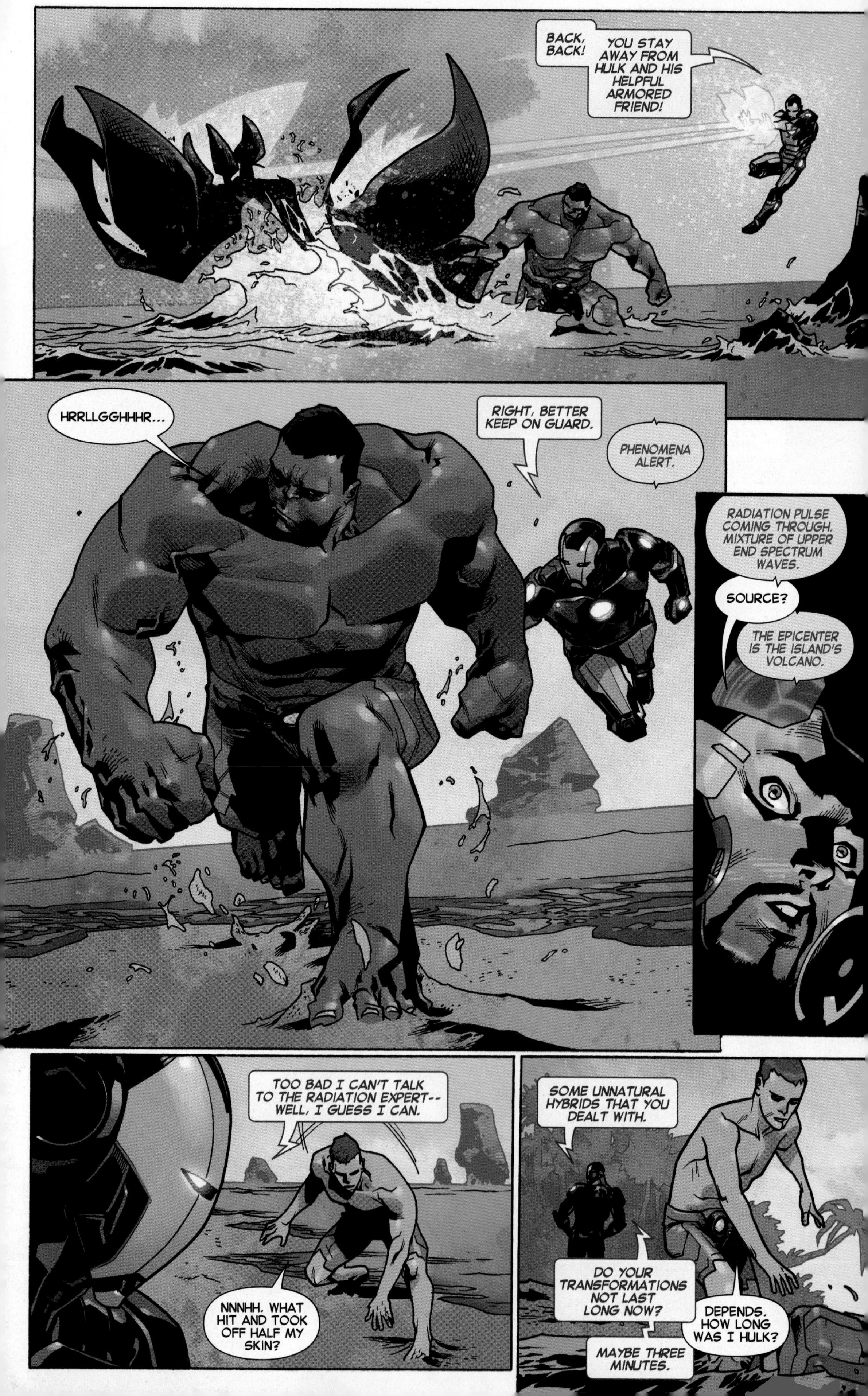
BACK, BACK!
YOU STAY AWAY FROM HULK AND HIS HELPFUL ARMORED FRIEND!
HRRLLGGHHHR...
RIGHT, BETTER KEEP ON GUARD.
PHENOMENA ALERT.
RADIATION PULSE COMING THROUGH. MIXTURE OF UPPER END SPECTRUM WAVES.
SOURCE?
THE EPICENTER IS THE ISLAND'S VOLCANO.
TOO BAD I CAN'T TALK TO THE RADIATION EXPERT-- WELL, I GUESS I CAN.
NNNHH. WHAT HIT AND TOOK OFF HALF MY SKIN?
SOME UNNATURAL HYBRIDS THAT YOU DEALT WITH.
DO YOUR TRANSFORMATIONS NOT LAST LONG NOW?
DEPENDS. HOW LONG WAS I HULK?
MAYBE THREE MINUTES.

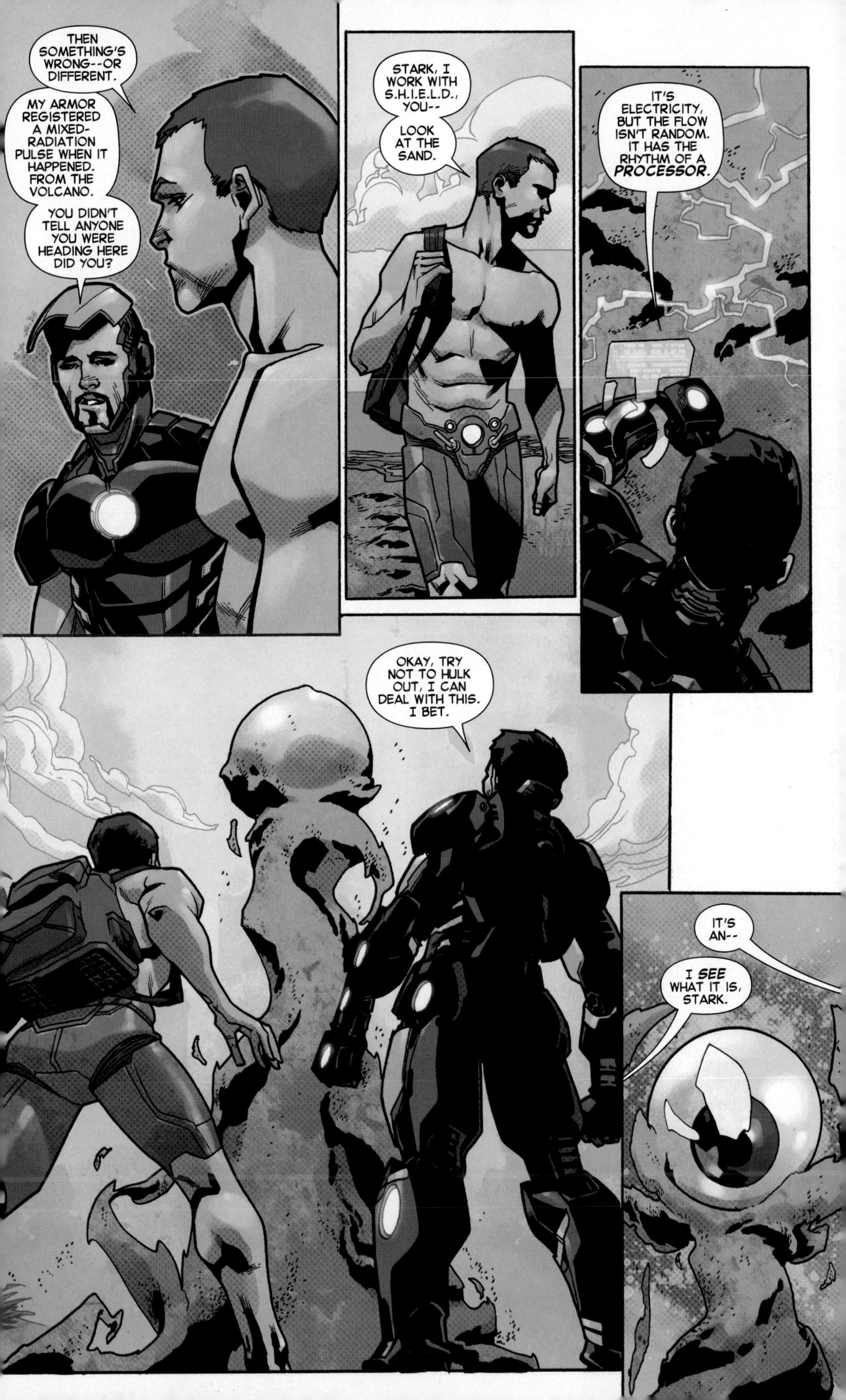

THEN SOMETHING'S WRONG--OR DIFFERENT.
MY ARMOR REGISTERED A MIXED-RADIATION PULSE WHEN IT HAPPENED. FROM THE VOLCANO.
YOU DIDN'T TELL ANYONE YOU WERE HEADING HERE DID YOU?
STARK, I WORK WITH S.H.I.E.L.D., YOU--
LOOK AT THE SAND.
IT'S ELECTRICITY, BUT THE FLOW ISN'T RANDOM. IT HAS THE RHYTHM OF A PROCESSOR.
OKAY, TRY NOT TO HULK OUT, I CAN DEAL WITH THIS. I BET.
IT'S AN--
I SEE WHAT IT IS, STARK.

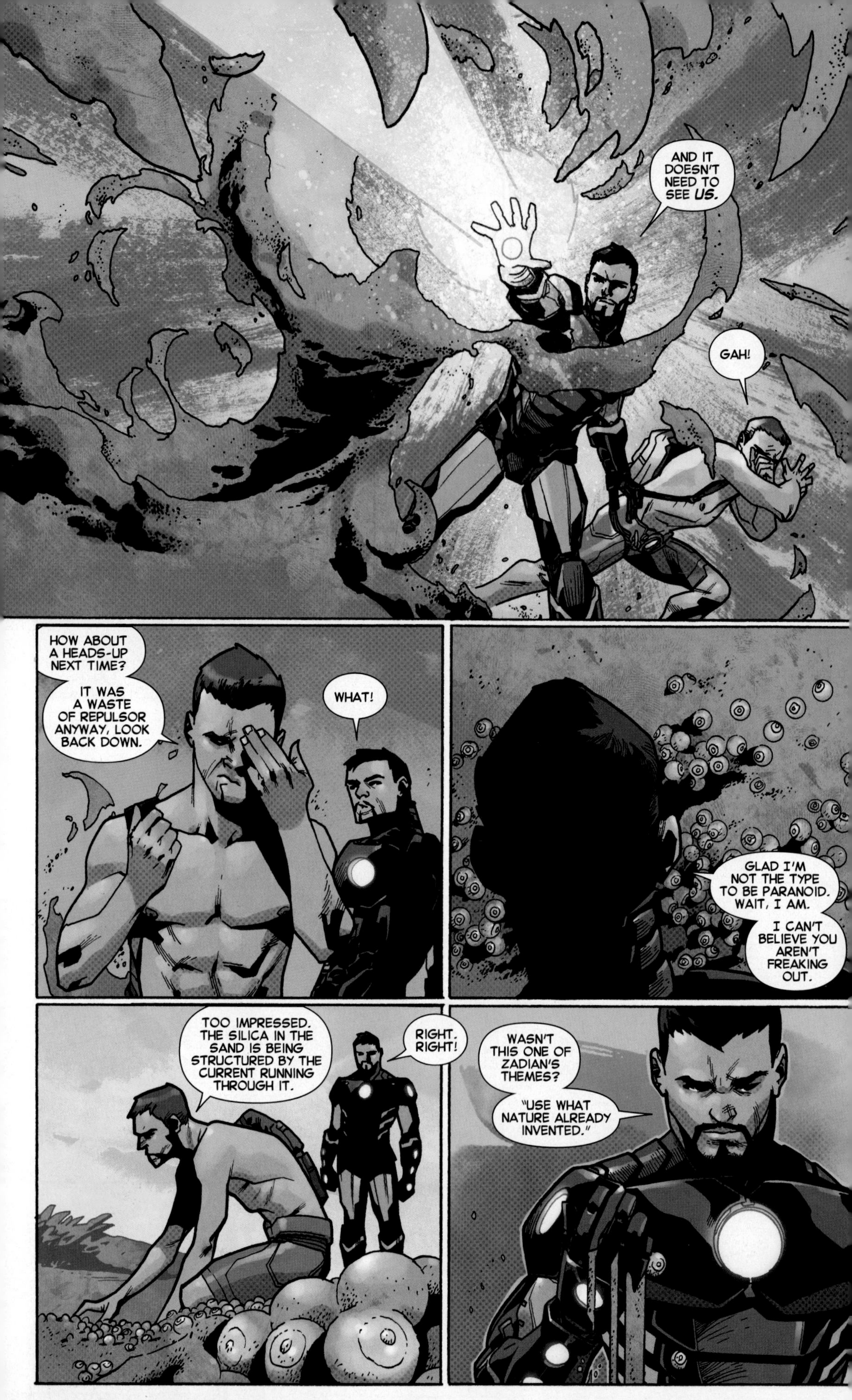
AND IT DOESN'T NEED TO SEE US.
GAH!
HOW ABOUT A HEADS-UP NEXT TIME?
IT WAS A WASTE OF REPULSOR ANYWAY, LOOK BACK DOWN.
WHAT!
GLAD I'M NOT THE TYPE TO BE PARANOID. WAIT, I AM.
I CAN'T BELIEVE YOU AREN'T FREAKING OUT.
TOO IMPRESSED. THE SILICA IN THE SAND IS BEING STRUCTURED BY THE CURRENT RUNNING THROUGH IT.
RIGHT. RIGHT!
WASN'T THIS ONE OF ZADIAN'S THEMES?
"USE WHAT NATURE ALREADY INVENTED."

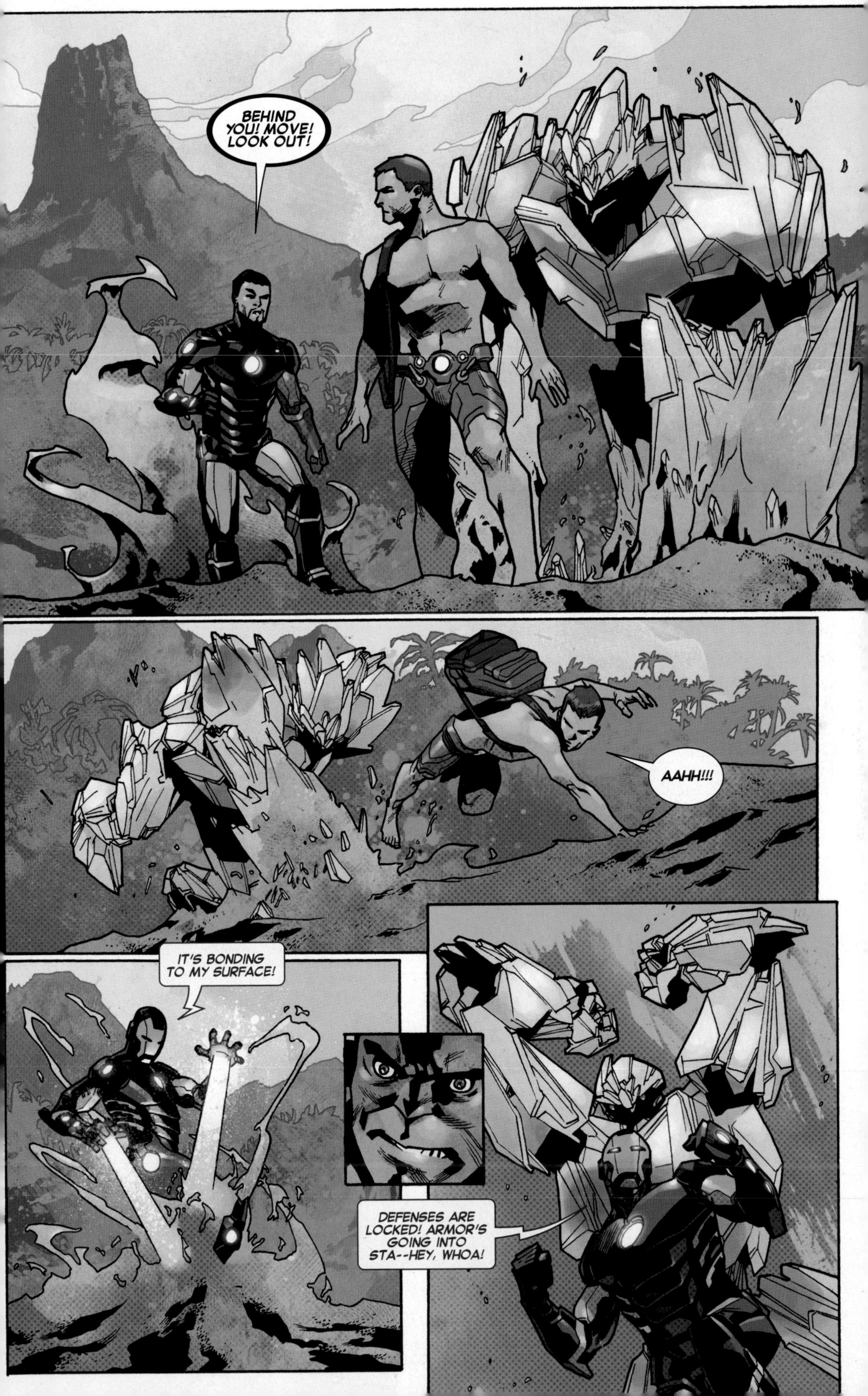
BEHIND YOU! MOVE! LOOK OUT!
AAHH!!!
IT'S BONDING TO MY SURFACE!
DEFENSES ARE LOCKED! ARMOR'S GOING INTO STA--HEY, WHOA!

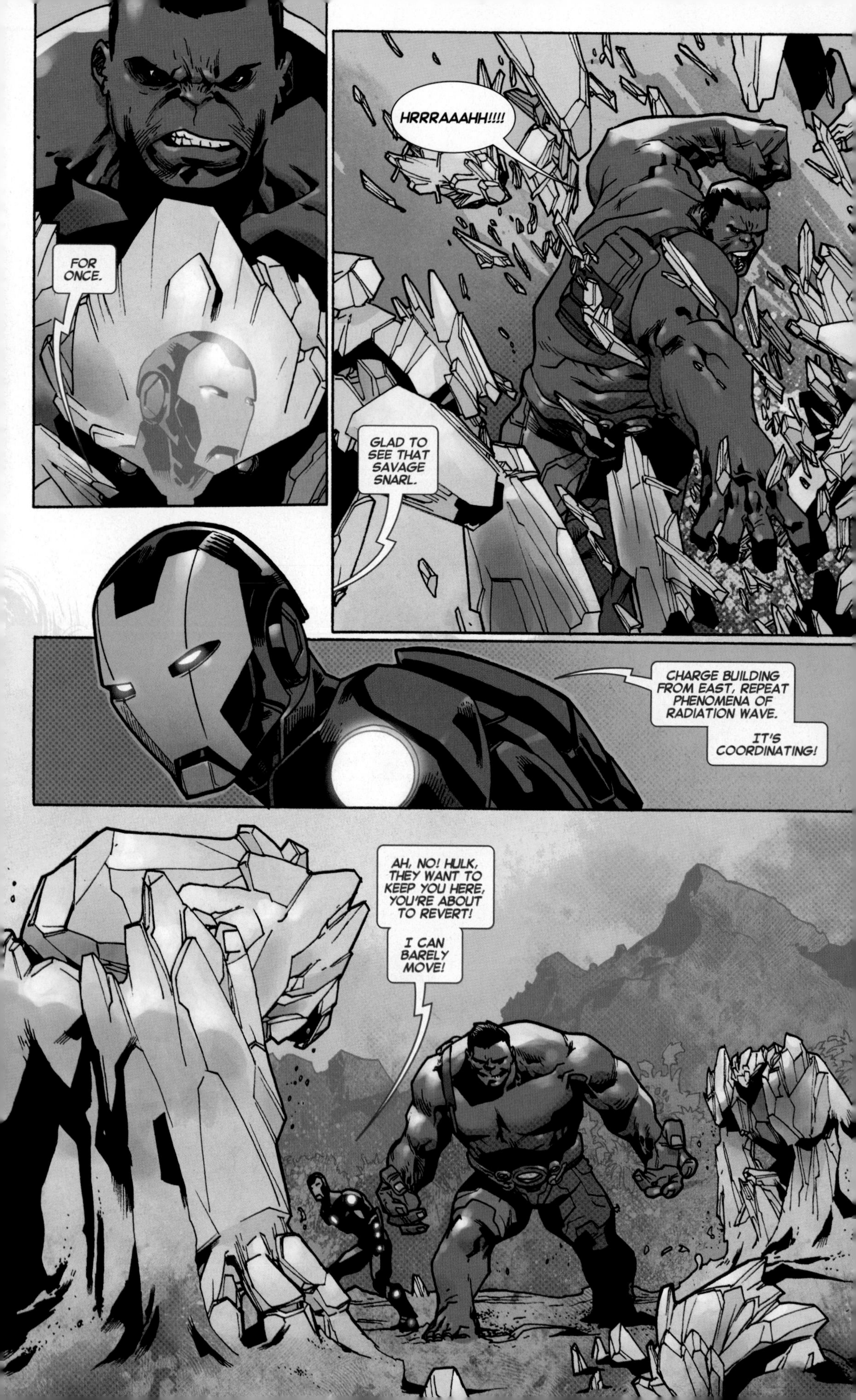
FOR ONCE.
HRRRAAAHH!!!!
GLAD TO SEE THAT SAVAGE SNARL.
CHARGE BUILDING FROM EAST, REPEAT PHENOMENA OF RADIATION WAVE.
IT'S COORDINATING!
AH, NO! HULK, THEY WANT TO KEEP YOU HERE, YOU'RE ABOUT TO REVERT!
I CAN BARELY MOVE!

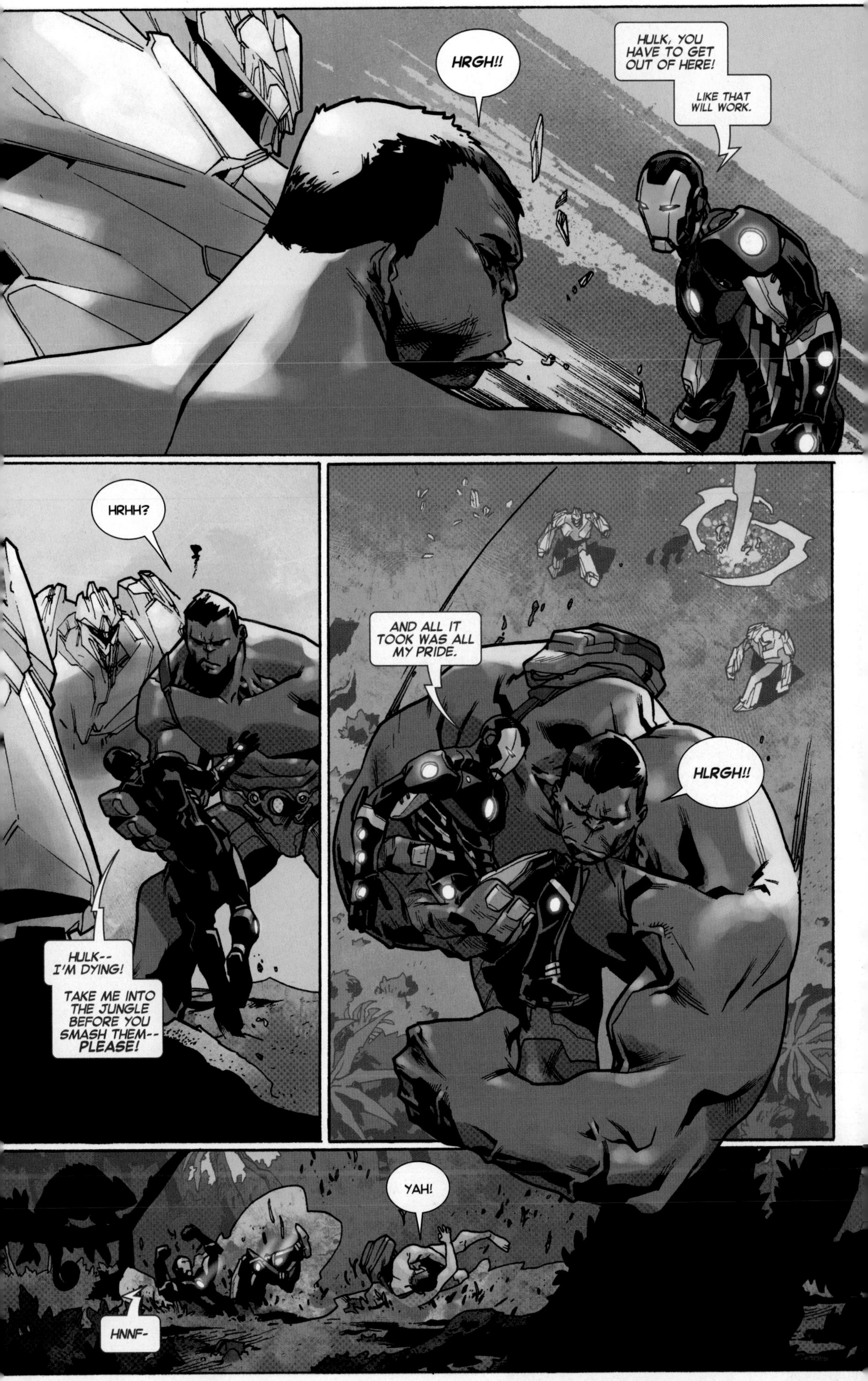
HRGH!!
HULK, YOU HAVE TO GET OUT OF HERE!
LIKE THAT WILL WORK.
HRHH?
HULK-- I'M DYING!
TAKE ME INTO THE JUNGLE BEFORE YOU SMASH THEM-- PLEASE!
AND ALL IT TOOK WAS ALL MY PRIDE.
HLRGH!!
YAH!
HNNF-

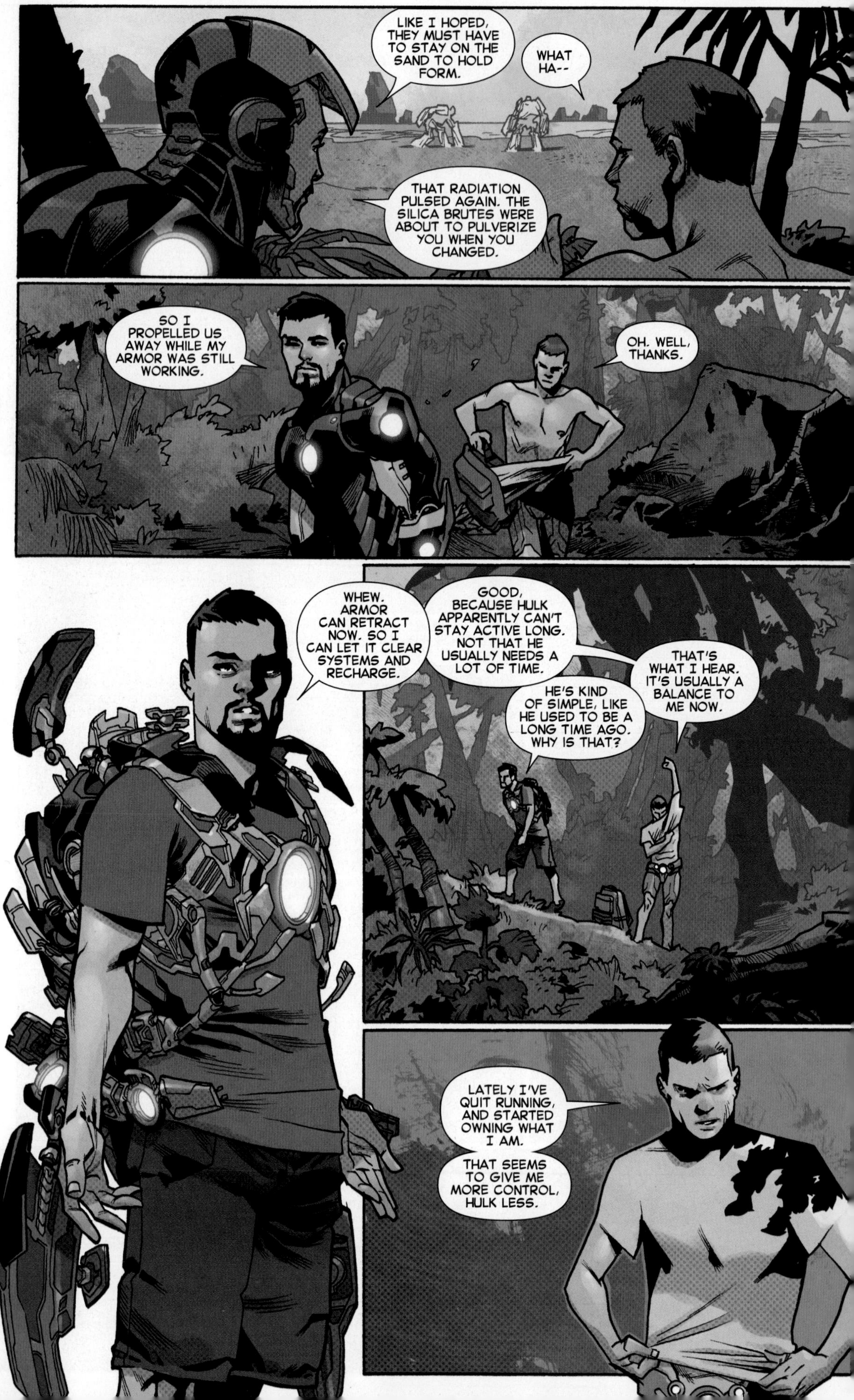
LIKE I HOPED, THEY MUST HAVE TO STAY ON THE SAND TO HOLD FORM.
WHAT HA--
THAT RADIATION PULSED AGAIN. THE SILICA BRUTES WERE ABOUT TO PULVERIZE YOU WHEN YOU CHANGED.
SO I PROPELLED US AWAY WHILE MY ARMOR WAS STILL WORKING.
OH. WELL, THANKS.
WHEW. ARMOR CAN RETRACT NOW. SO I CAN LET IT CLEAR SYSTEMS AND RECHARGE.
GOOD, BECAUSE HULK APPARENTLY CAN'T STAY ACTIVE LONG. NOT THAT HE USUALLY NEEDS A LOT OF TIME.
THAT'S WHAT I HEAR. IT'S USUALLY A BALANCE TO ME NOW.
HE'S KIND OF SIMPLE, LIKE HE USED TO BE A LONG TIME AGO. WHY IS THAT?
LATELY I'VE QUIT RUNNING, AND STARTED OWNING WHAT I AM.
THAT SEEMS TO GIVE ME MORE CONTROL, HULK LESS.

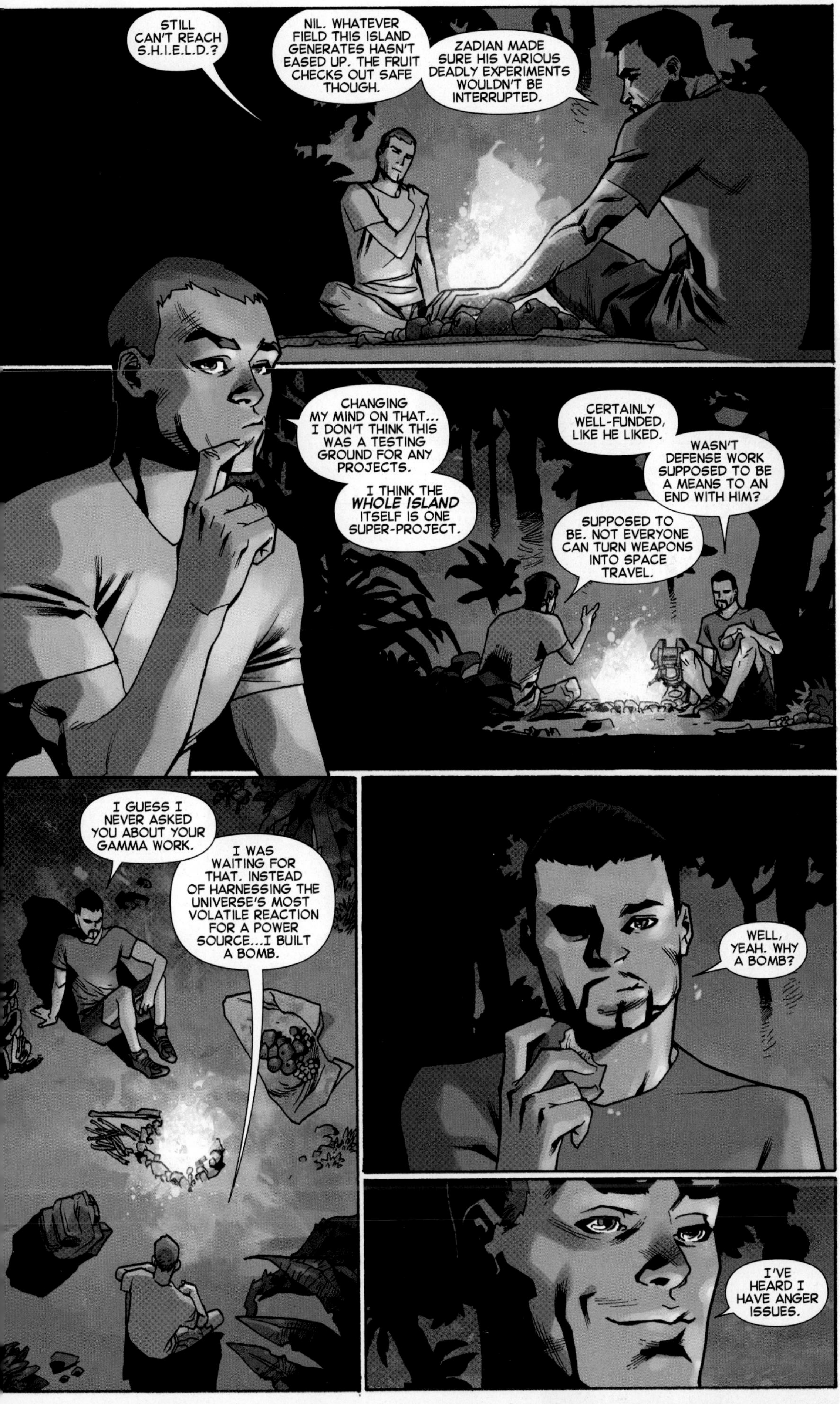
STILL CAN'T REACH S.H.I.E.L.D.?
NIL. WHATEVER FIELD THIS ISLAND GENERATES HASN'T EASED UP. THE FRUIT CHECKS OUT SAFE THOUGH.
ZADIAN MADE SURE HIS VARIOUS DEADLY EXPERIMENTS WOULDN'T BE INTERRUPTED.
CHANGING MY MIND ON THAT... I DON'T THINK THIS WAS A TESTING GROUND FOR ANY PROJECTS.
I THINK THE *WHOLE ISLAND* ITSELF IS ONE SUPER-PROJECT.
CERTAINLY WELL-FUNDED, LIKE HE LIKED.
WASN'T DEFENSE WORK SUPPOSED TO BE A MEANS TO AN END WITH HIM?
SUPPOSED TO BE. NOT EVERYONE CAN TURN WEAPONS INTO SPACE TRAVEL.
I GUESS I NEVER ASKED YOU ABOUT YOUR GAMMA WORK.
I WAS WAITING FOR THAT. INSTEAD OF HARNESSING THE UNIVERSE'S MOST VOLATILE REACTION FOR A POWER SOURCE...I BUILT A BOMB.
WELL, YEAH. WHY A BOMB?
I'VE HEARD I HAVE ANGER ISSUES.

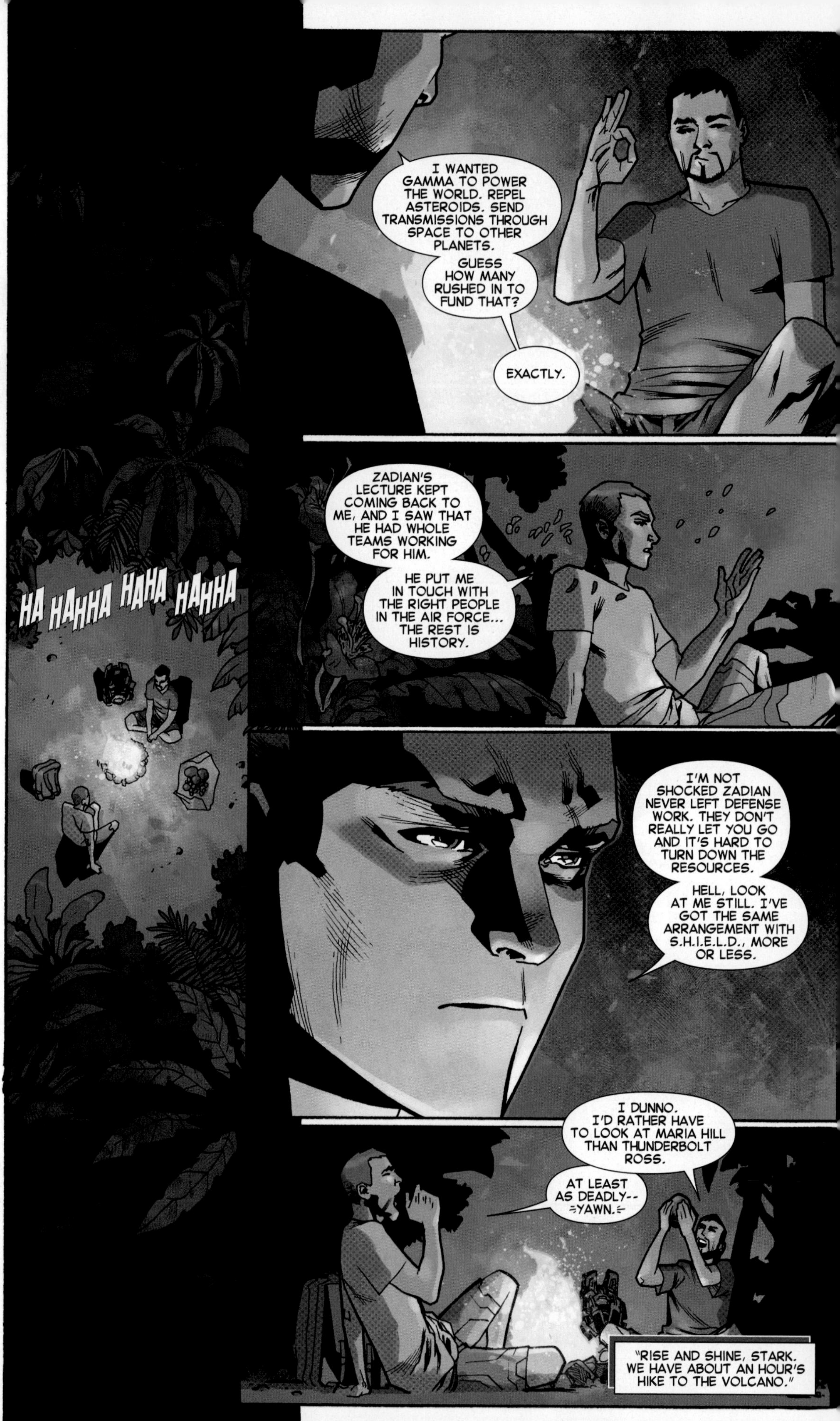
I WANTED GAMMA TO POWER THE WORLD. REPEL ASTEROIDS. SEND TRANSMISSIONS THROUGH SPACE TO OTHER PLANETS.
GUESS HOW MANY RUSHED IN TO FUND THAT?
EXACTLY.
HA HAHHA HAHA HAHHA
ZADIAN'S LECTURE KEPT COMING BACK TO ME, AND I SAW THAT HE HAD WHOLE TEAMS WORKING FOR HIM.
HE PUT ME IN TOUCH WITH THE RIGHT PEOPLE IN THE AIR FORCE... THE REST IS HISTORY.
I'M NOT SHOCKED ZADIAN NEVER LEFT DEFENSE WORK. THEY DON'T REALLY LET YOU GO AND IT'S HARD TO TURN DOWN THE RESOURCES.
HELL, LOOK AT ME STILL. I'VE GOT THE SAME ARRANGEMENT WITH S.H.I.E.L.D., MORE OR LESS.
I DUNNO. I'D RATHER HAVE TO LOOK AT MARIA HILL THAN THUNDERBOLT ROSS.
AT LEAST AS DEADLY-- YAWN.
"RISE AND SHINE, STARK. WE HAVE ABOUT AN HOUR'S HIKE TO THE VOLCANO."

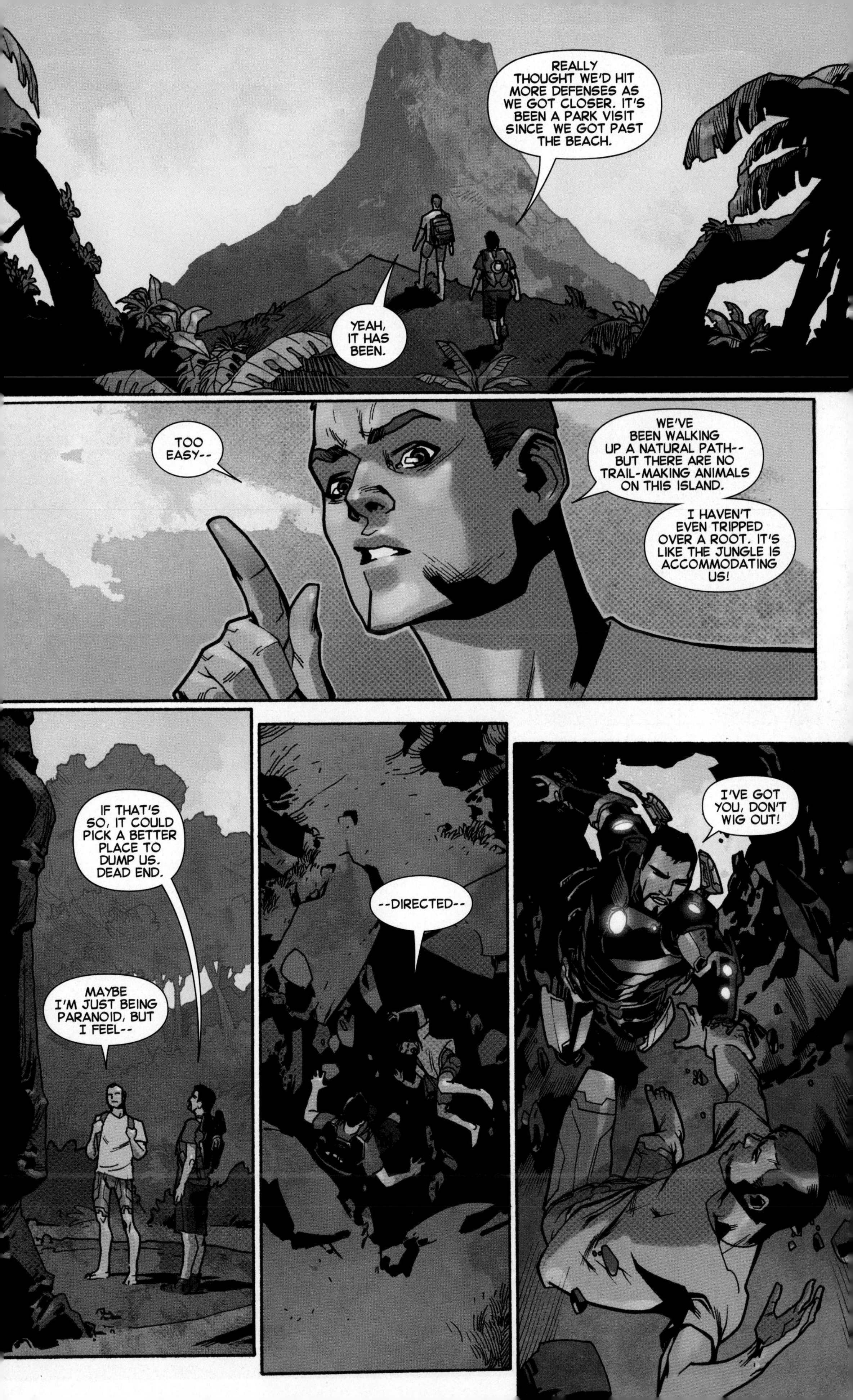
REALLY THOUGHT WE'D HIT MORE DEFENSES AS WE GOT CLOSER. IT'S BEEN A PARK VISIT SINCE WE GOT PAST THE BEACH.
YEAH, IT HAS BEEN.
TOO EASY--
WE'VE BEEN WALKING UP A NATURAL PATH--BUT THERE ARE NO TRAIL-MAKING ANIMALS ON THIS ISLAND.
I HAVEN'T EVEN TRIPPED OVER A ROOT. IT'S LIKE THE JUNGLE IS ACCOMMODATING US!
MAYBE I'M JUST BEING PARANOID, BUT I FEEL--
IF THAT'S SO, IT COULD PICK A BETTER PLACE TO DUMP US. DEAD END.
--DIRECTED--
I'VE GOT YOU, DON'T WIG OUT!

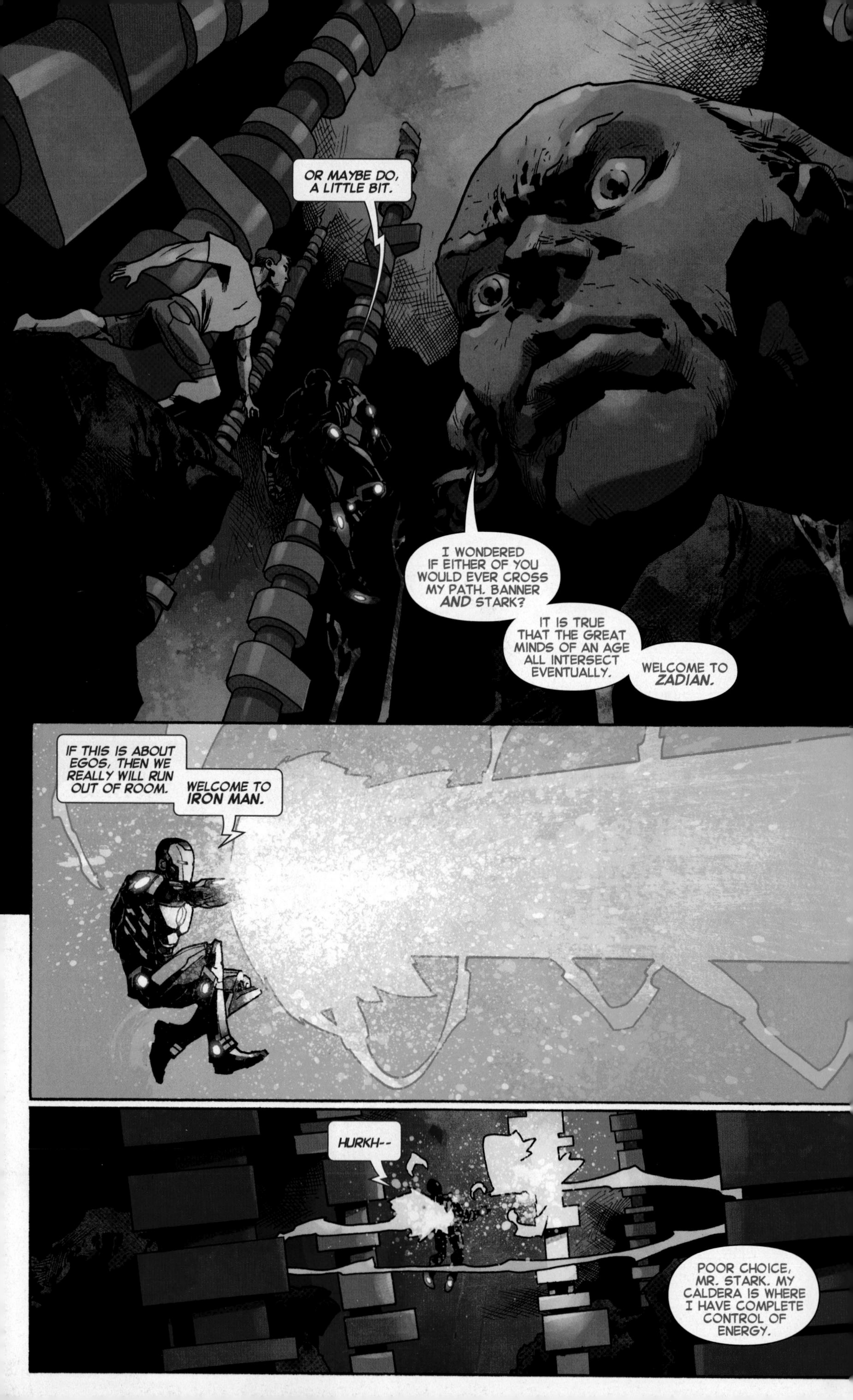

OR MAYBE DO, A LITTLE BIT.
I WONDERED IF EITHER OF YOU WOULD EVER CROSS MY PATH. BANNER AND STARK?
IT IS TRUE THAT THE GREAT MINDS OF AN AGE ALL INTERSECT EVENTUALLY.
WELCOME TO ZADIAN.
IF THIS IS ABOUT EGOS, THEN WE REALLY WILL RUN OUT OF ROOM.
WELCOME TO IRON MAN.
HURKH--
POOR CHOICE, MR. STARK. MY CALDERA IS WHERE I HAVE COMPLETE CONTROL OF ENERGY.

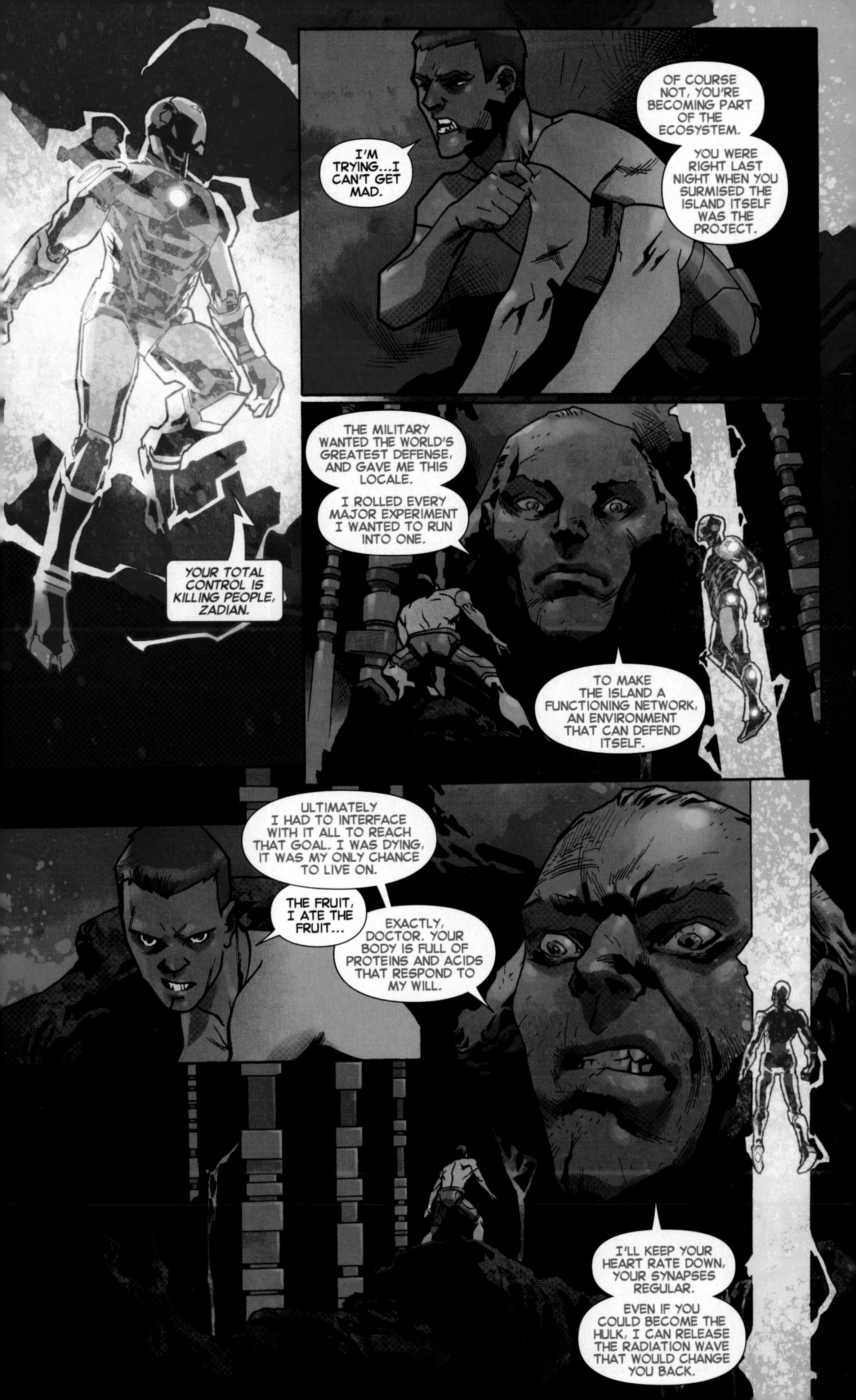
I'M TRYING...I CAN'T GET MAD.
OF COURSE NOT, YOU'RE BECOMING PART OF THE ECOSYSTEM.
YOU WERE RIGHT LAST NIGHT WHEN YOU SURMISED THE ISLAND ITSELF WAS THE PROJECT.
YOUR TOTAL CONTROL IS KILLING PEOPLE, ZADIAN.
THE MILITARY WANTED THE WORLD'S GREATEST DEFENSE, AND GAVE ME THIS LOCALE.
I ROLLED EVERY MAJOR EXPERIMENT I WANTED TO RUN INTO ONE.
TO MAKE THE ISLAND A FUNCTIONING NETWORK, AN ENVIRONMENT THAT CAN DEFEND ITSELF.
ULTIMATELY I HAD TO INTERFACE WITH IT ALL TO REACH THAT GOAL. I WAS DYING, IT WAS MY ONLY CHANCE TO LIVE ON.
THE FRUIT, I ATE THE FRUIT...
EXACTLY, DOCTOR. YOUR BODY IS FULL OF PROTEINS AND ACIDS THAT RESPOND TO MY WILL.
I'LL KEEP YOUR HEART RATE DOWN, YOUR SYNAPSES REGULAR.
EVEN IF YOU COULD BECOME THE HULK, I CAN RELEASE THE RADIATION WAVE THAT WOULD CHANGE YOU BACK.

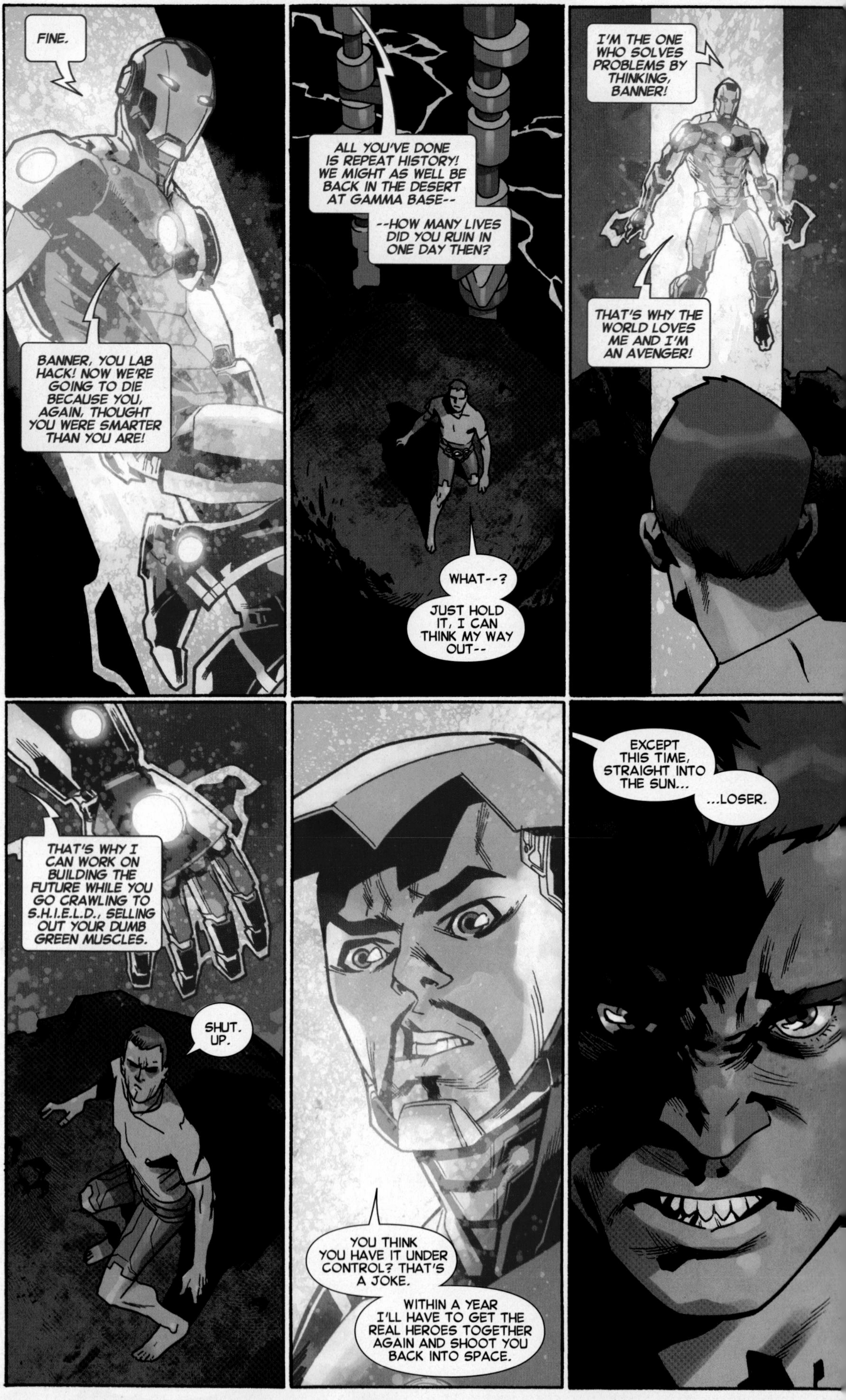
FINE.
BANNER, YOU LAB HACK! NOW WE'RE GOING TO DIE BECAUSE YOU, AGAIN, THOUGHT YOU WERE SMARTER THAN YOU ARE!
ALL YOU'VE DONE IS REPEAT HISTORY! WE MIGHT AS WELL BE BACK IN THE DESERT AT GAMMA BASE--
--HOW MANY LIVES DID YOU RUIN IN ONE DAY THEN?
WHAT--?
JUST HOLD IT, I CAN THINK MY WAY OUT--
I'M THE ONE WHO SOLVES PROBLEMS BY THINKING, BANNER!
THAT'S WHY THE WORLD LOVES ME AND I'M AN AVENGER!
THAT'S WHY I CAN WORK ON BUILDING THE FUTURE WHILE YOU GO CRAWLING TO S.H.I.E.L.D., SELLING OUT YOUR DUMB GREEN MUSCLES.
SHUT. UP.
YOU THINK YOU HAVE IT UNDER CONTROL? THAT'S A JOKE.
WITHIN A YEAR I'LL HAVE TO GET THE REAL HEROES TOGETHER AGAIN AND SHOOT YOU BACK INTO SPACE.
EXCEPT THIS TIME, STRAIGHT INTO THE SUN...
...LOSER.

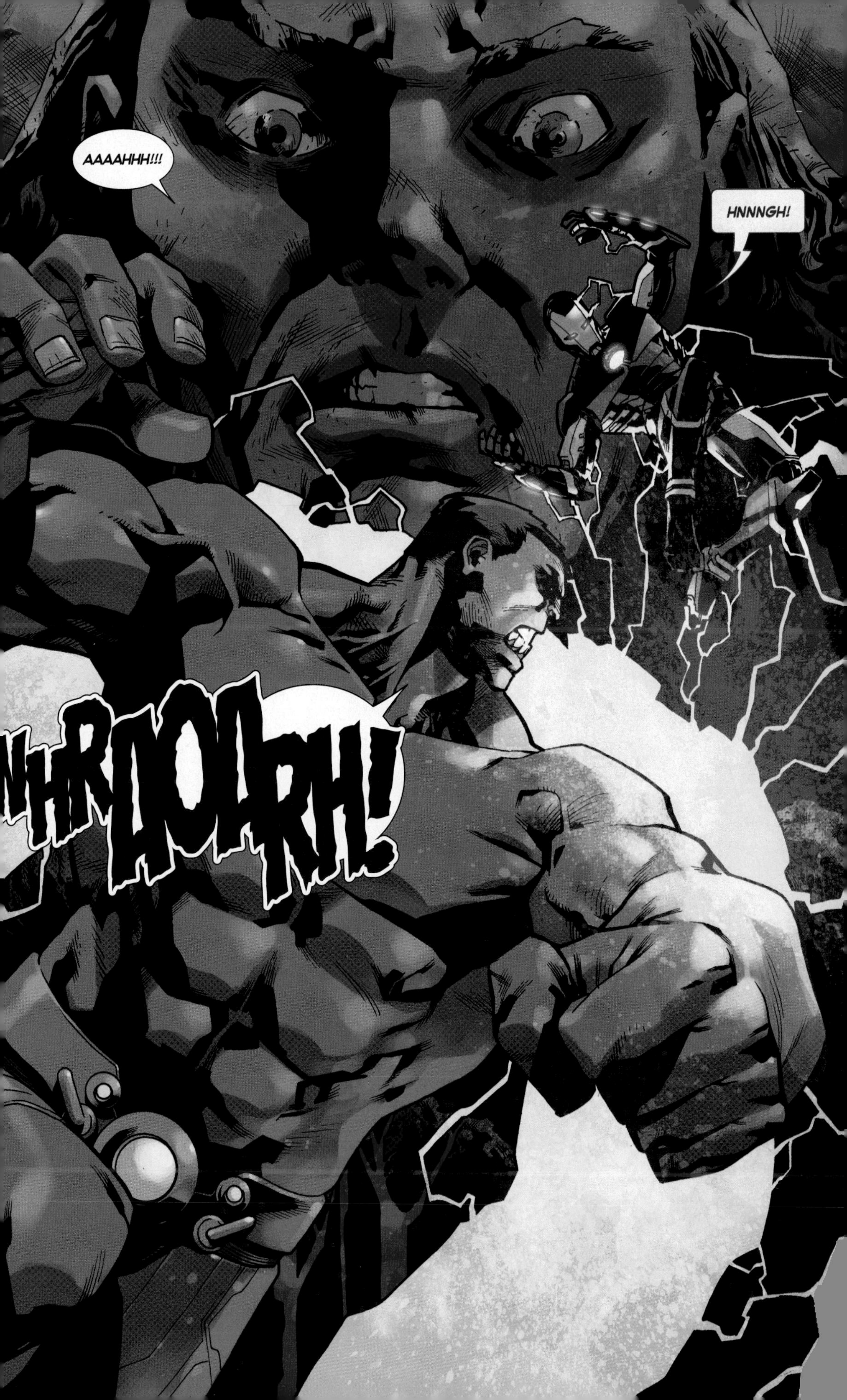
AAAAHHH!!!
HNNNGH!
WHRAOARH!

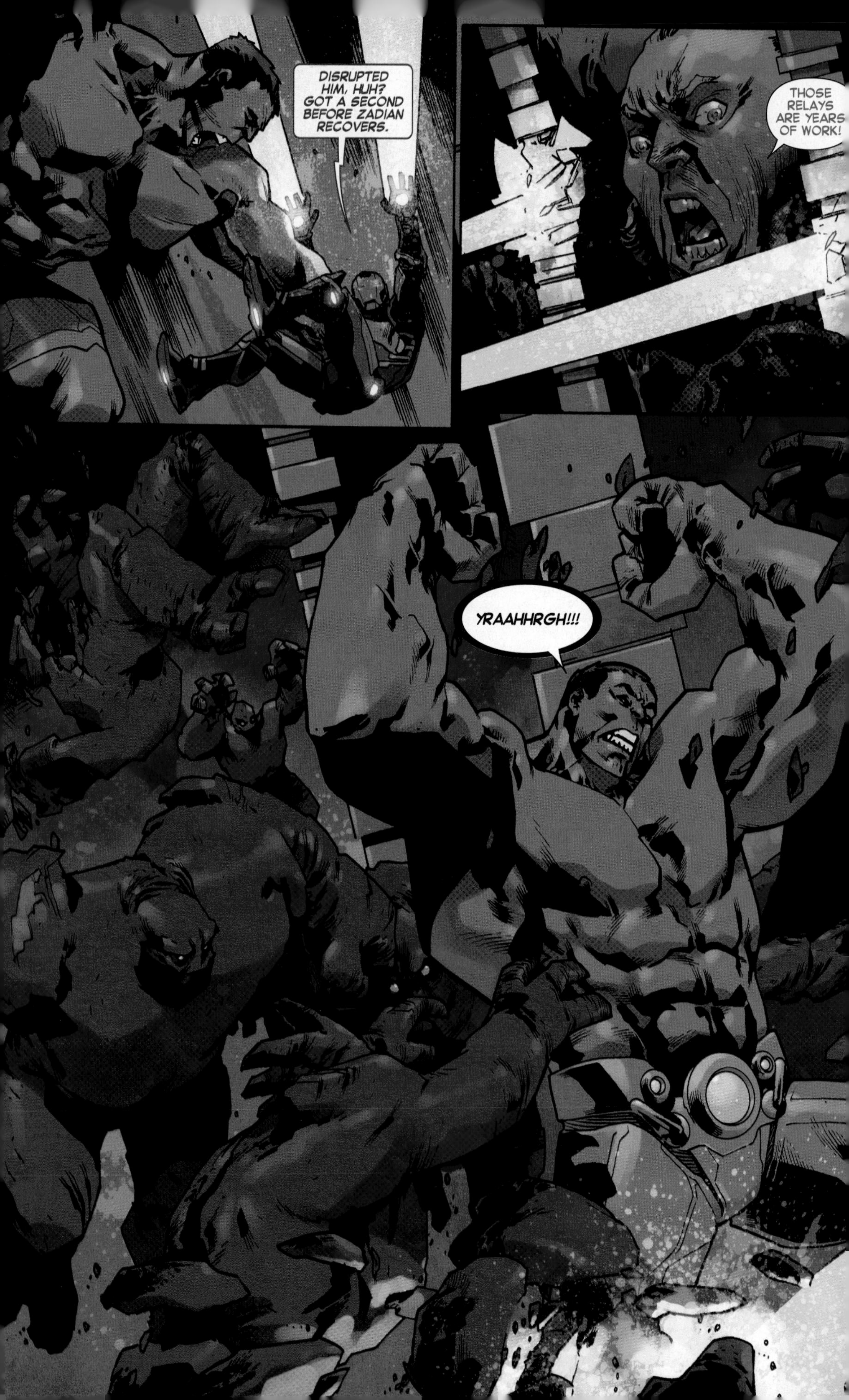
DISRUPTED HIM, HUH? GOT A SECOND BEFORE ZADIAN RECOVERS.
THOSE RELAYS ARE YEARS OF WORK!
YRAAHHRGH!!!

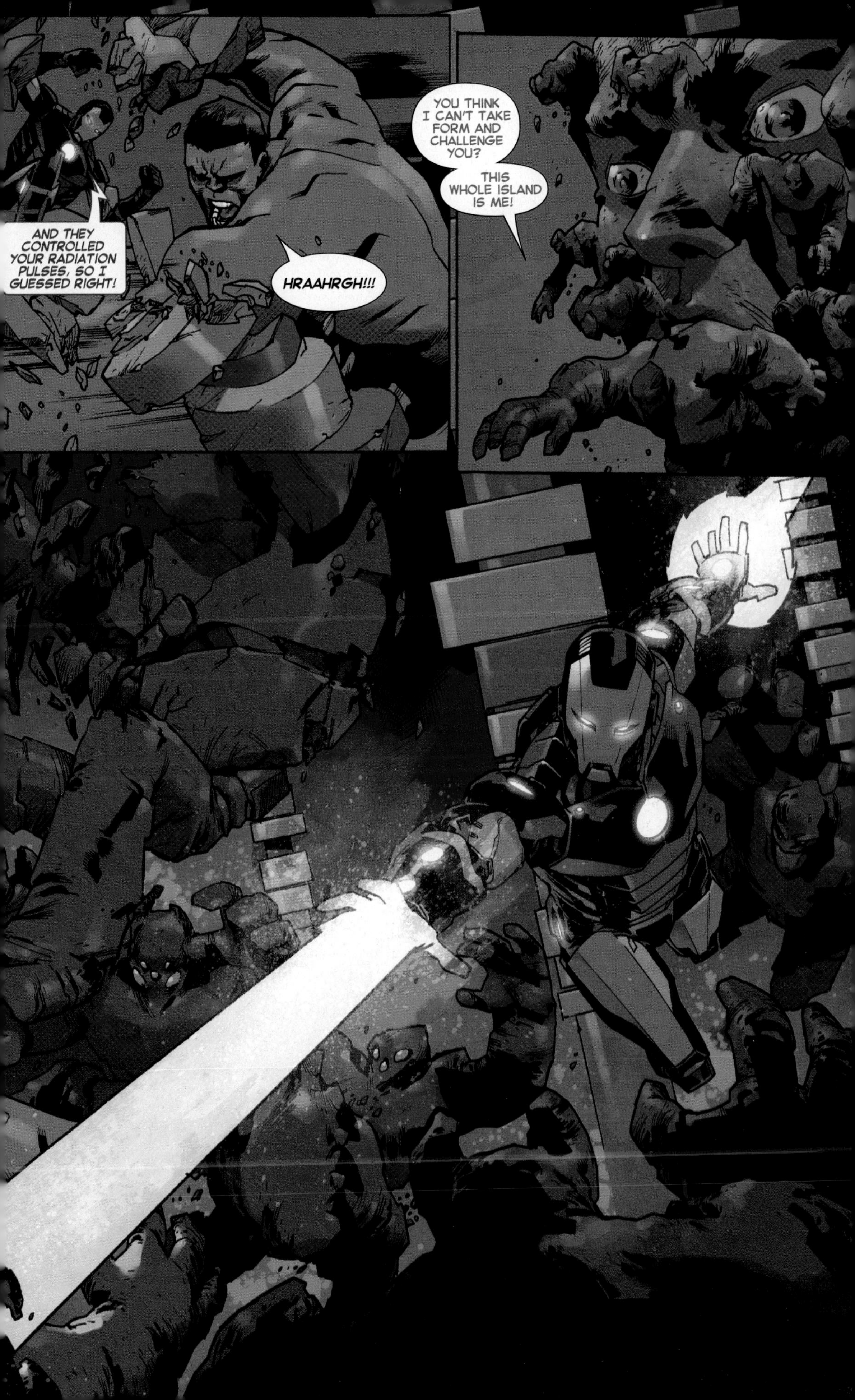
AND THEY CONTROLLED YOUR RADIATION PULSES, SO I GUESSED RIGHT!
HRAAHRGH!!!
YOU THINK I CAN'T TAKE FORM AND CHALLENGE YOU?
THIS WHOLE ISLAND IS ME!

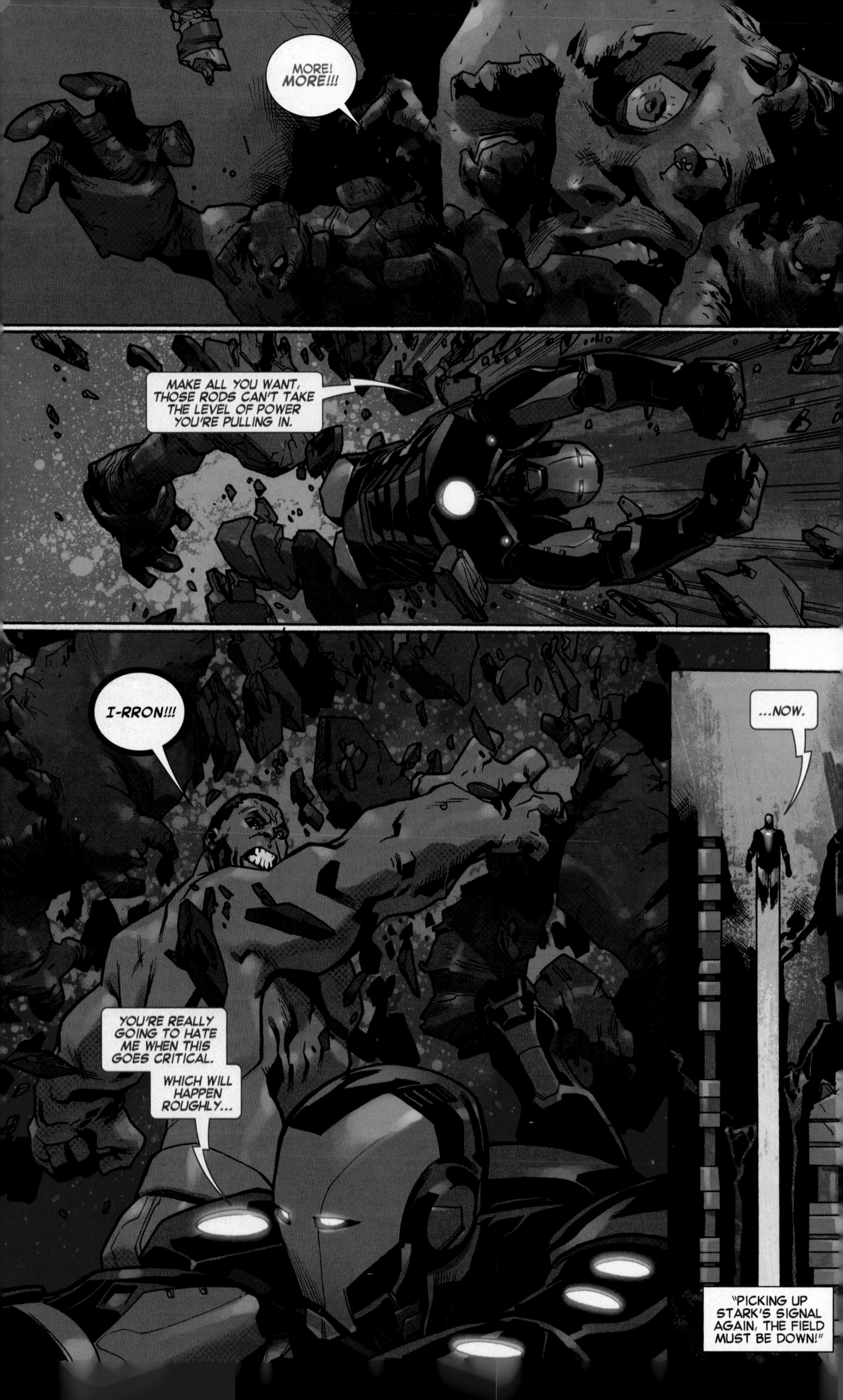
MORE! MORE!!!
MAKE ALL YOU WANT, THOSE RODS CAN'T TAKE THE LEVEL OF POWER YOU'RE PULLING IN.
I-RRON!!!
YOU'RE REALLY GOING TO HATE ME WHEN THIS GOES CRITICAL.
WHICH WILL HAPPEN ROUGHLY...
...NOW.
"PICKING UP STARK'S SIGNAL AGAIN, THE FIELD MUST BE DOWN!"

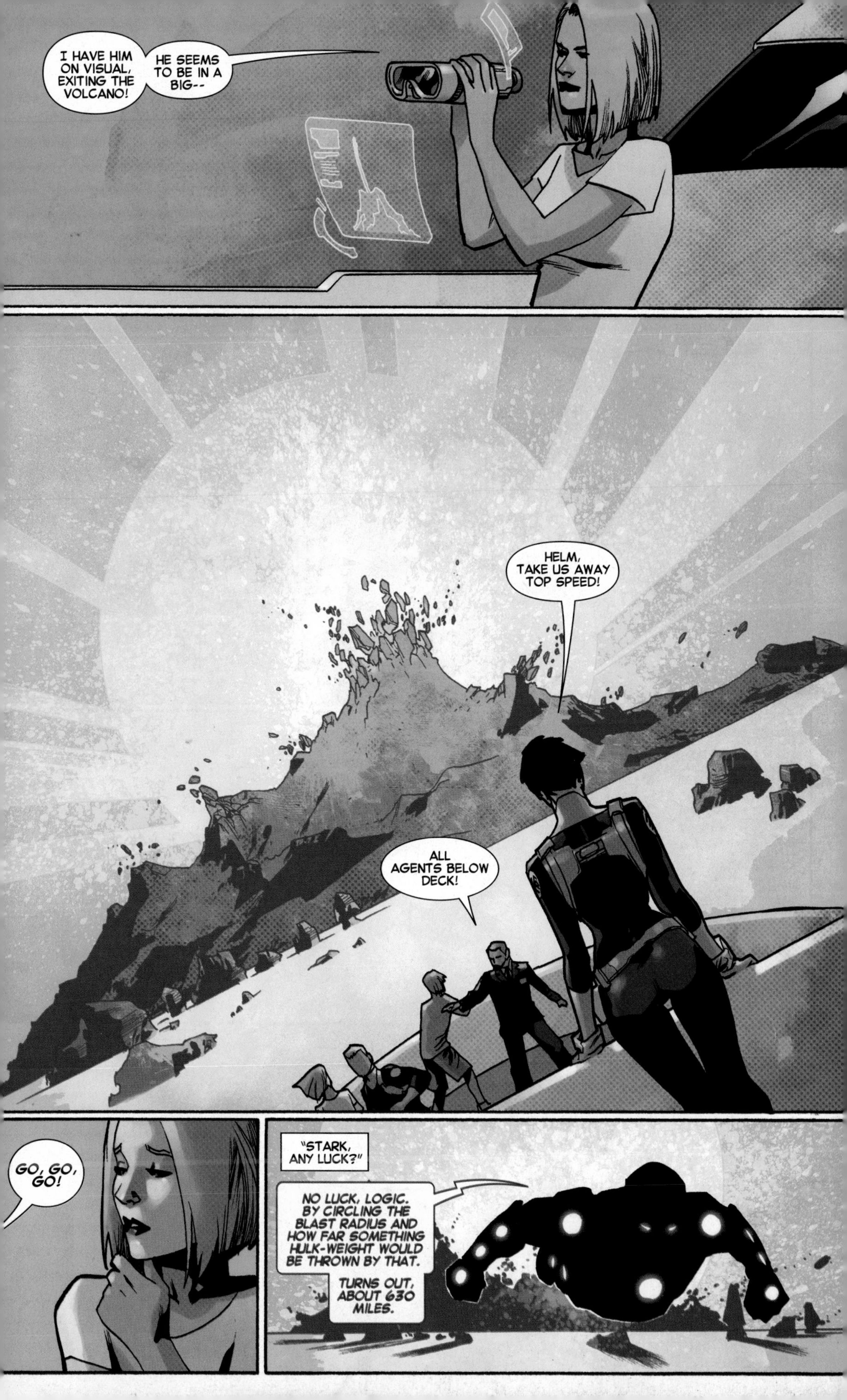
I HAVE HIM ON VISUAL, EXITING THE VOLCANO!
HE SEEMS TO BE IN A BIG--
HELM, TAKE US AWAY TOP SPEED!
ALL AGENTS BELOW DECK!
GO, GO, GO!
"STARK, ANY LUCK?"
NO LUCK, LOGIC. BY CIRCLING THE BLAST RADIUS AND HOW FAR SOMETHING HULK-WEIGHT WOULD BE THROWN BY THAT.
TURNS OUT, ABOUT 630 MILES.

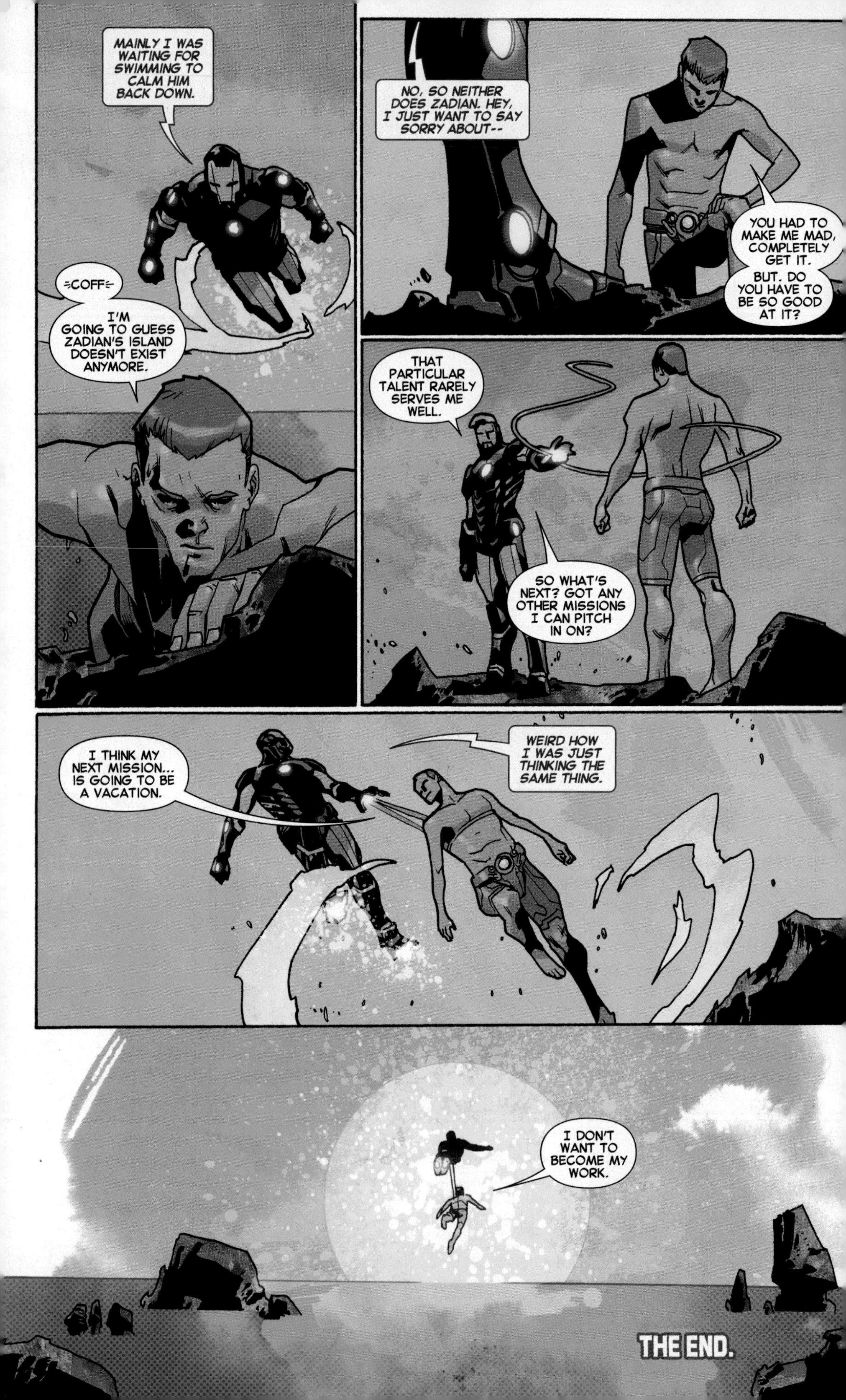
MAINLY I WAS WAITING FOR SWIMMING TO CALM HIM BACK DOWN.
≈COFF≈
I'M GOING TO GUESS ZADIAN'S ISLAND DOESN'T EXIST ANYMORE.
NO, SO NEITHER DOES ZADIAN. HEY, I JUST WANT TO SAY SORRY ABOUT--
YOU HAD TO MAKE ME MAD, COMPLETELY GET IT.
BUT. DO YOU HAVE TO BE SO GOOD AT IT?
THAT PARTICULAR TALENT RARELY SERVES ME WELL.
SO WHAT'S NEXT? GOT ANY OTHER MISSIONS I CAN PITCH IN ON?
I THINK MY NEXT MISSION... IS GOING TO BE A VACATION.
WEIRD HOW I WAS JUST THINKING THE SAME THING.
I DON'T WANT TO BECOME MY WORK.
THE END.

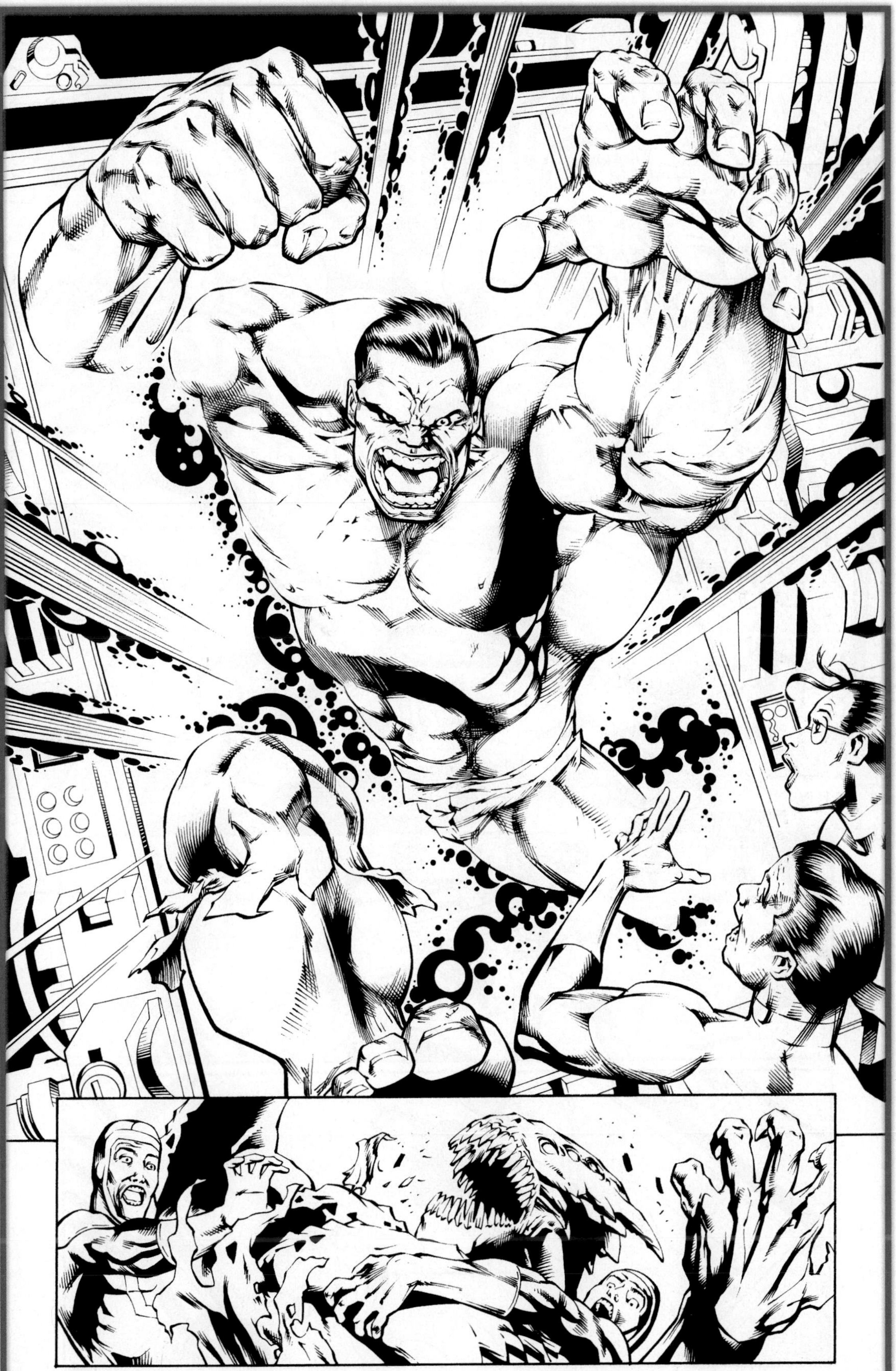

INCREDIBLE HULK #20, PAGE 7 ART BY JOE BENNETT & RUY JOSÉ

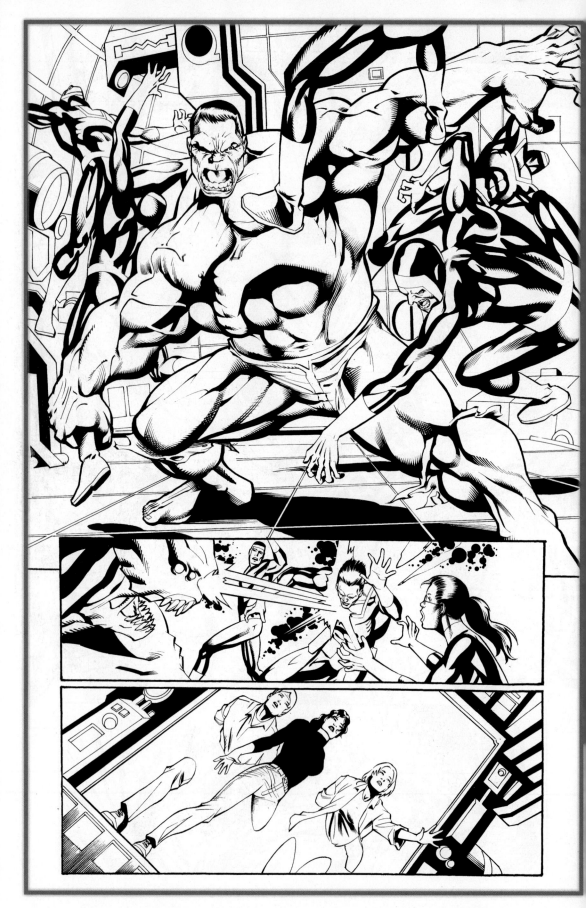

INCREDIBLE HULK #20, PAGE 8 ART BY JOE BENNETT & RUY JOSÉ

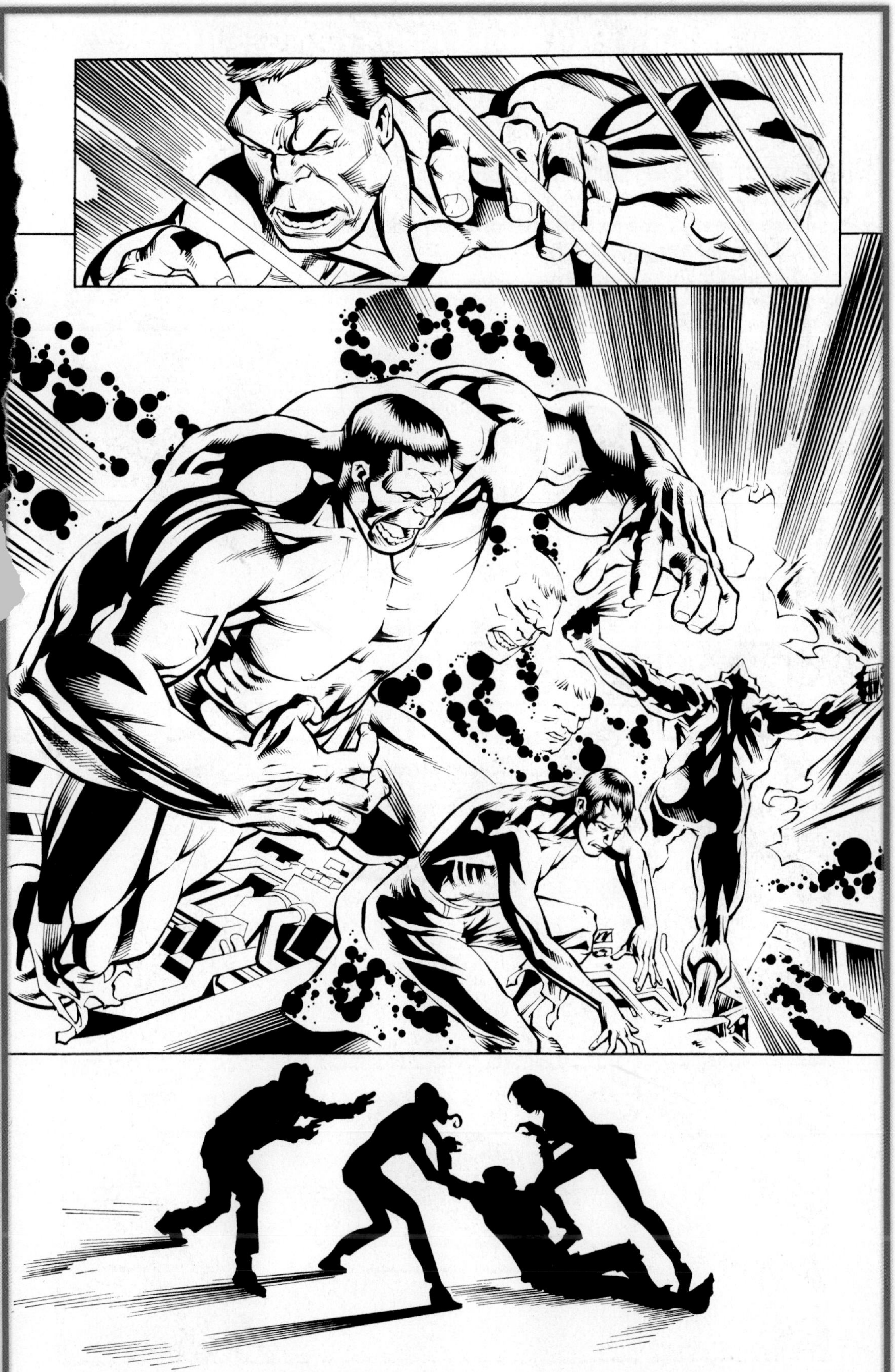

INCREDIBLE HULK #20, PAGE 13 ART BY JOE BENNETT & RUY JOSÉ

MARVEL AR AUGMENTED REALITY

MARVEL AUGMENTED REALITY (AR) ENHANCES AND CHANGES THE WAY YOU EXPERIENCE COMICS!

TO ACCESS THE FREE MARVEL AR CONTENT IN THIS BOOK*:

1. Locate the AR logo within the comic.
2. Go to Marvel.com/AR in your web browser.
3. Search by series title to find the corresponding AR.
4. Enjoy Marvel AR!

*All AR content that appears in this book has been archived and will be available only at Marvel.com/AR – no longer in the Marvel AR App. Content subject to change and availability.

INDESTRUCTIBLE HULK

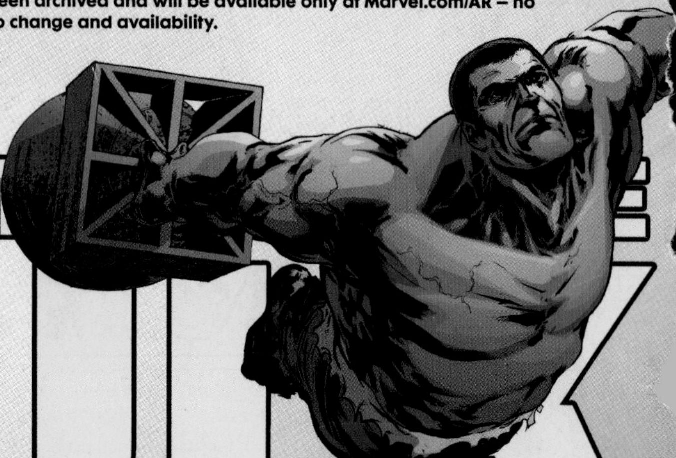

AR INDEX